QUEST FOR EMPIRE

*The Political Kingdom of God and the
Council of Fifty in Mormon History*

Dec 25, 1985

Dearest Clark;

Merry Christmas!

I hope this volume
will add 'info' to
your vast mental
file Box, Presented
with great love,

Ruth

QUEST FOR EMPIRE

---

*The Political Kingdom of God and the
Council of Fifty in Mormon History*

By KLAUS J. HANSEN

UNIVERSITY OF NEBRASKA PRESS · LINCOLN

First Bison Book printing: December 1974

Most recent printing shown by first digit below:

1   2   3   4   5   6   7   8   9   10

Bison Book edition reprinted by arrangement with Michigan State University Press.

Library of Congress Cataloging in Publication Data

Hansen, Klaus J
    Quest for empire.

    "A Bison book."
    Reprint of the 1970 ed. published by Michigan State
University Press, East Lansing; with new pref. by the
author.
    Includes bibliographical references.
    1. Church of Jesus Christ of Latter-Day Saints.
Council of Fifty. 2. Kingdom of God (Mormonism)
I. Church of Jesus Christ of Latter-Day Saints.
Council of Fifty. II. Title.
[BX8611.H295 1974]   289.3'3   74–8002
ISBN 0–8032–5769–4

And in the days of these kings
shall the God of heaven set up a kingdom,
which shall never be destroyed:
and the kingdom shall not be left to other people,
but it shall break in pieces and consume all these kingdoms,
and it shall stand for ever.

—Dan. 2:44

I calculate to be one of the instruments
of setting up the kingdom of Daniel
by the word of the Lord,
and I intend to lay a foundation
that will revolutionize the whole world.

—Joseph Smith, 12 May 1844

The Kingdom of God is actually organized
and the inhabitants of the earth do not know it.

—Brigham Young, 8 July 1855

Those of us who understood the situation were not nearly
as much opposed to polygamy as we were to the political
domination of the Church. We realized, however, that we
could not make those who did not come actually in contact
with it, understand what this political domination meant.
We made use of polygamy in consequence as our great weapon
of offense and to gain recruits to our standard. There was
a universal detestation of polygamy, and inasmuch as the
Mormons openly defended it we were given a very effective
weapon with which to attack.

—Frederick T. Dubois, Autobiography

TO JOAN

Preface
to the Bison Book Edition

For many reasons—the speculative nature of certain portions of this study, the continuing and lively debates that have engaged nineteenth-century American cultural historians in general and Mormon historians in particular, the greatly increased accessibility of Mormon sources, especially those at the Historical Department of the Church of Jesus Christ of Latter-day Saints in Salt Lake City—it might have been appropriate to subject this book to a major revision. Certainly the large number of studies in the social and intellectual history of the antebellum period that have appeared in the last decade might easily have dictated a revision of the first two chapters. The broader topic of the relationship between Mormonism and American culture, clearly, is a subject of the first magnitude. These chapters, however, are properly introductory; therefore, I have left them intact in the anticipation that I will be able to report on more detailed research in a book-length study. In the meantime, I refer the reader to some preliminary observations that have recently appeared elsewhere.[1]

That I have not rewritten the rest of the book is only in part due to the economics of paperback publishing. It is also because I believe that the growing and impressive body of facts pertaining to the political kingdom of God and the Council of Fifty has tended to confirm the basic premises and conclusions of my study. When the book first appeared in 1967, one leading historian, expressing "reservations" about "the frailness of some sources which are made to carry considerable weight, esp. the typed Council of Fifty minutes," voiced an opinion echoed in several reviews. Another regretted the paucity of "official" sources. While these are still most elusive, I am now at least able to assure readers that the typed versions of Council of Fifty minutes to which I had access are indeed copies of original manuscripts in the possession of the Mormon Church.[2]

If I seem unduly complacent regarding the accuracy of both facts and interpretation of this study, it is perhaps because I have been encouraged by a surprising scholarly consensus regarding the significance and role of the kingdom of God and the Council of Fifty in Mormon history. According to one commentator, who is critical of this consensus, "seldom have so many individuals from so many isolated and otherwise antagonistic 'camps' of Mormon scholarship shown such agreement in their interpretation of our tradition."[3] Having braced myself for the possibility of a heated debate, I was pleasantly surprised by the degree of equanimity if not open acceptance that scholars trained in and dedicated to the discipline of church history—with its implicit commitment to apologetics—brought to a work written from the secular perspective of the history of religion, a work that endeavors to treat Mormons with the same degree of "objectivity" as other secular historians might treat Catholics, or Buddhists, or worshipers of the Cargo Cult.

I can only guess at the reasons for this lack of controversy. First of all, Fawn Brodie's excessively maligned biography of Joseph Smith may well have preempted most of the shock value of the secular approach for Mormons.[4] What might have been cause for excommunication in 1945, was, in 1967, merely occasion for the privately expressed if stinging rebuke by a General Authority of the Mormon Church. Second, a generation of church historians trained in secular graduate schools clearly has gained a sufficient respect for "facts" and their role in the historical method not to allow suppression or dismissal of those that may prove uncomfortable, even painful. Third, it appears that on closer scrutiny, some "orthodox" or "conservative" scholars regarded these "facts" as not so painful, after all. Although my general theme, that the metamorphosis of the kingdom of God is one of the fundamental expressions of a transformation in Mormon values and Mormon culture, may seem disturbing to the "orthodox," particularly those who believe that "Americanism" and Mormonism have always been identical (in their opinion it was the persecutors of the Mormons that were "un-American"), a number of influential theologians and historians who have moved to a Mormon "neo-orthodox" position and who are, therefore, disturbed by what they see as evidence of a Mormon compromise with Babylon, clearly welcome the rediscovery of a Mormon past from its present Orwellian version as part of their attempt to redirect Mormonism to what they see as its fundamental values.[5] In even stronger agreement, of course, are various groups of "fundamentalist" dissidents who, because of their militant insistence on continuing the political kingdom, communitarianism, and polygamy, are beyond the pale of official Utah Mormonism and, if found out, are generally excommunicated.

This is not to say, of course, that what one critic has called "an entire 'school' of historical interpretation" would sweep the field without protest.[6] Significantly, however, this criticism has been lodged primarily by scholars with a sociological or anthropological orientation. One reason may well be that historians tend toward a somewhat literal and unsophisticated approach to "facts," however uncomfortable they may be. Certain sociologists and anthropologists, with their penchant for model building, seem to regard "facts" with less awe, particularly when they do not fit the model.

Gordon Thomasson's approach is a case in point. In his eagerness to prove "that the 'emperor' has no clothes on," he reduces "facts" to "assumptions," then neatly clinches his argument by stating that "it is not necessary to have recourse to an hypothetical political kingdom of God to understand

Church involvement in politics."[7] Thus history is reduced to a game of logic. To a historian, of course, the question is not whether it is *necessary* to have recourse to the concept of a political kingdom of God, but whether or not such a concept existed in the minds of nineteenth-century Mormon leaders. The logic of much of Mormon history, at least in its bowdlerized version, admittedly makes such a concept quite unnecessary. But I am still a sufficiently old-fashioned Rankean to believe that the first task of the historian is to find out not what is reasonable but what happened.

Not that this eliminates the necessity for evaluating circumstantial evidence and making informed guesses about what seems reasonable on the basis of the available evidence. My speculations regarding Joseph Smith's kingship are an example. Thomasson makes much of my lack of evidence, but ignores my qualifications, in which I recognize the possibility that the terms may be symbolic and metaphorical.[8] Thomasson, moreover, pushes conjecture much further in his own speculations regarding the connection between Smith's "kingship" and the Mormon temple ceremony of the "endowment," in which the faithful receive conditional promises of becoming "kings" in the next world. Thomasson argues that Smith, in a ceremony called the "Second Anointing," moved from these conditional blessings to a state of permanent assurance, "making him a 'king' indeed, and insuring that he would retain his kingship and his kingdom." But he emphatically insists that this "*in no way* implies that his kingdom was to be in any manner of this world."[9] This presentist approach is vulnerable on two counts. First of all, it ignores the possibility, even high probability, that the temple ceremony has undergone historical evolution. The corollary of this position, of course, is an a priori approach to the past that must conform to the theological and religious assumptions and experiences of the investigator. If this method is pushed to its logical conclusion, the historical approach, of course, becomes irrelevant.

On a more sophisticated level, the problem of the a priori assumptions of the "committed" scholar versus the open-ended approach of the secular historian of religion is raised by Professor John Sorenson, an anthropologist who takes issue with my thesis of cultural transformation.[10] Not that he quibbles about "facts." His summary of nineteenth-century Mormon history reads as if it is taken straight out of *Quest for Empire*. But when it comes to interpreting these events, we part company. On a superficial level the problem appears to be a question of definition. If only historians could be precise and define their terms, in this case the term "culture!" What Sorenson does not tell us, however, is that in their search for precision, anthropologists have transformed an analytic tool into a descriptive term, all their protestations to the contrary notwithstanding. It appears that each investigation of "culture" leads to a new "definition." If that remark seems uncharitable, one would like to have an alternate explanation for Alfred Kroeber's and Clyde Kluckhohn's discovery of more than three hundred definitions of the term "culture."[11]

Nevertheless, if I am to play the game, I will naturally play with balls of my own choosing. Implicit in my approach is a definition of culture as expressed by Lynn White, Jr., a historian of science: "People are organized into cultures by basic presuppositions—often unverbalized—that they share: their axioms. They put their intelligence, energy, and money into what they corporately consider good."[12] To nineteenth-century Americans, individualism and pluralism were axiomatic, leading to competition, laissez faire capitalism, "progress," at the end of which stood a vaguely defined concept of the millennium. Mormons also believed that their version of the millennium would be achieved through "progress." But their anti-individualistic, anti-pluralist means were anathema to Americans at large. Not until Mormons had given up their means —the political kingdom, communitarianism, and polygamy —were they considered as eligible to join the pluralistic American community. Sorenson may well argue that he is quite willing to follow me this far. Isn't it the end, after all, that is the crucial test of cultural values? My rejoinder is that it is the means that shape the ends, and that a culture cannot be identified properly without paying close attention to the means. It follows, then, that if one accepts my premises, Mormonism has experienced a profound cultural transformation.

But it does not, of course, require a great deal of ingenuity to come up with a definition of culture according to which no such transformation has occurred. All that is necessary is to look at contemporary Mormonism, check it off against its nineteenth-century counterpart, examine how much has been "preserved," and then apply these "constants" to the definition of Mormon culture. Mormonism, *mirabile dictu*, has not changed at all. Its essential spiritual teachings are defined neither by time nor place. Mormonism has been lifted out of history.

According to one passage in the Doctrine and Covenants, "culture" results from a corrupt application of history—"the tradition of their fathers."[13] As Professor Sorenson points out, from this perspective culture becomes "a negative force on men, reminiscent of Freud's characterization of culture ('civilization') as a burden imposed on the proper condition of man."[14] This imperfect world is in constant flux, for better or for worse. But the world that remains miraculously untouched, pure, is the world of ideas. In Sorenson's opinion, those "observers [Hansen and O'Dea] who hold that Mormon life has changed fundamentally over the years" are "precisely those . . . who pay least attention to ideology and other conceptual materials."[15]

Wishing, at this point, to speak only for myself, I believe that this view both oversimplifies and distorts what I have attempted to do. *Quest for Empire*, of course, is not intellectual history, at least not primarily history of ideas. Moreover, rather than making the interaction between ideas and society explicit, I have preferred to allow it to emerge through the dynamics of historical change implicit in my account. The model for my approach, of course, should be obvious to those familiar with Karl Mannheim's *Ideology and Utopia*.[16] Quite clearly, I have portrayed Smith and his collaborators as millenarians envisioning the establishment of a "utopia." As they "succeed" in their quest, the dynamics of change, inevitably, must be directed into more conservative channels. The original ideas that made the "utopia" possible now have to be transformed into an ideology, a rationalization of the existing order as it has historically evolved. If I may be permitted to steal some of my own thunder: "Mormonism in 1974, differs fundamentally from the Mormonism of 1890 even though no theoretical change in doctrine may have occurred."[17] Social change can sometimes be rationalized most effectively under the pretense that it isn't going on. But ideas, of course, do not exist in a vacuum. What is important about ideas is their social dynamics. There is a profound difference between treating ideas as "conceptual materials" and as "ideology." That distinction, however, can be made more effectively if one looks at ideas over time. The sociological and anthropological approach, therefore, with its potential for setting up timeless models, may be a more congenial tool than history in the hands of an apologist who is looking for the preservation of "essential spiritual teachings."

From the believer's point of view, this is of course fair enough. It is just that it virtually eliminates the need for any kind of searching historical investigation. It is supremely ironic, of course, that in spite of its well-meaning intentions, this particular brand of apologetics tends to diminish the pathos and heroism of nineteenth-century Mormon history. Thus, to complete the irony, it seems to me that the secular historian, who lets the chips fall where they may, can play a crucial part in restoring the dignity of the Mormon past. His comic (not comical!) or tragic vision of life may well provide a dimension the apologist will find difficult to sustain.

Kingston, Ontario
March, 1974

Notes

1. Klaus J. Hansen, "Mormonism and American Culture: Some Tentative Hypotheses," in F. Mark McKiernan et. al., eds., *The Restoration Movement: Essays in Mormon History* (Lawrence, Kansas, 1973), pp. 1–25.

2. Davis Bitton to author, August 11, 1967; S. Lyman Tyler, *Pacific Historical Review*, XXXVI (November 1967), 480–81.

3. Gordon C. Thomasson, "Foolsmate," *Dialogue: A Journal of Mormon Thought*, VI, No. 3 & 4 (1971), 148.

4. *No Man Knows My History: The Life of Joseph Smith the Mormon Prophet* (New York, 1945).

5. O. Kendall White, Jr., "The Transformation of Mormon Theology," *Dialogue: A Journal of Mormon Thought*, V, No. 2 (1970), 9–24. The leading neo-orthodox interpretation of the political kingdom is Hyrum L. Andrus's *Joseph Smith and World Government* (Salt Lake City, 1958).

6. Thomasson, "Foolsmate," pp. 148–49.

7. *Ibid.*

8. See *infra.*, pp. 66–67.

9. Thomasson, "Foolsmate," pp. 150–51.

10. John L. Sorenson, "Mormon World View and American Culture," *Dialogue: A Journal of Mormon Thought*, VIII, No. 2 (1973), 17–29.

11. *Culture: A Critical Review of Concepts and Definitions* (New York, 1963).

12. "Technology Assessment from the Stance of a Medieval Historian," *The American Historical Review*, 79 (February 1974), 1.

13. Section 93: 38–40.

14. Sorenson, "Mormon World View and American Culture," p. 28.

15. *Ibid.*, p. 25.

16. (London & New York, 1936).

17. *Infra.*, p. 188.

Preface

Polygamy, contrary to popular opinion, probably seduced few men into the seraglio that was Mormonism in the mind of a prurient, Victorian America. Yet it lured several generations of historians—not to speak of journalists and popular novelists—into believing that its theory and practice provided the major key to an understanding of the Mormon question. Not all disciples of Clio succumbed to this point of view; nevertheless, further evidence requires another look at the problem, suggesting that the idea of a political kingdom of God, promulgated by a secret "Council of Fifty," is by far the most important key to an understanding of the Mormon past. The polygamy conflict, as I hope to confirm, was merely that part of the iceberg visible above the troubled waters of Mormon history. Some church leaders, for example, once they had reconciled themselves to the inevitability of the attack on polygamy, subtly invited assaults on the "relic of barbarism" in order to shield an institution of infinitely greater significance for Mormon history, the political kingdom of God.

When, in 1890, Mormon president Wilford Woodruff issued the so-called "Manifesto" ostensibly ending the practice of polygamy, he did so apparently to save not only the church but also the kingdom of God. The semantic distinction between the two terms—the first denoting strictly an ecclesiastical body, the second a political organization intended to prepare the world for a literal, political government in anticipation of Christ's millennium—originated with the Mormon prophet Joseph Smith, who taught those attending the secret sessions of the Council of Fifty in Nauvoo that the kingdom of God and the church were separate organizations. As our understanding of the history of this kingdom unfolds, it will be apparent that, if the Manifesto marked a watershed in the 1890's because it heralded the beginning of the end for polygamy, the following twenty years, though lacking the dramatic impact of Woodruff's pronouncement, divided Mormon history even more conclusively and permanently because they witnessed the decline and virtual disappearance of the idea of the political kingdom of God, so vigorously promoted by the Council of Fifty in the nineteenth century. Because this kingdom had existed for the most part *sub rosa*, its death— though accompanied by much agony—failed to attract as much public attention as the death of plural marriage. Polygamy died with a bang, the political kingdom of God with a whimper. The life and death of that kingdom, and of the organization that was its government, is the story of this book.

Because the historical implications of the political kingdom and the Council of Fifty are of the greatest magnitude, their detailed treatment would require a multivolume work, amounting to nothing less than a complete rewriting of nineteenth-century Mormon history. This I have not attempted to do. Yet I do hope that my study, tentative as it is, may perhaps be of some value to whosoever will undertake that Herculean task.

It is a pleasure to acknowledge the aid of the many people and institutions who facilitated this study. I am particularly indebted to Edward Lurie, who directed an earlier version of this work as a doctoral dissertation at Wayne State University, for his constant encouragement and invaluable criticism of both content and style; to Russel B. Swensen and Clinton F. Larson of Brigham Young University, who directed a master's thesis that became the nucleus for further research; and to Russel B. Nye, for reading the manuscript and encouraging its publication. I am grateful to Lee Benson, Raymond C. Miller, and Goldwin Smith, all of whom had a patient ear and gave advice freely; to Richard D. Poll, who nurtured and stimulated an early interest in Mormon history, and who provided helpful suggestions; to Leonard J. Arrington, Alfred L. Bush, Eugene Campbell, S. George Ellsworth, and Gustive O. Larson, for their careful and critical readings of the manuscript; to S. George Ellsworth and Juanita Brooks for freely sharing their extensive knowledge of Mormon history and sources; to B. Carmon Hardy, James R. Clark, Everett Cooley, and Robert B. Flanders, for their readiness to provide invaluable information. Alfred L. Bush, Curator of the Rollins Collection of Western Americana at Princeton University, first called my attention to the significance of the kingdom of God and the Council of Fifty for Mormon history. He has been an unfailing friend, supporting this project from its inception both with his enthusiasm and extensive knowledge of Mormon sources.

I also wish to thank the staffs of the following archives and libraries for their cooperation: Brigham Young University Library and Archives, particularly Chad Flake, Special Collections Librarian, for his unfailing help; the University of Utah Library, where Mrs. Ruth Yeaman went beyond the call of duty in providing access to manuscripts; the Utah State University Library; the Church Historian's Office of the Church of Jesus Christ of Latter-day Saints; the Utah State Historical Society, particularly John James, Librarian; the New York Public Library; Houghton Library at Harvard University; Yale University Library, particularly Archibald Hanna, Curator of Western Americana; The Library of Congress; The National Archives; Wayne State University Library; and finally the Ohio State University Library, particularly for providing me with a cell where I could work undisturbed.

I am also grateful to the College of Arts and Sciences of The Ohio State University and the History Department of Utah State University for facilitating the typing and completion of the manuscript.

I wish to thank the editors of *Brigham Young University Studies, Michigan History,* and *Dialogue,* for permission to use material from articles of mine which first appeared in these journals.

To my parents I am grateful for their many years of support and encouragement.

To my wife Joan I owe a special debt of gratitude for putting up with the itinerant life of an historian, carrying the major burden of caring for a growing family, and still finding time to be a perceptive critic of style and content.

If, with the help of such a large number of persons and institutions, this book is less than perfect, only the author is to blame.

Klaus J. Hansen

Logan, Utah, 1966.

Contents

Contents

QUEST FOR EMPIRE

*The Political Kingdom of God and the
Council of Fifty in Mormon History*

The Kingdom of God
and the Millennial Tradition

I

WHEN VICTORIA WAS crowned Queen of Great Britain and Ireland in Westminster Abbey on June 28, 1838, the Mormons took little notice of an event whose pomp and ceremony prompted the Turkish ambassador Sarim Effendi, more out of awe than contempt, to mutter repeatedly: "All this for a woman!" Confident that they were instruments in the hand of God to create on earth that kingdom which they believed Daniel had predicted some 2300 years earlier, the Saints had little awe for secular monarchs of either sex. In a letter addressed to the Queen in 1841, Mormon apostle Parley P. Pratt wrote: "Know assuredly, that the world in which we live is on the eve of a REVOLUTION, more powerful in its beginning—more rapid in its progress—more lasting in its influence—more important in its consequences—than any which man has yet witnessed upon the earth." The present political and religious establishments, the letter solemnly affirmed, were destined to vanish, and God was about to set

3

up "a new and universal Kingdom, under the immediate administration of the Messiah and his Saints." [1]

It is doubtful that Pratt's letter caused the Queen any sleepless nights. If she took notice of it at all, she most likely dismissed it as the work of merely another religious crank. In any case, the pious Victoria could take comfort in the Bible, which, as interpreted by the Church of England, assured her that Christ's kingdom was not of this world, and the Second Coming a decidedly spiritual event. Yet if the young monarch had read another letter, written three years later, by Pratt's fellow apostles Brigham Young and Willard Richards, to Reuben Hedlock, leader of the British Mormons, informing him that the kingdom of God was "organized and although as yet no bigger than a grain of mustard seed, . . . in a flourishing condition, and our prospects brighter than ever," [2] she might have done well to pause and reflect that her predecessor by two hundred years, Charles I, had lost his head at the hands of a band of religious fanatics who dreamed of establishing the kingdom of God on earth, acting out of the fervent conviction that they were carrying out the will of God. Not that the Mormons were thinking of regicide. Far from it. And yet the political implications of the kingdom of God Pratt and his fellow religionists hoped to establish were, potentially at least, a greater threat to Victoria's crown than all the turmoil stirred up by Chartists and anti-corn-law leagues which so annoyed and perplexed the Queen in the restless 1840's.

But Victoria was hardly the only one who failed to realize this. Even among the Mormons, few were themselves aware of the revolutionary implications inherent in the concept of the political kingdom of God as taught by their prophet Joseph Smith to a small group of faithful followers, after he had initiated them into a secret Council of Fifty in the spring of 1844. The majority of church members might well have been startled by the letter addressed to Hedlock. For faithful Latter-day Saints generally believed that, when Joseph Smith organized or rather restored the Church of Christ in 1830, he had also begun the establishment of the kingdom of God on earth, a kingdom that was to be identical with the church in the minds of most followers. The announcement of the establishment of *this* kingdom to Hedlock in 1844, after it had struggled valiantly against fourteen years of Gentile persecution, clearly would not have made any sense.[3] Had Christ, then, perhaps appeared in secret to prepare for His millennial reign? To most Mormons such a supposition would have been the only alternative answer and yet a highly improbable one since too many of the predicted signs of the times had not yet been fulfilled. Indeed, if few Mormons, in 1844, knew what kind of kingdom their prophet had organized that year, fewer know today. Therefore, in order to understand more fully what kingdom Young and Richards were referring to in their letter to Hedlock, we must first examine briefly the development of the idea of the kingdom of God in Mormon thought.

In April, 1829, Joseph Smith issued a revelation which announced that "a great and marvelous work is about to come forth unto the children of men. . . . Behold, the field is white already to harvest; therefore, whoso desireth to reap, let him thrust his sickle in with his might, and reap while the day lasts, that he may treasure up for his soul everlasting salvation in the kingdom of God." [4] In this context the term kingdom of God clearly had a spiritual connotation. Christians had traditionally regarded the salvation of the soul as being within the province of the church; to the faithful, generally, the kingdom of God on earth became a visible metaphor to enable man's entrance into the invisible kingdom of God in heaven. In the days of Joseph Smith this concept was so much a part of the Christian tradition that the terms "church" and "kingdom of God" were used rather loosely and interchangeably. Although Joseph Smith repudiated this tradition, he continued to use the term "kingdom of God" with some lack of precision.

When Smith organized the "Church of Christ" on April 6, 1830, in Peter Whitmer's farmhouse in Fayette, New York, he asked the six charter members of the new religion "whether they accepted us [Smith and Oliver Cowdery] as their teachers in the things of the kingdom of God, and whether they were satisfied that we should proceed and be organized as a church."[5] The new religion thus became an ecclesiastical organization consisting of those who had accepted the tenets of the "restored Gospel" and had submitted to the rites and ceremonies necessary to gain membership. To this day, Mormons regard baptism and the "laying on of hands" for the gift of the Holy Ghost as essential prerequisites for membership in the church or kingdom of God.[6] In this ecclesiastical sense, Mormons, like most Christians, hardly took the term "kingdom" literally, but considered it little more than an elevating metaphor.

The Saints, however, tended toward a certain literalmindedness, and regarded metaphors with some suspicion. The most startling fact about Joseph Smith's first vision, which he experienced as a boy of fourteen, was perhaps not that he had seen God and Christ, but that these were separate beings possessing—as he later learned—bodies of flesh and bone. Although the Christian ministers in Smith's neighborhood regarded his story as little more than a crude expression of anthropomorphism, to Smith it became the cornerstone of Mormon metaphysics. For the development of one of the major philosophical ideas of Mormonism resulted in its rejection of the mind-matter dualism of Cartesian philosophy. "There is no such thing as immaterial matter," proclaimed Smith. "All spirit is matter, but it is more fine or pure, and can only be discerned by purer eyes; we cannot see it; but when our bodies are purified we shall see that all is matter."[7] In an even stronger expression of this same idea, the Mormon *Millennial Star* quoted the prophet as saying that "God the father is material, Jesus Christ is material. Angels are material. Space is full of materiality. Nothing exists which is not material."[8] The established Christian churches, by worshiping an immaterial God, were thus, in fact, guilty of atheism.[9]

The Mormon concept of materialism, however, was more than a metaphysical construct. More concretely, it found expression in a strong emphasis on temporal matters in Mormon society. Although the mixing of the sublime and the mundane was a peculiarity of nineteenth-century American religion not reserved for Mormonism alone, the followers of Joseph Smith went further than most sects in this direction. Thus, when the editor of a Pittsburgh Universalist publication visited Kirtland, Ohio, in 1837, he could not refrain from observing that the Saints had "too much worldly wisdom connected with their religion—too great a desire for the perishable riches of this world—holding out the idea that the kingdom of Christ is to be composed of 'real estate, herds, flocks, silver, gold,' etc. as well as of human beings." [10] This concern for both the spiritual and the temporal welfare of man has become one of the chief characteristics of Mormonism.

The dual emphasis on the spiritual and the temporal is also strongly reflected in the priesthood organization of the Mormon church. On May 15, 1829, Smith and Cowdery announced to their followers and to the world that none other than John the Baptist had returned from heaven to ordain them priests in the order of Aaron. Several months later, in the summer of the same year, the founder of Mormonism and his disciple claimed to have been ordained apostles under the hands of three other heavenly visitors who had identified themselves as Peter, James, and John. The apostleship held the keys to the Melchizedek or higher priesthood. Thus, priestly duties were shared by two distinct groups, with the Melchizedek priesthood officiating primarily in spiritual matters and the Aaronic priesthood administering to the temporal needs of the church.[11] Smith inferred that this priesthood organization, as combined in its spiritual and temporal branches, was called the kingdom of God.[12] Brigham Young was even more explicit on the matter:

I will say to you with regard to the kingdom of God on the earth—Here is the Church of Jesus Christ of Latter-day Saints, organized with its rules and regulations and degrees, with the quorums of the holy Priesthood, from the First Presidency to the teachers and deacons; here we are; an organization. God called upon Joseph, he called upon Oliver Cowdery, then others were called through Joseph, the Church was organized, he with his two counselors comprised the First Presidency. In a few years the Quorum of the Twelve was organized, and the Priests' quorum, the Teachers' quorum and the Deacons'. This is what we are in the habit of calling the kingdom of God.[13]

This interpretation of the kingdom of God as a synonym for the church in both its spiritual and temporal connotations seems always to have been the one most generally accepted by the followers of Joseph Smith. It has found expression from the pulpit to this day and is, in fact, about the only interpretation most Mormons are aware of at the present time.[14]

Yet Latter-day Saints would acknowledge that the kingdom of God need not necessarily encompass a formal and complete church organization. Joseph Smith introduced this concept in a sermon given at Nauvoo in 1843. In an attempt to refute Alexander Campbell, who held that the kingdom of God had not been set up until the day of Pentecost, Smith argued that John the Baptist had been a legal administrator of the kingdom of God by virtue of his priesthood. The prophet expanded this idea into the doctrine that "whenever men can find out the will of God and find an administrator legally authorized from God, there is the kingdom of God." In this sense, according to Smith, the kingdom had existed on earth "from the days of Adam to the present time." [15]

Finally, the Mormon prophet equated the kingdom with the city of Zion to be built on this earth. The establishment of such a Zion had been a favorite dream of the radical Reformation; and the desire to build a Zion in the wilderness had become a peculiarly American expression of this dream. The Mormons were not the first to leave homes, friends, and civilization behind them in exchange for a wilderness where, in the words of William Bradford—an earlier migrant—there were "no friends to welcome them, nor inns to entertaine or refresh their weather beaten bodys, no houses much less townes to repaire too, to seke for succoure." [16] But the Mormon search for a city of Zion represents the strongest expression of this idea in nineteenth-century America.

Originally, the Mormons had envisioned their Zion as a literal and physical gathering place for the elect. Through his agent Joseph Smith, the Lord's finger had pointed to Jackson County, Missouri, as the locale for the building of the city of the Saints. Soon, however, the twin forces of persecution and increasing church membership forced the prophet to expand the idea of Zion. In a metaphor he saw the church as a gigantic tent supported by stakes. The center stake of Zion was to be driven in Jackson County. Radiating from this core, "Stakes of Zion" could be erected as needed to support the ever growing tent of the kingdom, until it would cover the entire North and South American continents, and finally the world.[17]

But as the "Stakes of Zion" grew and expanded, the concept of Zion as a physical and geographical reality was transformed into a spiritual ideal. Latter-day Saint theology was readily adaptable to this change. If in Mormon metaphysics there was nothing spiritual that did not also have material substance, it was also true that things material had spiritual qualities. Zion was therefore not only bricks, mortar, and real estate; inevitably, it also had its seat in the hearts of the faithful. That this concept may have gradually increased in importance through necessity is not an unreasonable assumption; for, when bricks and mortar crumbled under Gentile hands, there seemed but one place left where the "pure in heart" could keep their Zion inviolate.[18] Nevertheless, as long as the Saints were actively engaged in building their physical Zion, the concept of the "pure in heart" might ennoble the idea of an earthly kingdom of God, but it could not supplant it. As long as the "pure in heart" gathered to Zion, the physical reality was at least as important as the ideal of a spiritual Zion. Only when the Saints no longer felt a need to gather did the idea of Zion as the "pure in heart" become another illustration of the gradual spiritualization of Mormon doctrine. Yet even at the present time faithful Mormons tend to refer in a special sense to Salt Lake City as their Zion. There lingers, then, the kernel of a physical concept which has not been entirely lost.

It is true, however, that time has diluted the notion of Zion as a physical entity to such an extent that the letter written by Brigham Young and Willard Richards to Hedlock in 1844 would be unintelligible to most present-day Mormons. And many Latter-day Saints even in the days of Joseph Smith may well have been puzzled by its contents. Was not Nauvoo a physical manifestation of Zion, of a social and material kingdom of God? Did not the Saints, inevitably, hold political power in their own communities? What other sort of Kingdom, then, had to be organized? That it could not have been the millennial kingdom seemed obvious to most of the faithful, as previously indicated. Too many prophecies describing events leading to its establishment simply had not been fulfilled in 1844. Nevertheless, the political kingdom of God organized by Smith in that year grew directly out of the concept of an earthly Zion and represented one of the strongest expressions of millennialism in Mormon history.

True to the apocalyptic seekers for the millennium such as the Montanists, John of Leyden in Munster, and the Fifth Monarchists in Cromwell's England, the Mormons repudiated Saint Augustine's doctrine that the kingdom of God and the millennium had, in fact, been ushered in with Christ's ascension. Even in its least radical phase, Mormon theology held that the millennial kingdom was destined to come in the future. In its more revolutionary earlier period, Pratt's letter to Queen Victoria represents a typical example of a more enthusiastic millennialism that pointed to a day when, as an editorial in the *Millennial Star* put it, "all the political, and all the religious organizations that may previously exist, will be swallowed up into one entire union—one universal empire—having no laws but God's law, and Saints to administer them." [19]

The Mormon church, in both its spiritual and temporal manifestations, thus existed to prepare its followers for the advent of the messianic kingdom. Ultimately, the earthly and spiritual kingdoms would be one; but, in the meantime, a dichotomy between reality and aspiration was inevitable. Yet, in their letter to Hedlock, Young and Richards were referring to neither of these manifestations of the kingdom of God. Rather, the Lord had revealed to Joseph Smith that still another manifestation of the "kingdom" was required to usher in the millennial reign of Christ. This was the political kingdom of God, destined to bring about the political transformation of the world, just as the church was intended to change the world religiously. Christ, at His coming, would usher in not only the ecclesiastical reign of a world church, but also of a political world government. And in order to prepare the world for the reign of the Son of God, the Saints would have to establish a political government on earth prior to His coming. As apostle George Q. Cannon admonished an audience of Mormon missionaries, the time would come when the elders of the church would go out to the world not only as representatives of an ecclesiastical organization, but also as literal ambassadors of the Mormon kingdom of God, accredited to foreign governments. For the kingdom of God was "to become a political power, known and recognized by the powers of the earth," before the nations of the earth would have met with the ultimate destruction decreed by the Almighty, preparatory to the arrival of Christ the King Himself.[20] The Mormon concept of the political kingdom of God, and the activities and aspirations of its governing body, the Council of Fifty, can only be understood, then, in the context of Mormon millennialism. In fact, the evolution and metamorphosis of the millenarian ideal in Mormon history was inextricably intertwined with the rise and fall of these two organizations.

Walter Nigg and Norman Cohn have demonstrated that

the pursuit of the millennium antedated Christianity and had its origins in Hebrew nationalism. The writings of Isaiah and the Book of Daniel stirred the nationalistic imagination of the Jews from Judas Maccabaeus to Simon bar-Cochba. They hoped to establish a messianic kingdom through the hands of a "saving remnant of Israel" which would survive the judgment of the Lord, and live with Him in the New Jerusalem, the spiritual and political capital of a new world of peace and abundance. The Christians added to this messianic vision certain passages from the New Testament, especially from the Book of Revelation. They also continued to draw upon Old Testament prophecies whenever the adversities of life could be countered by the belief that the time was near at hand when all wrongs would be righted and all enemies made prostrate under the triumphant feet of the Saviour and his victorious Saints.[21]

Although the philosophy of Saint Augustine effectively suppressed millennialism in the Roman Catholic Church—which from then on merely carried along the idea as so much excess baggage—the apocalyptic tradition "persisted in the obscure underworld of popular religion." [22] It was here that the seeds of millennialism could be effectively nurtured until they bore fruit in the Protestant Reformation, much to the distress of John Calvin and Martin Luther, both of whom condemned Anabaptist excesses in the harshest terms. In the orthodox Christian view, the examples of the Anabaptists Jan Matthys and Johann Bockhold could hardly be held up as models for the future. The same was true of the excesses of certain left-wing Protestants in the English Revolution, who, far from being deterred by the fate of their Munster predecessors, attempted to establish the Fifth Monarchy in Oliver Cromwell's England.[23]

Although the New England Puritans recoiled from such "gangrena," the millenarian tradition continued in America in less extreme forms. John Winthrop emphatically believed in the nearness of the Second Coming; and John Davenport anticipated the Mormons by some two hundred years when he declared that "There is another, a *political Kingdom of Christ* to be set up *in the last times*."[24] As Ira V. Brown has pointed out, the "millenarian faith in one form or another was entirely respectable socially and intellectually well into the nineteenth century."[25] The early part of that century was in fact a fruitful period for the promulgation of variegated millennial doctrines. For the Shakers, formally known as the Millennial Church of the United Society of Believers in Christ's Second Appearing, the millennium had already begun with the incarnation of "Mother Ann" Lee as a female Christ. John Humphrey Noyes, leader of the Oneida Perfectionists, could seriously nominate Jesus Christ for the presidency of the United States. The followers of George Rapp at New Harmony believed that the kingdom of God was already at hand. Indeed, chiliasm became a major article of faith in most communitarian sects. Even Robert Owen, though repudiating the transcendent character of the kingdom of God, believed in the possibility of establishing a secular millennium.[26]

When Joseph Smith moved with his family from Vermont to that part of western New York known to historians as the "Burned-over District,"[27] such expectations were very much in the air. Although Smith did not identify the millennialism of his church with that of any other sect, it is not surprising that the belief in the immediacy of the parousia became one of the chief motivating forces of the new religion. In spite of the fact that Smith, in his millenarian ideas, differed significantly from most of his contemporaries, he shared with such millennialists as Alexander Campbell and William Miller —who originally predicted the coming of the Lord for the year 1843—the belief that Christ's coming would *precede* the millennium.

This doctrine of pre-millennialism was interdependent with the logic and the assumptions of the cataclysmic history of evil in the world. According to this eschatology, the millennium could not be ushered in until the wicked had been burned and assigned to a temporary hell, to a kind of purgatory. Thereafter, Christ would personally bind Satan so that the righteous could enjoy a thousand years of peace and happiness under the reign of their Saviour. At the end of this period, Satan would burst his chains temporarily and turn men once again to wickedness. Shortly thereafter, the Lord would consume the entire earth in a general holocaust from which only the righteous would escape by being "caught up" into heaven. After the conflagration, God would summon all men before His bar of Judgment and assign to them their just rewards. To the righteous He would deed a renewed earth as a permanent inheritance, the "celestial glory" or kingdom of heaven, to which all Latter-day Saints aspired. The millennial kingdom, then, itself only prepared the elect for that ultimate kingdom which transcended all others in glory.[28]

Although the kingdom of heaven might surpass the millennial kingdom in grandeur, it was too remote to inspire the immediate hopes of the Saints. These aspirations the Mormons reserved for that kingdom which—in the typical fashion of all chiliasts—they believed to be immediately at hand. This conviction dominated the hopes of the early Saints. And because the followers usually could afford to be more uncritical in their enthusiasm than their leaders, expectations tended to increase as chiliasm worked its way down into the ranks. Martin Harris, one of the three witnesses for the *Book of Mormon*, undoubtedly catering to the rank and file, predicted in 1831 that the faithful would see Christ in fifteen years while non-believers would be damned.[29]

The urgency and literal-mindedness of the millennial hope, as expressed among many ordinary Mormons, is illustrated by the account of a Saint's purported dream in the *Millennial Star*. The enthusiastic believer had been transported to the year 1945. The millennium had long since arrived, as attested to by some archaeological relics, dug up at the former site of the city of New York, during the excavations for the temple in the 124th city of Joseph.[30] A guide, conducting the Saint on a tour of the city of Zion, pointed out dwellings that had "The appearance of 'precious stones,'" and streets that "glittered like gold." At noon, more than three hundred thousand Saints assembled for lunch in the "grove of Zion," with Jesus Christ sitting at the head of the table:

> After the feast . . . we stepped into the News Room, and the first article in the Pure News, which attracted our attention, was, the Minutes of the General Conference, held in Zion, on the 14th day of the first month, A.D., 1945, when it was motioned by Joseph Smith and seconded by John the Revelator, "That forty-eight new cities be laid out and builded, this year, in accordance with the prophets which have said, 'who can number Israel? who can count the dust of Jacob? Let him fill the earth with cities.'" Carried unanimously. . . . The paper contained a notice for the half yearly conference, as follows: "The general half yearly conference will be held at Jerusalem on the 14th day of the seventh month, alternately with the yearly conference in Zion. It is proposed that the high way cast up between the two cities of our God, be decorated with fruit and shade trees between the cities and villages, which are only eighty furlongs apart, for the accommodation of wayfaring men of Israel. Gabriel has brought from paradise some seeds of fruit and grain which were originally in the Garden of Eden, and will greatly add to the comfort and convenience of man. . . ."
>
> Many things which we saw are not lawful to utter and can only be known as we learned them, by the assistance of the guardian angel.[31]

Such accounts hardly qualified as church doctrine, yet many of the early Saints took them quite seriously.

Although Joseph Smith refrained from such fanciful speculations, he should not have been too surprised that his followers showed less restraint. For many of his revelations predicted the nearness of the day of the Lord.[32] A close reading of these prophecies indicates, however, that the Saints may not have observed the pronouncements of their own prophet very acutely. Smith usually avoided pinpointing a time for the return of Christ. As early as 1831 he had dampened the millennial enthusiasm of Martin Harris and others by revealing that if the signs of the times were "nigh at hand," it was "speaking after the manner of the Lord." [33] Because a day, in the Lord's reckoning, was like a thousand years on earth, this scripture gave the Saints little comfort. As a result, they tended to ignore it and clutched to some of the less equivocal though unofficial opinions of the prophet not included in the Mormon canon. In an unguarded moment he had once declared that "there are those of the rising generation who shall not taste death till Christ comes." [34] And in 1835 he predicted to a group of Mormon elders that "fifty-six years should wind up the scene." [35] With this statement, the prophet had moved perilously close to appointing a time. But later on he reneged.[36] At any rate he felt perfectly safe in refuting William Miller's revised prediction that the Second Coming would occur on October 22, 1844: "I prophesy, in the name of the Lord, that Christ will not come in forty years; and if God ever spoke by my mouth, He will not come in that length of time." [37]

Smith had received this negative assurance in 1842. While "praying very earnestly to know the time of the coming of the Son of Man," he heard a voice repeat the following: "Joseph, my son, if thou livest until thou art eighty-five years old, thou shalt see the face of the Son of Man; therefore let this suffice, and trouble me no more on this matter." He felt that about the only conclusion he could draw from a statement as equivocal as this was that "the coming of the Son of Man will not be any sooner than that time." [38] Since the prophet was born in 1805, he believed that the parousia would not occur before 1890. Thus, when another watcher for the millennium, Cyrus Redding, reported seeing the sign of the Son of Man, in 1843, the founder of Mormonism declared that "notwithstanding Mr. Redding may have seen a wonderful appearance in the clouds one morning about sunrise (which is nothing very uncommon in the winter season), he had not seen the sign of the Son of Man, as foretold by Jesus. . . . Therefore hear this, O earth: The Lord will not come to reign over the righteous, in this world, in 1843, nor until everything for the Bridegroom is ready." [39]

Such caution prevented the Mormons from rushing headlong into the disastrous enthusiasm of such groups as the Millerites. It also caused considerable preoccupation among them with attempts to determine just when everything would be ready for the Bridegroom. Yet the Saints had not been cast upon a sea of entire uncertainty. The signs of the times, like beacons, would guide them through the dark and troubled waters until the light of Christ would reappear. To the Gentiles these beacons were to be warning lights if not the fires of judgment. For the signs included calamities of nature, railroad accidents, fires, steamboat explosions, wars, revolutions, and signs in the heavens. Because there was never any difficulty in finding such catastrophes in abundance, the *Millennial Star* faithfully recorded them in each issue under a special section headed "Signs of the Times." So did Smith in his personal history. Every calamity in the world was looked upon as a signpost of and contribution to the end of the world. "One and all," observed T. B. H. Stenhouse, "are, to the Saint, so many cheering confirmations of his faith, and intimations of the triumphant recognitions of . . . [the] 'Kingdom.' " [40]

War was to play a special role in the ushering in of the millennium. For Christ would not be a ruler over the wicked; likewise, all nations and their governments would have to be destroyed because it was unlikely that they would acknowledge an abridgment of their sovereignty and give homage to "Him whose right it is to reign." [41] This destruction of both men and nations was conditional; but even the most sanguine optimist among the Saints did not expect a large-scale conversion of the world to Mormonism, a feat which alone could have saved mankind. As it was, the Sword of Laban, which Joseph Smith and Oliver Cowdery purportedly had seen unsheathed in the Hill Cumorah as a symbol for the impending destruction, was "never to be sheathed again until the kingdoms of this world [had] become the kingdom of our Lord and His Christ." [42]

Divine judgments alone, however, could not bring about this final consummation. The cleansing fires of the Lord could rid the world of corruption, but the planting for a millennial harvest required new seed. Christ would not return unless a chosen people had prepared itself to receive Him. If the Lord's word was to go forth from Jerusalem, and the law from Zion, the foundations for the spiritual and the political world capitals would have to be laid. Not until the Jews had returned to their ancient homeland, and not until a modern Israel in North America had created a viable nation from which the law could "go forth," would the eyes of the faithful behold the glory of the coming of the Lord.[43]

These were positive signs and thus, in the long run, fraught with even more portent than the judgments of God. Most important, these were signs the Saints had to bring about themselves. Joseph Smith taught his followers that, although the Second Coming was an act of divine intervention, Christ would not return until the Saints had established moral, social, and political conditions congenial with the presence of a divine ruler on earth. Jedediah Grant tersely summed up the attitude of most Mormons: "If you want a heaven, go and make it." [44]

Mormon millennialism, therefore, differed significantly from most antecedent and contemporary forms, even from its own earliest chiliastic enthusiasm. It might even be the case that the Mormons, by assigning to man the primary responsibility for creating the millennium, interjected into this optimistic doctrine an insurance clause against a remote possibility that the Lord, perhaps, might fail to reappear. The concept of the political kingdom of God, regardless of its utopian character, suggests that Mormonism, by the early 1840's, had already undergone a shift toward what might be termed religious realism. From a psychological perspective, it was more prudent to doubt that the millennium, irrespective of human agency, would be ushered in miraculously.[45] It was no accident that Smith failed to set a time for Christ's return. Calendar watchers, inevitably, repaired to caves or mountains, only to be sorely disappointed when the miracle failed to occur. "The Mormons appointed a place" instead.[46]

As a result of this attitude the Saints were spared the intensity of the disappointments that led to the disintegration of those movements awaiting the Bridegroom in ascension robes. Mormonism, even in its radical phase of millennial enthusiasm, contained enough elements of stability to enable it, in the words of Richard Niebuhr, "to survive and to form a really distinctive and important religious denomination." [47] Yet it was also true that a certain degree of disillusion was inherent in the very nature of millennialism.[48] The Saints, therefore, did not escape an inevitable psychological letdown. Many of Smith's followers, especially in the early years, fervently hoped for a miraculous, catastrophic transformation of the world. A man as close to the prophet as Patriarch Benjamin F. Johnson, an original member of the Council of Fifty, revealed his disappointment by recalling in 1903: "We were over seventy years ago taught by our leaders to believe that the coming of Christ and the millennial reign was much nearer than we believe it to be now." [49]

By the early twentieth century, however, church leaders had worked out an effective rationalization to explain Christ's failure to appear. They asserted that the Saints had simply lacked a proper perspective of the historical process through which the kingdom was to be realized. This allegation could either have meant that the early Saints had not worked hard enough to push history along or that in spite of strenuous efforts much more work had to be accomplished before the Saviour would appear. Obviously, most Mormons favored the second interpretation. As early as 1850, Orson Pratt had suggested that the stupendous tasks of raising a nation, building cities, erecting temples, and "great feats" required the Saints to perform two days' work in one. "You can do it," he had admonished the faithful, perhaps failing to realize that he was asking for nothing less than miracles.[50]

Yet Pratt was consistent. Miracles, in Mormon theology, were nothing more than natural laws not yet discovered by man. Even the laws of God could not contradict those of Newtonian physics because God could not contradict Himself. The Mormon God was subject to natural law; more than this, He was subject to a process of cosmic evolution from which no part of the universe was exempt. Every Saint, therefore, might aspire to godhood: "As man is God once was: as God is man may become," became a favored maxim of Mormons.[51] To a later generation of Latter-day Saints, Joseph Smith had clearly anticipated Charles Darwin.[52]

Such an exegesis was of course a gross misinterpretation of both Mormonism and Darwinism. Still, Mormonism was in many ways very much in the mainstream of Western thought, as illustrated by its melioristic doctrine of eternal progression. The secular progressives had exchanged the idea of salvation for the idea of progress. Mormonism did not go this far. It was both secular *and* salvationist. But salvation was part of an evolutionary process that involved not only prayer but also hard work and study. Joseph Smith insisted that man could be saved no faster than he gained knowledge. It is understandable that revivalists could find little in Mormonism to recommend it.[53]

Ralph Waldo Emerson had called Mormonism an "afterclap" of Puritanism, and in a sense he was right. The Saints had little in common with Free Will Baptists, Methodists, Presbyterians, or the followers of Alexander Campbell. Rather, they reflected in their theology certain religious ideas which had found expression by such seventeenth-century divines as Joseph Mede, Henry More, and Thomas Burnet. These optimistic millennialists harnessed the Second Coming to the idea of progress, and they believed that the transformation of the world into a utopia would be brought about by natural laws, with the result that even Cotton and Increase Mather thought not only of burning witches but also of beginning a program for inoculation against smallpox.[54] This was the tradition impelling Timothy Dwight of Yale who, while enjoying a strong interest in natural science, could yet insist as late as 1813 that "the Millennium, in the full and perfect sense, will begin at a period, not far from the year 2000," because it would be established gradually, through man's own efforts. To Dwight as to Joseph Smith the utopian society would be realized "not by miracles, but by means." [55]

The political kingdom of God as envisioned by Joseph Smith and Brigham Young was one of the strongest expressions of this progressive meliorism in Mormon history. As indicated, church leaders believed that earthly governments would not vanish overnight and be replaced immediately by the government of God. They believed that there would be an intermediate period when the political kingdom of God and the other governments of the earth would exist side by side. The leaders thought Christ would not return and destroy the nations of the earth until the kingdom of God had become a prosperous nation.

The role of the kingdom of God in the framework of a progressive philosophy of history caused considerable intellectual difficulties for the kingdom and the Saints. Although Mormons believed that the kingdom could not be built without exerting all the efforts of which they were capable, they also knew that it would never be accomplished until the Lord lent His hand. Believing that God inspired the history of man, they had assurance that such aid was forthcoming. But it had to come through natural means. The will of the Lord, then, had to be read in the processes of history. Here were revealed signs of the times more significant than steamboat explosions and hurricanes.

Discerning the will of God in history, however, was like walking a tightrope, even for a prophet; for prophets, like their followers, were too prone at times to read the future into the present. The Saints, moreover, soon learned that the will of God could not be influenced. Yet they also knew that the Lord's hand would not move unassisted. Guiding the kingdom of God through history, therefore, proved a difficult task for its leaders. At the beginning of the Civil War, for instance, the Saints were sure that the political kingdom of God was about to become independent of the United States. But by 1864, it was all too obvious that they had misread the signs. God's purposes clearly had not coincided with the wishes of the Saints. Thus it had been earlier, and thus it would be later. At one moment the growth of the kingdom of God was expected to be rapid; at another its development was believed to be gradual and difficult.[56] As the years wore on, the Saints grew understandably weary of attempting to usher in the millennial kingdom through their own efforts. They believed repairing to the mountain tops might have its advantages, after all. Therefore, it was not persecution alone that prompted the Saints to postpone to an undetermined future their attempts to establish the political kingdom. In fact, persecution generally heightened the millennial expectations of the Saints. In this respect, they were no different from the Jews and early Christians, who frequently turned to millennialism as an escape from persecution, hoping that the messianic kingdom and its apocalyptic imagery might help solve present difficulties.[57]

As Therald Jensen observed, Mormon millennial expectations moved in cycles. In times of crisis, chiliastic anticipations usually ran high, while periods of political and economic stability witnessed a dampening of these hopes.[58] According to this theory, millennialism among the Mormons should have been on the rise during the late 1880's and early 1890's when the Gentiles, aided by the United States Government, made an all-out effort to finish off once and for all the recalcitrant Mormons. Indeed, at least one Saint regarded the Edmunds Law, which outlawed polygamy, as a harbinger of the end.[59] And in 1890, not a few Mormons, remembering the earlier predictions of Joseph Smith, felt sure that Zion was to be redeemed in 1891. Whereupon the leaders of the church assured their followers that no such event was contemplated for that year. Nobody, as the scriptures had indicated, would know the hour or the day when the Lord would come as a thief in the night. Again, the leaders felt they could be more positive than their overeager followers because too many of the predicted signs had not yet occurred.[60]

One of the most important of these evidences, the establishment of the political kingdom of God, was farther from realization than ever in the last decade of the nineteenth century. In fact, the political kingdom of God was a major cause of Mormon persecution because of its suspected un-American, even anti-American, nature. In 1890, therefore, the Saints could not hope that the kingdom could be realized through natural means in the near future. The chiliasm of 1890 was rather a popular expression of the desire for a miraculous event, for a sudden deliverance of Zion from its enemies. But this kind of millennialism could not serve as a springboard for the establishment of a political kingdom of God. When it became apparent that the enemy was willing to retreat in return for some painful concessions, and that the Lord was not about to destroy the adversaries of the kingdom, hopes for a miraculous delivery receded. The decline of millennialism in Mormon history thus coincided with the decline of the belief in the political kingdom of God. After the Saints had come to terms with the world, they took a more philosophic view of history. To this day, Mormons have held on to the millennial dream, but it has become a calm anticipation which they hope to realize through a kingdom of God that is synonymous with the church; missionary activity and welfare work are the means through which this kingdom is to grow and fill the earth. When Victoria died in 1901, most Latter-day Saints knew considerably more about her kingdom than about the one their prophet Joseph Smith and his successors had struggled so hard to establish in the nineteenth century.

Mormonism and the American Dream

II

CERTAIN NON-MORMONS, curiously enough, seem to have known more about the political ambitions of Joseph Smith and Brigham Young than most faithful Latter-day Saints. Again and again, these Gentiles accused the Mormon leaders of seeking to set up a theocratic imperium within or without the United States. Understandably, such alleged attempts were viewed as being thoroughly un-American. And yet, no American religion professed greater allegiance to the principles of the Constitution than Mormonism. Only through an examination of the political theory of the kingdom of God and its relationship to American democracy will it be possible to understand this seeming paradox.

Mormons take considerable pride in the knowledge that "their movement shares with Christian Science the distinction of being the most striking indigenous major American religion." [1] They are fond of relating a conversation between Andrew Dickson White, during his term as United States minister to the Court of St. Petersburg, and Count Leo Tolstoi on the subject of religion in America. The Count had asked for White's opinion about "the American religion"; whereupon the minister informed his host that in the United States no church enjoyed preferential treatment by the state. Becoming somewhat impatient, Tolstoi replied that of course he knew that America had no state church. Yet, he continued, "the Church to which I refer originated in America and is commonly known as the Mormon Church. . . . The Mormon people teach the American religion." [2]

Tolstoi was neither the first nor the last observer to comment on the peculiarly American nature of Mormonism, and to understand that the characteristics of Mormonism differed significantly from other American religious movements. As Whitney Cross observed, the religious fervor of the Burned-over District, which gave birth to Mormonism, also influenced the perfectionism of a Charles Grandison Finney and a John Humphrey Noyes, and produced a William Miller as well as a host of lesser religious enthusiasts.[3] Although these cults and sects, and especially the more firmly established Methodists, Baptists, and Presbyterians, acquired peculiarly American characteristics in their new environment, the historical and intellectual roots of their religious persuasions had their origins in Europe and its Judaeo-Christian heritage.

Although Joseph Smith did not repudiate this heritage entirely, he attempted to divest it from its form and its historical background. Mormonism was not to be merely another Christian sect. "It was a real religious creation, one intended to be to Christianity as Christianity was to Judaism: a reform and a consummation." [4] The analogy, however, cannot be pushed too far, since Christianity repudiated the ideas of a chosen people and of religious nationalism and substituted for them a catholic world church. Mormonism also claimed to be a world religion, applicable to all mankind, but its mission was to be fulfilled through a peculiar identification with American nationalism. This force, in turn, was to be the catalyst for a specific Mormon nationalism expressed through the ideas of a chosen people and a political kingdom of God that was to rule the world.

As a secular dream, this concept was not, of course, original. The founding fathers had been inspired by the belief that they were creating a new government and acting out a providential pageant in the promised land. As John Adams put it: "I always consider the settlement of America with reverence and wonder, as the opening of a grand scene and design in providence for the illumination of the ignorant and the emancipation of the slavish part of mankind all over the earth." [5] James Madison wrote somewhat ironically of Gouverneur Morris that "he flattered himself he came here in some degree as a Representative of the whole human race." [6] And Thomas Jefferson, writing to Joseph Priestley, affirmed: ". . . we feel that we are acting under obligations not confined to the limits of our own society. It is impossible not to be sensible that we are acting for all mankind." [7] As a secular dream, this "American Idea of Mission" has always persisted in national values.[8]

This secular notion, moreover, was subject to significant theological influences. As Sherwood Eddy observed, "the religious ideal of the Kingdom of God was causally related to the American Dream." [9] The Protestant churches took up the battle cry, and few institutions in American life have been able to equal them as vehicles of nationalism. Mormonism, understandably, shared in this enthusiasm. More than this, it provided a religious foundation for the American idea of mission going far beyond the religious nationalism of most Protestant churches. The nationalism of Protestantism always remained the handmaiden of a secular American faith. Joseph Smith reversed this relationship by repudiating the historical forms of the Judaeo-Christian heritage, and by substituting for them a framework that provided both Christianity and American history in general with pre-Columbian native roots. Smith, in a sense, produced America's religious declaration of independence. As A. Leland Jamison observed, Mormonism was "at once an irreconcilable Christian heresy and the most typically American theology yet formulated on this continent." [10]

The repudiation of old world religious origins was already foreshadowed when Smith, as a boy of fourteen, had his first vision in a small grove behind his father's farm. Following the advice of Jas. 1:5, he had retired there to find out whether he should join the Methodists, Baptists, or Presbyterians.[11] No one was more startled than Smith himself when God the Father and Jesus Christ purportedly appeared to him, informing him that he "must join none of them, for they were all wrong; and the Personage who addressed me said that all their creeds were an abomination in his sight; that those professors were all corrupt." [12]

Smith had this vision in the year 1820. Yet the Lord made him wait ten years for permission to restore the Gospel of Jesus Christ in unadulterated form. This restoration signified a complete break with the traditions of European Christianity. Most Protestant churches had of course broken the apostolic succession, but they also affirmed that the Bible contained the sole and complete record of the Word of God, serving as an authoritative guide after which Christians could pattern their lives and as a source of inspiration to those who believed in the priesthood of all believers. European Protestantism in its transplanted American form thus was paradoxical. Its break with the past, though inherently radical, lacked consistency. In the absence of a central authority and the tradition of an apostolic succession, churches and sects proliferated, each claiming to be the only one interpreting the Bible correctly. Biblical exegesis, however, was itself part of the historical development of Protestantism. The reformers, insisted Smith, would never be able to arrive at the original intentions of Christ through the Bible alone, especially since it had been adulterated through faulty translations.[13] The "great and abominable church, which is the mother of abominations, whose foundation is the devil" had corrupted the tree of

Christianity; [14] the sects and churches of the reformers were branches of this tree. How, implied Smith, could the branches succeed in restoring the trunk to its former vigor? He believed it impossible. A new tree had to be planted, uncontaminated by the "great and abominable church." The true Gospel could be restored only by the transmission of the apostolic authority through heavenly messengers commissioned by Jesus Christ. It was in this manner, Smith affirmed, that he received divine sanction to organize the "Church of Christ" in 1830.[15]

The primary requirements for the restoration of the Gospel were thus fulfilled. A church without a past, however, was like a tree without roots. Since faulty translation had impaired the authenticity of the Bible, a new scripture was required to provide historical authority for the Word of God.[16] The *Book of Mormon* filled this gap. Having sprung from native American soil, where Smith claimed it had rested for about fourteen hundred years, uncontaminated by human hands, it provided American Christianity with a scripture presumably superior to that of the old world.

Theologically, the *Book of Mormon* claimed to be a new witness for Christ in America. The central story of the book revolves around Lehi, a Hebrew prophet living in Jerusalem around 600 B.C., who was warned by the Lord to flee with his family in order to escape the impending Babylonian captivity of the Jews. God's hand guided the refugees across desert and ocean to a promised land, America. Here Lehi's descendants became a mighty people, building cities and cultivating the soil. As true Israelites, they adhered to the prophetic tradition of their forefathers, which included belief in the coming of a Messiah. After his death and resurrection in Palestine, Christ appeared to the inhabitants of the New World, preached and performed miracles, and laid the foundation of a church, just as he had done in Palestine. Before his departure he ordained twelve disciples who were to preach the Gospel to their fellow Americans. This church flourished for several centuries until a fratricidal war destroyed it along with an advanced civilization after the people had departed from its Christian precepts. Only a degenerate race which had refused to accept the Gospel survived; these were the ancestors of the modern Indians. The civilized half of the Israelitic descendants had kept records of metal; before the final destruction of this group, one of the last survivors buried these records in a hill, where they were found by Joseph Smith through guidance by a heavenly messenger in 1823. Here, Joseph Smith taught, was further proof of the divinity of Christ; but here, also, was a more perfect account of Christ's ministry, unspoiled by human corruption.

Viewed superficially, the *Book of Mormon* is an obvious and, for some historians, not a very original attempt to explain the origin of the American Indians. That the *Book of Mormon* assigned the ancestors of the American Indians to the Near East and claimed they were descendants of the House of Israel was very much in keeping with ideas prevalent in Smith's time.[17] But unlike previous attempts to explain the origin of the Indians, Smith's account was merely incidental to a more fundamental concept. For if the Indians were the descendants of a civilized race, American history could equal in tradition that of the Old World. German historian Peter Meinhold sees in the *Book of Mormon* the expression of an American quest for a usable past which represents a native American historical consciousness unrivalled to this degree and intensity in the entire range of American historical thought.[18]

Smith continued the historical logic of the *Book of Mormon* through a revelation in the *Doctrine and Covenants,* which explained that these Israelite ancestors of the native Americans were themselves only transplanted Americans. For the Garden of Eden had been in the New World. After Adam was cast out of Paradise, he had dwelt in the land of Adam-ondi-Ahman, located in the Mississippi Valley, in Daviess County, Missouri. The presence of the patriarchal Old Testament cultures in the Near East found a very simple explanation in the Flood; that is, Noah had drifted on the water for many days and obviously he would not land at the same spot where he had embarked. Thus, the *Doctrine and Covenants* assigned the entire antediluvian history of the Old Testament to the New World. The term "New World" was a misnomer because America was really the cradle of man and of civilization. The historical vision of Joseph Smith thus made it possible to conjure from the bones of an American Adam and his pre-Columbian descendants an image of America that could motivate those who believed in this past to recreate the Garden of Eden in its original setting. It was no accident that the Mormons dreamed of building the New Jerusalem in the vicinity of the location where Adam presumably had dwelt after his expulsion from the Garden of Eden, in Jackson County, Missouri.[19] To the Mormons, the search for a usable past was thus inseparably connected to the quest for an American paradise to be established in the future.[20] The organization of the political kingdom of God was an integral part of this quest.

This kingdom was to be the true expression of an American political heritage which, like its religious heritage, no longer had to look for European precedents after the establishment of Mormonism. From its very beginning, taught the *Book of Mormon*, America was destined to be a land of freedom. The first immigrants to the New World were told that God was sending them to "a land of promise, which was choice above all other lands, which the Lord God had preserved for a righteous people . . . and whatsoever nation shall possess it, shall be so free from bondage, and from captivity, and from all other nations under heaven, if they will but serve the God of the land, who is Jesus Christ." [21] Because the Nephites, as the major group of Lehi's descendants are called in the *Book of Mormon*, failed to obey this injunction, they were destroyed. Thus, destruction would be the fate of all who turned from the true religion and who would pervert the ancient American ideals of political freedom.[22]

The American continent was to be the stage for the restoration of the Gospel of Jesus Christ and of the ancient liberties of mankind in the latter days. Hence God had purposely hidden the knowledge of its existence from the rest of the world until the time had ripened for the fulfillment of His purposes. When that time came, God's spirit sent Columbus to the promised land to open it to a new race of free men: "This land shall be a land of liberty unto the Gentiles, and there shall be no kings upon the land . . . For it is wisdom in the Father that they should be established in this land and be set up as a free people by the power of the Father." [23] Thus, the American Revolution was part of a plan decreed by God to achieve the freedom of the New World, a freedom to be preserved through a constitution drafted by divinely inspired men specifically "raised up unto this very purpose." [24]

Mormonism was to be the culmination of this grand design. "The United States of America," wrote Parley P. Pratt, "was the favoured nation raised up, with institutions adapted to the protection and free development of the necessary truths, and their practical results. And that Great Prophet, Apostle and Martyr—JOSEPH SMITH was the Elias, the Restorer, the presiding Messenger, holding the keys of the 'Dispensation of the fulness of times.' " [25] Without the United States, continued Pratt, this consummation would not have been possible. For the "grain of mustard seed," the nucleus of the kingdom of God, needed "a land of free institutions, where such organizations could be legally developed and claim constitutional protection. No other country in the world provided the necessary conditions for the establishment of the Kingdom of God." [26]

The divine origin and destiny of the American Republic was thus one of the most basic Mormon values. It is, therefore, one of the almost tragic ironies of American history when

Protestant ministers, after the Civil War, believed they had received a divine commission not only to "Christianize" but also to "Americanize" the reputedly disloyal Mormons. Why these ministers believed such a mission to be necessary becomes partially intelligible through an examination of the political theory of the Mormon kingdom of God.

One accusation Christian ministers, government officials, and professional and amateur anti-Mormon crusaders repeated again and again, and one that stood at the top of their anti-Mormon syllabus of errors, was that the Mormons had violated the sacred American principle of the separation of church and state. Many accusations the Mormons bore without protest. Others they proudly and defiantly acknowledged. But of all the charges levelled against them they denied none more vehemently than the one that in their society church and state were one. Yet, to the Gentiles, no fact was more openly established. Were not Joseph Smith and Brigham Young spiritual as well as political leaders of their people? Did not most of the members of the hierarchy hold important political offices? Did not the Mormon priesthood, in fact, rule the Saints both spiritually and temporally? To the Gentiles, these facts were too obvious to be denied. The Mormon disavowals thus even lacked the grace of elegant lies. If black was to appear as white, the Gentiles hinted, the Mormons had to use more clever tactics.

Yet the Saints honestly believed that they were being truthful. "No people," thundered George Q. Cannon at a general conference of the church, "are less open to the charge of mingling the two and seeking to destroy the distinctions between church and state than the Latter-day Saints; any attempt on the part of any one to say that we have any such design, is the attack of an enemy and is untrue." [27] To the Gentiles, such denials were merely a proof of Mormon hypocrisy.

Cannon preferred to accept the charge of hypocrisy rather than to prove to his adversaries the truthfulness of his position. He could point to the Mormon scriptures and show that the *Doctrine and Covenants* prohibited an established church.[28] He could further point to the Mormon reverence for the Constitution of the United States. But, to the Gentiles, neither of these examples was proof. It was primarily because opponents of the Mormons in Congress believed that Cannon, as territorial delegate, came to Washington not only as an elected representative but also as the emissary of the Mormon priesthood that he was denied his seat in the House in 1882. His polygamy merely provided a better pretext to oust him. In defense of his right to his seat, Cannon had insisted that he represented no church, but served in Washington strictly as the legally qualified political representative of Utah Territory.[29] But his protest was of no avail.

Part of the difficulty was that he could not be as open with Congress as he was with his own people. To the Saints, he tried to explain as much as possible about the Mormon theory of separation of church and state without revealing secrets which he had sworn to keep when he became a member of the Council of Fifty. For only in the sessions of this council did the church leaders amplify on important ramifications relating to the Mormon theory of separation of church and state. The fact is that to Congress and the Gentiles in general the practical application of the Mormon theory of the separation of church and state would no doubt have been even more distressing than the supposed union of the two. For the Mormon idea of the separation of church and state could be put into operation only through the realization of the political kingdom of God. Therefore, the Mormon leaders preferred that the Gentiles believe in distorted and even totally erroneous interpretations of Mormon doctrine if correction of the error would result in revealing the secrets of the political kingdom of God and the Council of Fifty. That organization had to remain secret at all costs,[30] for the suspected activities of the Council were the major cause of conflict between Saints and Gentiles.

Church leaders, nevertheless, occasionally hinted strongly at the existence of the political kingdom in order to clarify important points to their followers. The theory of the separation of church and state was one of them. Cannon amplified on this doctrine in a sermon to the Saints:

> We have been taught from the beginning this important principle, that the Church of God is distinct from the Kingdom of God. Joseph gave us the pattern before he died. He gave his brethren an example that has not been forgotten to this day. He impressed it upon them, that men, not members of the church, could be members of the kingdom that the Lord will set up when he reigns. He picked out the youngest among them, and told them to be sure and remember this. In the midst of all of us who understand this matter there is a clear distinction between the church in its ecclesiastical capacity and that which may be termed the government of God in its political capacity.[31]

Gentiles, understandably, would have been reluctant to become members of such a kingdom. But their theoretical inclusion was indispensable to Mormonism in order to uphold the idea of separation of church and state. More than that, if the idea were to be followed to its logical conclusion, the Gentiles would even have the right to sit in the governing council of the political kingdom. "Though a man may not even believe in any religion," insisted Brigham Young, "it would be perfectly right, when necessary, to give him the privilege of holding a seat among that body which will make laws to govern all the nations of the earth and control those who make no profession of religion at all." [32]

Therefore, Mormons reasoned that, if the congressional representative from Utah Territory also happened to be a Latter-day Saint, this fact was nothing more than a highly probable coincidence since the majority of the inhabitants of the territory were Mormons. Separation of church and state, the Saints insisted, did not imply that "religious people should not soil their hands in political affairs." Such a policy would ultimately leave the control of civil government to irreligious men.[33] Still, in a state controlled by one church, union of church and state would be almost an inevitable result. The political theory of the kingdom of God, therefore, was nothing less than a heroic attempt to reconcile kingdom building with the American political tradition.

The attempt was not entirely successful. A theoretical separation of the political kingdom and the church was one thing, its practical application quite another. The members of the Council of Fifty could insist with vehemence that the combination of ecclesiastical and political office in the hands of one man did not represent union of church and state, but they would not have convinced the Gentiles, especially if the latter had known the whole truth. The fact remained that the Mormon hierarchy also held most of the important political offices from the early days of the church in Kirtland and Missouri, until the abdication of political control around the turn of the century.

That the idea of separation of church and state was more of a semantic distinction than even its originators probably wished it to be is revealed through the role both the church and the Mormon priesthood were to play in establishing the political kingdom of God. For if the church were separate and distinct from the political kingdom, the former was, nevertheless, the precursor of the latter. According to Brigham Young, the political kingdom was to grow "out of the Church of Jesus Christ of Latter-day Saints."[34] John Taylor, elaborating on this idea, insisted that "before there could be a kingdom of God, there must be a church of God," because it would be impossible to introduce "the law of God among a people who would not be subject to and be guided by the spirit of revelation."[35] The political programs of the various utopian societies would utimately fail because they lacked the guidance of the Spirit of God.

The government of the kingdom of God, fortunately, was to be spared this fate because it was subject to the jurisdiction of the priesthood. If Parley P. Pratt is to be believed, the powers of the Mormon priesthood were indeed vast. It held "the right to give laws and commandments to individuals, churches, rulers, nations and the world; to appoint, ordain and establish constitutions and kingdoms: to appoint kings, presidents, governors or judges." [36]

Pratt's brother Orson, whose influence on Mormon theology was to be even more pervading and lasting, developed this idea into a theory of legitimacy that was not to sit very well with the Gentiles:

> The kingdom of God . . . is the only legal government that can exist in any part of the universe. All other governments are illegal and unauthorized. God, having made all beings and worlds, has the supreme right to govern them by his own laws, and by officers of his own appointment. Any people attempting to govern themselves by laws of their own making, and by officers of their own appointment, are in direct rebellion against the kingdom of God. [37]

Church and kingdom thus had come full circle. For the most part, they were separate in theory only. Ultimately, no distinction could be drawn between the two. The priesthood that controlled the church also controlled the state. Parley P. Pratt even went so far as to insist that "any system of religion should include every branch of government that [a people] could possibly need for dwelling with each other." The fact that the religions of the world insisted upon a distinction between themselves and the "policy of civil government" was an indication not only of their ineffectiveness but also of their lack of divinity. [38] A true religious system also provided for a political government. Pratt continued:

> When I say a religious system, I mean that which unites principles of political government and religious. . . . Whether men realize it or not, when they say "Thy Kingdom come, thy will be done in earth as it is in heaven," it is as much to say "O God, sweep away all the falsehood and abuses of power

there are in the world, whether religious or political; . . . And
in the place of all these false governments and religions, in
political and social life, introduce that eternal government, that
pure order of things, those eternal principles and institutions,
which govern society in those better worlds, the worlds of im-
mortality and eternal life." [39]

If lacking the Mormon priesthood, a Gentile member of the
governing council of the political kingdom would have found
himself in an extremely tenuous position under such a system,
however tolerantly the priest-legislators might have exercised
their authority.

Still, in theory, the political kingdom of God was to be a
pluralistic society that granted wide latitude to the individual
differences of its prospective members. Such a latitude was
only possible if the kingdom and the church were separate organizations. In no other way could the political kingdom of
God have become the vehicle for a distinctive Mormon interpretation of the relationship between natural law and individual rights.

This interpretation was the response of a suppressed
minority against majority rule. The rule of the majority was
based on a natural rights philosophy wedded to the idea of
natural law. The Mormons believed with Alexis de Tocqueville that this concept of natural rights frequently and para-
doxically led to the denial of these rights to a minority
group.[40]

The Mormons could talk from first-hand experience about
the tyranny of the majority. As a result, they looked with considerable distaste on the idea of natural rights and its natural
offspring, majority rule. They substituted for it a doctrine of
individual rights that was also ultimately grounded in natural
law, but with the important qualifications that under its
provisions the individual did not have to bow to the will of
the majority.[41] This idea was analogous to Calhoun's doctrine
of concurrent majority, although the Mormons did not cite
him as an authority.

Through the individual rights philosophy of the political kingdom of God, the Saints hoped to show their intolerant fellow Americans how they expected to be treated by indicating how they themselves would act toward minority groups. According to Brigham Young, the political kingdom of God was

> . . . to send forth those laws and ordinances that shall be suitable and that shall apply themselves to the Church of Jesus Christ of Latter-day Saints; that will apply themselves to the mother Church, "the holy Catholic Church"; they will commend themselves to every class of infidels, and will throw their protecting arms around the whole human family, protecting them in their rights. If they wish to worship a white dog, they will have the privilege; if they wish to worship a man they will have the privilege, and if they wish to worship the "unknown God" they will have the privilege; This kingdom will circumscribe them all and will issue laws and ordinances to protect them in their rights—every right that every people, sect and person can enjoy, and the full liberty that God has granted to them without molestation . . . the kingdom of God will protect every person, every sect and all people upon the face of the whole earth in their legal rights.[42]

Young, no doubt, here was engaging in overly optimistic rhetoric. It seems doubtful that the Gentiles would have been eager to have their rights protected by such a kingdom. Furthermore, the harsh realities of life made the application of such theories difficult even by the Saints themselves. When Gladden Bishop, who had started a rival Mormon sect, brought some of his followers to Salt Lake City in an attempt to proselytize for his version of the kingdom of God, Young seems to have ignored his theories temporarily, as attested to by the rapid departure of the Gladdenites from the Territory.[43]

The doctrine of individual rights reinforced the Mormons in their rejection of the idea of majority rule and of its underlying assumption, the sovereignty of the people. More fundamentally, the idea of popular sovereignty and majority rule was incompatible with the notion of priesthood government. By its very definition, the priesthood obtained its authority from God, and not from the people. The priesthood, therefore, had a divine right to rule. As a result, the Mormons believed it to be "the best legislative body there is upon the face of the earth." [44] It followed that Mormon leaders, like their Puritan predecessors, had little faith in the ability of the people to govern themselves. Joseph Smith once declared that "all, all speak with a voice of thunder, that man is not able to govern himself, to legislate for himself, to protect himself, to promote his own good, nor the good of the world." [45] John Taylor's reservations about popular sovereignty were even more pointed: "We talk sometimes about *vox populi, vox Dei* . . . the voice of the people is the voice of God; yet sometimes it is the voice of the Devil, which would be more proper by *vox populi, vox Diaboli;* for the voice of the people is frequently the voice of the Devil." [46]

But Taylor was apparently carried away by his rhetoric. The *Book of Mormon,* discussing the matter with more restraint, reflects more accurately the position of the Mormon hierarchy. When the sons of King Mosiah refused the kingship, the aged ruler thought it wise to establish a republic in spite of his belief that "it would be expedient that [the people] should always have kings to rule over them" if they governed justly and in accordance with the will of God. But, unfortunately, kings frequently ruled according to their whims. A republic, therefore, would be more desirable because the majority of the people usually desired that which is right. If ever the time should come "that the voice of the people doth choose iniquity," then the "judgments of God" would be poured out among the people.[47]

Although the people, however, had a right to choose under the political theory of the kingdom of God, they did not have a right to direct government. Parley P. Pratt made this quite clear when he observed that the voice of the people "is rather a sanction, a strength and support to that which God chooses. But they do not confer the authority in the first place, nor can they take it away." [48] The practical results of such a philosophy, to the Gentiles at any rate, seemed singularly un-American. When William H. Hooper, for example, "campaigned" for the seat of territorial delegate to Congress in 1865, apostle George A. Smith, who accompanied the aspirant on his election campaign, informed the Saints of Mount Pleasant: "What we do we should do as one man. Our system should be Theo-Democracy—the voice of the people consenting to the voice of God." [49] Needless to say, Hooper was "elected." So were all political candidates nominated by the hierarchy as long as the church controlled politics. For over fifty years, Mormon elections were hardly anything more than a "sustaining" of the official candidates. If, however, on rare occasions the people might actually nominate a candidate not approved of by the hierarchy, "counsel" by the leaders usually sufficed to bring about the desired results.[50]

Such a system, the Mormons believed, made political parties both unnecessary and undesirable. Brigham Young was thus only consistent by claiming that "when political opposition is permitted, we admit the existence of error and corruption somewhere." [51] If a man, therefore, opposed the official church candidate, he was questioning the divine sanction under which this candidate had been nominated. Such a man was clearly on the road to apostasy.[52] The world, too, would be better off without political parties. They contained the "seeds" of the destruction of the [United States] government. Young concluded that "every government lays the foundation of its own downfall when it permits what are called democratic elections." [53] Since there is one absolute truth, and only one source for this truth, editorialized the *Deseret News*, the "people only disagree where they have not sufficient knowledge of the subject under consideration, or through wickedness, which is itself the offspring of ignorance." [54] Yet the

Saints were neither ignorant nor wicked, as attested to by a description of Mormon theo-democracy in the *Millennial Star:*

> At mass meetings, held in all the principal precincts, delegates are chosen by unanimous vote to meet in a convention, and select the names of individuals to fill the various vacant offices. In case of any dispute or dubiety on the mind of the convention, the Prophet of God, who stands at the head of the Church, decides. He nominates, the convention endorses, and the people accept the nomination. . . . So in the Legislature itself. The utmost freedom of speech free from abuse is indulged in; but any measure that cannot be unanimously decided on, is submitted to the President of the Church, who, by the wisdom of God decides the matter, and all the Councillors and Legislators sanction the decision. There are no hostile parties, no opposition, no Whig and Tory, Democrat and Republican, they are all brethren, legislating for the common good, and the word of the Lord, through the head of the Church, guides, counsels, and directs.[55]

To the Gentiles, such theories and practices were, if not proofs of disloyalty, an indication that the Mormons had departed significantly from the American political tradition. These accusations the Saints vehemently denied. In fact, the leaders of the political kingdom of God professed to believe that their political system came closer to the original intention of the founding fathers than the political system of the United States under men like Martin Van Buren. The latter, particularly, by failing to come to the aid of persecuted minorities, had made a mockery of the American dream.[56]

The Mormons thus attempted to reconcile their divergence from the generally accepted standards of American democracy by looking to a mythical past and pointing to an idealized future. The Saints saw themselves as a bulwark against the present perversion of the American values by corrupt politicians. They felt the time would come when the political kingdom of God would be the only power left in America capable of preserving the ideals of liberty. They also thought the time would come when the Constitution, "hanging by a thread," would be preserved by the elders of the church.[57] What the Saints failed to realize was that even if they had been able to discern the purposes of the founding fathers, events had made many of these purposes irrelevant by the 1830's.

The Saints, therefore, were not overly bothered by the apparent discrepancy between the political kingdom of God and the realities of American political institutions, at least not as far as this discrepancy might adversely reflect on the Americanism of the Mormons. Brigham Young insisted that under ideal conditions the government of the political kingdom of God closely resembled the government of the United States. He declared:

> But few, if any understand what a theocratic government is. In every sense of the word, it is a republican government, and differs but little in form from our National, State and Territorial Governments: . . .
>
> The Constitution and laws of the United States resemble a theocracy more closely than any government now on earth. . . . Even now the form of Government of the United States differs but little from the Kingdom of God.[58]

The main difference between the two, according to Young, was that the subjects of the kingdom of God recognized *"the will and dictation of the Almighty."* [59] But Young failed to perceive that this precisely was the most important difference between the two. The crux of the matter was that the ideas of divine sovereignty and popular sovereignty were mutually exclusive. The Saints were thus divided between the absolute claims of revealed religion and a social and political heritage which revelation had declared to be divinely inspired. This was a paradox that seemed insolvable. The Mormons thus had to temporize and claim that the paradox did not exist; by surrounding themselves with the trappings of democratic government, they could pretend that in fact they were carrying out the true intentions of the founding fathers.

The solution of the dilemma lay in the melioristic, evolutionary view of history adopted by the Mormons. Brigham Young made this clear in a discourse delivered to the Saints in 1860:

> The signers of the Declaration of Independence and the framers of the Constitution were inspired from on high to do that work. But was that which was given them perfect, not admitting of any addition whatever? No; for if men know anything, they must know that the Almighty has never yet found a man in mortality that was capable, at the first intimation, at the first impulse, to receive anything in a state of entire perfection. They laid the foundation, and it was for after generations to rear the superstructure upon it.[60]

But the superstructure being reared by Democrats and Whigs was little to Young's liking. The edifice Young had in mind was to be raised by the statesmen of the kingdom of God. Although the Saints considered the Constitution of the United States the best man had ever devised, it was to be but "one of those stepping stones to a future development in the progress of man." [61] After the kingdom of God had achieved "domination over all the earth to the ends thereof," the Constitution and the laws governing this kingdom would "emanate from the throne of God." [62] In fact, the constitution of the political kingdom of God had been revealed to Joseph Smith before he organized the government of God. That it resembled that of the United States closely should not be surprising. In fact, Joseph Smith suggested that the revisions would only be minor.[63] It was no doubt this revised, revealed version the Mormon prophet had in mind when he told his followers that the time would come when all nations would adopt "the God-given Constitution of the United States as a Paladium of Liberty and Equal Rights." [64] Ultimately, therefore, all contradictions between Mormonism and Americanism would disappear, if only the Saints could themselves determine what Americanism meant, and if the Gentiles would adapt themselves to Mormonism.

As long as the majority decided on the values of American democracy, however, the Mormons were a little like the soldier on parade whose proud mother found him to be the only one in step. But who was in step depended entirely on the point of view. More than that, it depended on whose point of view could be enforced. The Saints' point of view contained a final paradox, for their version of the American dream could be enforced only through the destruction of the United States in its present form. "The day will come," exulted Parley P. Pratt, "when the United States government, and all others, will be uprooted, and the kingdoms of this world will be united in one, and the kingdom of our God will govern the whole earth." [65] In the meantime, the Gentiles did their best to uproot the kingdom of God. That they failed to destroy Mormonism in the process was largely due to the fact that the leaders of the kingdom finally bowed to the superior strength of the Gentiles and relegated to an undisclosed future date the aspirations of the government of the kingdom to rule the United States and the world.

The Establishment of the
Government of God

III

IN THE SPRING OF 1844, the future of the kingdom of God looked bright—so bright, indeed, that Joseph Smith, though not without hesitation, embarked upon one of the most momentous ventures of his entire career. On May 12, he declared before an assembly of Saints in Nauvoo: "I calculate to be one of the instruments of setting up the kingdom of Daniel by the word of the Lord, and I intend to lay a foundation that will revolutionize the whole world."[1] It is probable that only a few members of his audience understood the full meaning of his words. Fewer still knew—most likely identifying the foundation of the kingdom of God with the origins of the Mormon church in 1830—that Smith had begun the establishment of a literal, temporal government for the "kingdom of Daniel" two months earlier.

It was, of course, no accident that Smith waited until 1844 before building his nucleus world government. For although the political kingdom of God and the church were to be two separate organizations, one could not proceed without the other. Indeed, some of the ideas behind the "kingdom of Daniel" can be traced to the very beginnings of the Mormon church in 1830. When First Counselor Sidney Rigdon informed the Saints at the general conference of the church in April, 1844, that he did "not know that anything has taken place in the history of this Church which we did not then [1830] believe," he was exaggerating in an obvious attempt to impress the congregation with his own power and importance.[2] Yet much of what he said that day can be verified through an analysis of Smith's character and career. According to Rigdon, the leaders of the church held secret meetings as early as 1830.

> We were maturing plans fourteen years ago which we now can tell. . . . There we sat in secret and beheld the glorious visions and powers of the kingdom of heaven pass and repass. . . . We talked about the people coming as doves to the windows, and that nations should flock unto it; that they should come bending to the standard of Jesus, . . . and of whole nations being born in one day . . . and we began to talk about the kingdom of God as if we had the world at our command.[3]

Whole nations, however, could be born in a day only through the magic of rhetorical enthusiasm. The establishment of the kingdom of God, let alone of Mormon world rule, required more than talk. Even the creation of the modest government of the kingdom of God in 1844 was possible only through years of planning and preparation, trial and error, and much disheartening defeat. Again and again, the prophet had to postpone his dream of setting up the kingdom predicted by Daniel. The establishment of the political kingdom of God in 1844 was the culmination of efforts that had seemed on the verge of realization more than once, only to be dashed to pieces before their consummation.

Fundamental to all these efforts was the idea of Zion and its related concept of the "gathering." As early as 1830 Smith revealed to his followers that he had been "called to bring to pass the gathering of mine elect . . . unto one place upon the face of this land." [4] Land and people were the obvious and primary requirements of an earthly kingdom of God. Mormon missionaries, fanning out to the far corners of the earth, instructed their converts that gathering to Zion was one of the basic tests of orthodoxy. "None of the Saints," admonished Orson Pratt, "can be dilatory upon this subject, and still retain the spirit of God. To neglect or be indifferent about gathering, is just as displeasing in the sight of God as to neglect or be indifferent about baptism for the remission of sins." [5]

It was at Kirtland, Ohio, that Smith first attempted to establish an earthly kingdom of God through gathering the Saints. In the autumn of 1830, a group of Mormon missionaries had converted almost the entire Campbellite congregation of Sidney Rigdon to the new faith. These and other converts rapidly transformed Kirtland into a Mormon settlement, a haven for the Saints in the eastern United States. According to one reporter, "Kirtland presented the appearance of a modern religious Mecca. Like Eastern pilgrims [the Mormons] came full of zeal for their new religion. They came in rude vehicles, on horseback, on foot. They came almost any way, filling on their arrival every house, shop, and barn to the utmost capacity." [6]

The Mormon prophet, however, intended Kirtland only as a temporary gathering place, or at best as a corner stake of the tent of Zion. The Ohio country was too crowded for the establishment of a Mormon empire. The kingdom would have to be set up in a more uninhabited region. Indeed, Smith had taken the first steps in this direction in the summer of 1831, when he designated the town of Independence in Jackson County, Missouri, as the location for the New Jerusalem. Here, in the regions where Adam had presumably dwelt after his expulsion from the Garden of Eden, the Lord, through his mouthpiece Joseph, promised the Saints an eternal inheritance. A first group of Mormon colonists, arriving in the summer of 1831, pooled their resources to buy as much land as possible and began life together under a communitarian system called the United Firm.[7]

The projected center stake of Zion never was fully raised, however, and the inheritance in Jackson County was only of short duration. The events of 1833 doomed the immediate hopes of Smith and his followers. In that year, a Missouri mob damaged Mormon homes and smashed W. W. Phelps's printing press. The elaborate plan of the city of Zion which Joseph Smith had sent to Missouri in June of 1833 had to be realized elsewhere.[8]

When Oliver Cowdery reported news of these Missouri disorders to Smith in Kirtland, the prophet at first counselled the Saints to obtain redress in the courts. The Mormons hired the firm of Wood, Reese, Doniphan, and Atchison to represent their interests.[9] But when the Missouri rabble, on learning of Mormon intentions, resorted to new and even greater violence in the winter of 1833–34, the Mormon leader resolved to meet force with force. In a revelation given on February 24, 1834, in Kirtland, the prophet proclaimed thus the will of the Lord: "Behold, I say unto you, the redemption of Zion must needs come by power; therefore, I will raise up unto my people a man, who shall lead them like as Moses led the children of Israel; for ye are the children of Israel, and of the seed of Abraham, and ye must needs be led out of bondage by power, and with a stretched out arm." [10]

The Mormon leader commissioned Parley P. Pratt and Lyman Wight to gather an army that would hopefully number five hundred men. Under the command of Smith himself, they were "to go up . . . unto the land of Zion . . . and organize my kingdom upon the consecrated land, and establish the children of Zion upon the laws and commandments which have been, and which shall be, given unto you." [11] Pratt and Wight marshalled their men without delay. On May 5, 1834, Zion's Camp, as the expedition had been named, left Kirtland. However, when the army of about two hundred men reached Missouri, it became apparent that the Mormon cause in Jackson County was lost. Military operations clearly would be of no aid to the Saints and would only aggravate an already untenable situation. Smith realistically disbanded his army; for the time being, the dispossessed Saints resettled in the Missouri counties of Clay and Caldwell.

Judged from its immediate results, Zion's Camp was a quixotic adventure, and yet one of long-range significance for the future development of the political kingdom of God because it set the precedent for the establishment of the military arm of the kingdom. All future Mormon military organizations, including the Nauvoo Legion, and the governing structure of the "Army of Israel" that directed the exodus to Utah, were patterned after Zion's Camp. The Mormons had thus achieved one of the important prerequisites of a nation-state. Moreover, Zion's Camp provided valuable training and experience for future leaders of the church such as Brigham Young, Heber C. Kimball, Orson and Parley P. Pratt, Charles C. Rich, George A. Smith, Wilford Woodruff, and many more.[12] As Young recalled, "I would not exchange the experience gained in that expedition for all the wealth of Geauga county." [13] Few of the participants forgot that they had been charged to "organize my kingdom"; many of them participated in the organization of the political kingdom of God in Nauvoo in 1844.

In 1836, most of the Saints abandoned Clay in favor of Caldwell County, which the Missouri legislature had created specifically for settling the Mormons. And two years later those of the Kirtland Saints who were still faithful to the prophet (after the collapse of the Kirtland Safety Society Bank Company in 1837) joined their Missouri brethren to establish the new Zion with Far West in Caldwell County as the center. More than five thousand Mormons flocked to the new gathering place. All available men volunteered their labor for the excavation of a temple site. Again, the Saints entertained high hopes for the establishment of the kingdom of God.

Supported by Governor Lilburn Boggs's cruel extermination order, hostile mobs who hardly needed such encouragement, once again ejected the Saints from their hoped-for Missouri Zion. Not until the Mormons found hospitality in the neighboring state of Illinois in the winter of 1839–40 at Commerce, a swampy town located at a bend of the Mississippi, did it appear that the Saints had finally found peace, and sufficient real estate to transform their dream into reality. It was here that the prophet, for the first time, could fully realize the plans for the city of Zion which he had originally dreamt of establishing in Jackson County.[14]

Smith issued a call to all Mormons to gather to the new Zion. Swelled by a tide of new converts from England, the Saints poured into the promised land. The prophet had changed the name of the village to Nauvoo, "the Beautiful." By 1844 it boasted a population of over twelve thousand. A charter granted to the Mormons by the Illinois legislature turned Nauvoo into a virtual city-state, authorizing the city council to enact any kind of ordinance "not repugnant to the Constitution of the United States or of this state." A municipal court under the jurisdiction of the mayor was empowered to grant writs of *habeas corpus* "so widely as to enable Mormons to escape trial under gentile jurisdiction." A municipal militia, the Nauvoo Legion, was separate from the state militia, subject only to the authority of the governor. Joseph Smith, with the imposing rank of Lieutenant General—the only one in the United States—became the commanding officer.[15]

The celebration of the eleventh anniversary of the organization of the church, on April 6, 1841, gave Smith and his followers an opportunity for an impressive display of their newly won temporal power. The day's events culminated in a full-dress review of the Nauvoo Legion by Smith, resplendent in his general's uniform. The kingdom of God, it seemed, was at last becoming a reality. And, as Nauvoo grew, so did the enthusiasm of the Saints. An article in the *Millennial Star*, published a year later, entertained sanguine hopes for the mission of the Legion. The time would come, hoped the editor, when it would be strong enough "to rescue the American Republic from the brink of ruin." [16]

Understandably, Gentiles viewed the Legion with considerable suspicion. The extravagant hopes entertained by the Saints for the future of Nauvoo also increased the apprehensions of non-Mormons. According to the *Millennial Star*, Nauvoo was

> . . . the nucleus of a glorious dominion of universal liberty, peace and plenty; it is an organization of that government of which there shall be no end—of that kingdom of Messiah which shall roll forth, from conquering and to conquer until it shall be said, that *"the kingdoms of this world are become the kingdoms of our Lord, and of His Christ."* "AND THE SAINTS OF THE MOST HIGH SHALL POSSESS THE GREATNESS OF THE KINGDOM UNDER THE WHOLE HEAVEN." [17]

Joseph Smith was riding the crest of power. The apostate John C. Bennett, who took every chance to blacken the reputation of his erstwhile leader and denounce him publicly, charged that the prophet had dreamt of making Nauvoo the base of operations for a Mormon empire that was at first to include Missouri, Illinois, and the Territory of Iowa. "The remaining states were to be licked up like Salt, and fall into the immense labyrinth of glorious prophetic dominion, like the defenceless lamb before the mighty king of the forest!" [18] Bennett greatly distorted the aims of the Mormons. Smith had made it emphatically clear that "it will not be by the sword or gun that this kingdom will roll on." [19]

But the prophet's dreams of empire were nevertheless true. On March 1, 1844, there appeared in the Nauvoo *Times and Seasons* the so-called Great Acrostic: "Joseph The Great Prophet of the Western Empire of States." The Gentiles could not quite comprehend how such an empire could be established without violence. In the same year Thomas Gregg, editor of the *Warsaw Message*, had written of Joseph Smith as "that hoary monster who rules at Nauvoo; whose black heart would exult in carnage and bloodshed, rather than yield one iota of what power he has obtained by his hellish knavery." [20] Gregg's editorials became increasingly vitriolic: "We claim not to be a prophet nor the son of a prophet, yet we tell you that your career of infamy cannot continue but a little longer! Your days are numbered!" [21]

Smith may have guessed that such threats would sooner or later come true. One thing he knew; if Gregg and those of his ilk would learn of the projected future of the kingdom of God, the situation of the Mormons in Illinois would be even worse, if that was possible. As long as the Saints were forced to live among the Gentiles the prophet felt he could not confide his innermost dreams even to his followers. "Brother Brigham," he once remarked to Young at Kirtland, "if I were to reveal to this people what the Lord has revealed to me, there is not a man or a woman that would stay with me." [22] What, then, could he expect if the Gentiles got wind of such doctrines?

The revelation outlining the organization of the political kingdom of God was, therefore, political dynamite. Although the revelation was dated April 7, 1842, the prophet waited for almost two years before he organized the government of that kingdom in 1844.[23] Such hesitation suggests that Smith may well have been aware that the time would come when the Saints would have to leave Nauvoo if they wanted to build a permanent political kingdom. Activities of such magnitude simply could not be kept secret for very long.

Another compelling reason for removing the Saints from Gentile contact was the increasing difficulty the prophet faced in hiding and denying some rather unorthodox marriage practices which, it was whispered in Nauvoo, he and some of his intimate followers had engaged in. Rumors that Smith and some of his associates were practicing polygamy can be traced back as far as the Kirtland period. Significantly, in August, 1835, the church made the first of a number of pronouncements denying the charges of polygamy at a time when rumors were spreading that Smith had taken up with Fannie Alger, a seventeen-year-old orphan.[24] One Mormon faction, the Reorganized Church of Jesus Christ of Latter Day Saints, denies even today that Smith ever taught or practiced plural marriage.[25] This denial, however, is untenable in the face of overwhelming evidence. Fawn Brodie has shown quite conclusively that Smith had inaugurated plural marriage at the latest on the eve of the eleventh anniversary of the church on April 5, 1841, when he married Louisa Beaman.[26] There is, moreover, considerable evidence that the prophet had taken several wives even before that date. And according to some prominent Mormons, a revelation foreshadowing plural marriage was given to Smith as early as 1831.[27]

In Nauvoo, Smith also began to initiate some of his close and trusted associates into the practice. Among these people the initial shock was considerable. Brigham Young later confessed that "it was the first time in my life that I desired the grave, and I could hardly get over it for a long time." [28] Smith himself claimed that he instituted the practice only after God had repeatedly commanded him to do so. According to Eliza R. Snow, one of the most renowned of his numerous wives, and an individual destined to become one of the leading women in Mormon culture after his death, the prophet hesitated to carry out the fateful commandment "until an angel of God stood by him with a drawn sword, and told him that, unless he moved forward and established plural marriage, his priesthood would be taken from him and he should be destroyed." [29]

Smith apparently realized that polygamy could tear Mormonism asunder. Privately, he insisted that "it eventually would prove the overthrow of the church and we should be obliged to leave the United States, unless it could be speedily put down." [30] Consequently, he *publicly* denied and condemned the practice until his death. He was intelligent enough to foresee the consequences if he would openly admit the existence of polygamy, given the climate of opinion in Illinois.[31]

Yet plural marriage was part of the social order of the political kingdom of God. It is reasonable to assume that Smith believed it the wisest policy to defer the public announcement of polygamy until the establishment of the kingdom on firmer ground either in Nauvoo or elsewhere. It may be more than coincidental that the official though secret revelation concerning polygamy was given more than a year after the revelation pertaining to the political kingdom of God.[32] The political kingdom, of course, did not depend upon polygamy for its survival, but plural marriage could only be practiced in ethical and moral terms within the kingdom. It was, therefore, no accident that Brigham Young deferred the public announcement of polygamy until he had established a quasi-independent kingdom of God in the Rocky Mountains.[33]

Polygamy was also to have a direct effect on the fortunes of the political kingdom. It could serve as a rallying point and symbol of identification for a people who, in spite of all the special qualities of their faith, shared most of the basic cultural characteristics of their fellow Americans. More than anything else, polygamy could stamp these folk as a "peculiar people" and thus aid them in establishing a national identity for the kingdom of God. Perhaps even more important, polygamy irrevocably tied a man to Mormonism. For a polygamist it was virtually impossible to defect from the kingdom. As will be demonstrated in Chapter VIII, many opponents of Mormonism realized these facts only too well and conducted the anti-polygamy crusade of the 1880's not only on moral grounds, but more importantly as a way of destroying the political kingdom of God.[34]

The idea of a political kingdom of God can be traced back to the Kirtland period of the church. If the official revelation on polygamy was foreshadowed as early as 1831, one may assume that the secret revelation pertaining to the political kingdom of God, likewise, had its precedents. But the idea of a special, secret governing body for this kingdom, separate from the Mormon hierarchy, apparently was not conceived by Smith until he established his temporal kingdom on relatively firm foundation (at least so he had hoped) in Nauvoo. John C. Bennett, the brilliant charlatan who had insinuated himself into the confidence of the prophet in Nauvoo and became his chief lieutenant, claimed after his defection from Mormonism that, in a revelation dated April 7, 1841, Smith had commissioned him to organize a para-monarchical organization called the Order of the Illuminati after the prophet's death as a means of perpetuating the kingdom of God.[35] In view of Bennett's character it would seem strange if he had not embellished the truth. Yet, although the Order of the Illuminati, established by Bennett after Smith's death in James Strang's schismatic Mormon kingdom of God on Beaver Island in Lake Michigan, was largely born of Bennett's own vivid imagination, the connection to a revelation by Smith is not improbable. That revelation was dated just one day after the impressive celebration of the eleventh anniversary of the church on April 6, 1841.[36]

Bennett's secret order bore some remarkable similarities to certain masonic rituals and practices. This was also true of Smith's Council of Fifty. In its early period, Mormonism was strongly anti-masonic; the *Book of Mormon* condemned secret societies and combinations in the strongest terms.[37] But John C. Bennett was able to convince Smith that a masonic lodge in Nauvoo might be a considerable asset to the Saints. Bennett, himself a master mason, obtained a dispensation for a lodge in Nauvoo. On March 15, 1842, the Grand Master of Illinois, Abraham Jonas, installed the lodge. Most of the leading Mormons joined the organization. Smith himself was initiated as a master mason on the following day, March 16. Many other members of the hierarchy, likewise, advanced within the craft at a rate that seemed quite irregular to members of the non-Mormon lodges in Illinois, particularly since the Mormon lodge, officially, never proceeded beyond the dispensation stage. As a result, friction between Mormons and Gentiles increased, contrary to Smith's expectations.[38]

The Nauvoo Lodge seems to have been of some service for the consolidation of Smith's power. A secret oath-bound society could serve as an effective mechanism to enforce solidarity and discipline, and could be useful in keeping the secrets of polygamy contained within a group of men Smith felt he could trust. It is not mere coincidence that some of the most prominent members of the Nauvoo Lodge also were among the first to be initiated into the practice of polygamy. Thus, William Clayton, personal secretary of the prophet and one of the first polygamists, became secretary of the Lodge. Later, in 1844, he became clerk of the Council of Fifty.[39]

Whether or not there existed any direct connection between the government of the kingdom of God and Freemasonry cannot be determined. But it is significant that the Nauvoo Lodge was installed three weeks before Smith received his revelation about the political kingdom of God. The oaths of secrecy administered in the Lodge in 1842 could serve as a means of preparation and of testing to determine to whom the prophet could entrust the more important and potentially more dangerous secrets revealed to the Council of Fifty in 1844. It is, therefore, to be expected that many charter members of the Council of Fifty in 1844 belonged to the Nauvoo Lodge.[40] Whether or not this relationship between Freemasonry and the Council of Fifty had any influence on the secret rituals practiced by those belonging to the government of God is again only a moot-question. But members of the Council of Fifty, like the Freemasons, donned special robes in their private ceremonies, and "offered up" secret signs.[41]

If Smith hesitated to publicize the explosive doctrine of polygamy it is understandable that he drew back even more in openly proclaiming the political kingdom of God; in fact, he seems to have been indecisive about establishing it. At worst, polygamy was a highly unorthodox and detestable moral and social practice to the Gentiles. The secret meetings and activities of the Council of Fifty, especially if misinterpreted by the Gentiles, might well have made Smith vulnerable to the charge of treason. As a result, the prophet moved with extreme caution. Even a two-year testing period was by no means too long to determine whom he could trust. It had taken the prophet that long to decide that he "wished Bennett was in hell!" [42] To come to that conclusion about a man initiated into the Council of Fifty might well prove fatal not only to the Council but to the church as well.

Although the Bennett episode revealed Smith as a man who trusted his fellow men somewhat naively, it also taught him a lesson. The apprenticeship of the prophet's most trusted associates whom he initiated into the Council of Fifty lasted considerably longer than two years. As already indicated, one of the earliest testing grounds for loyalty was Zion's Camp. Another was the embattled Mormon counties in Missouri during the persecutions of 1838–39.

By the summer of 1838, rumors began to circulate in the town of Far West, the new Mormon gathering place in Missouri, about a secret society variously called the Daughters of Zion, the Destroying Angels, the sons of Dan, and the Danites. Although such rumors inevitably exaggerated and distorted the truth, they had some factual basis. Sampson Avard, with the connivance and encouragement of Sidney Rigdon, had organized a secret military organization bound together by oaths and secret passwords. According to John D. Lee, who was to become a prominent member of the Council of Fifty, "the members of this order were placed under the most sacred obligations that language could invent. They were sworn to stand by and sustain each other; sustain, protect, defend, and obey the leaders of the church under any and all circumstances unto death." [43] Ostensibly, Avard had organized the band in self-defense against the depredations of the Missourians. But his real intentions went farther, and must be identified with Smith's ambitions to establish the political kingdom of God. Although the prophet repudiated Avard's excessive zeal and excommunicated him from the church, there can be no question that the germ for Avard's ideas must be sought in ideas that originated with the leader of Mormonism himself. In his personal history, Smith recorded an account of Avard's address to his captains:

> Know ye not, brethren, that it soon will be your privilege to take your respective companies and go out on a scout on the borders of the settlements, and take to yourselves spoils of the goods of the ungodly Gentiles? For it is written, the riches of the Gentiles shall be consecrated to my people, the house of Israel; and thus you will waste away the Gentiles by robbing and plundering them of their property; and in this way we will build up the kingdom of God, and roll forth the little stone that Daniel saw cut out of the mountain without hands, and roll forth until it filled the whole earth. For this is the very way that God destines to build up His kingdom in the last days.[44]

Purged of this lust for plunder and vengeance, many of the men attracted to Avard's service could be even more useful in establishing the legitimate kingdom of God. Proven loyalty in one secret organization could be advantageous to another. As a result, several important Danites were among those initiated into the Council of Fifty in 1844.[45] In fact, the aura of secrecy surrounding the Council, and the method of enforcing it, thus had a precedent going beyond the somewhat symbolic significance of the masonic oaths and rituals. But although Smith had initiated several Danites into the Council of Fifty, there is no evidence that the Council was in any sense a continuation of the Danite organization. Rumors circulating in Nauvoo during 1844 that Smith had revived the Danite band cannot be substantiated and are most likely a result of the suspected purposes and activities attributed to the Council of Fifty by the uninitiated.[46]

This veil of secrecy makes it difficult to obtain not only full information on the Council of Fifty itself, but also on the events and circumstances leading to its organization. It is clear, however, that Smith did not limit the preparation of the future members of his council to the performance of masonic rituals. In a number of special council meetings between 1842 and 1844, recorded in the *History of the Church* in a rather cryptic fashion, the prophet and some of his close associates conducted business that was apparently other than ecclesiastical.[47] Of special interest is a council held by Smith on September 28, 1843, in a conference room above his store in Nauvoo. The reasons for calling the council and the nature of its deliberations remain obscure. After listing the names of those attending, Smith simply remarks that "by the common consent and the unanimous voice of the council, I was chosen president of the special council."[48] Others present were John M. Bernhisel, Amasa Lyman, George Miller, Willard Richards, Smith's brother Hyrum, his uncle John Smith, John Taylor, Newel K. Whitney, and Lucien Woodworth. When the council met again in the evening, William Law and William Marks also attended. What makes the council interesting is that of all those present, only one, William Law, did not become a member of the Council of Fifty in 1844, most likely because he had by then defected from the church.[49] It is also significant that most of those present would take a prominent part in the activities of the Council of Fifty in 1844.

Though it cannot be documented fully, it is quite probable that this particular council was to deliberate on the political future of the church, especially in view of the impending 1844 national elections. On October 1, 1843, three days after this council first met, the *Times and Seasons* published an editorial entitled, "Who shall be our next President?"[50] The Council of Fifty decided in favor of the Mormon prophet in 1844.

The council may also have been convened to commission elder George J. Adams for a special mission to Russia, of which the *Times and Seasons* informed its readers under the same date. As the newspaper pointed out, this assignment was to be more than an ordinary church mission. To it were "attached some of the most important things concerning the advancement and building up of the kingdom of God in the last days, which cannot be explained at this time." [51] If Adams had been sent on a routine church mission, it is doubtful that Smith would have been constrained to give such an explanation. Hundreds of Mormon missionaries were travelling throughout the world to preach the Mormon gospel to "every people, kindred, tongue, and nation." This was common knowledge to both Saints and Gentiles. Adams's mission most likely was in behalf of the political kingdom of God, rather than the church, with the intention of sounding out Russia's attitude regarding an independent Mormon state, which the Council of Fifty would attempt to establish half a year later. At that time, the Council would send quasi-diplomatic representatives to other nations. But the trip to Russia would be considerably more expensive, longer, and fraught with much more uncertainty. Timely preparation would be of the essence.

Another noteworthy fact about this document is that, since the commission to Adams was issued by the First Presidency of the church, it should have been signed not only by Joseph and Hyrum Smith, but also by Sidney Rigdon and William Law. Yet the signatures of the latter two are conspicuously absent. This omission is especially significant because neither Rigdon nor Law became members of the Council of Fifty. Is it possible that Smith was already separating the functions of the church and of the kingdom, and, having lost some confidence in Rigdon and Law, was unwilling to initiate them into matters regarding the political kingdom of God that required the utmost secrecy and discretion? In the absence of further evidence, this supposition seems the most logical one. [52]

When, on March 11, 1844, Smith began the organization of the Council of Fifty in the lodge room over Henry Miller's house, he had the reasonable assurance that the men he convened for that purpose would not be overly startled by the doctrines he was about to propound. By that time they had become accustomed to the startling doctrines their prophet would from time to time expound; they had also become acquainted, in part at least, with many of the ideas to be promulgated in the secret sessions of this body. The prophet, moreover, had reason to believe that he could expect unswerving loyalty from these men since he had moved cautiously and selected them slowly and judiciously.[53]

The name of the Council, as given by revelation in 1842, was "The Kingdom of God and His Laws with the keys and powers thereof and judgment in the hands of his servants." [54] The authenticity of this document was corroborated by John D. Lee, who recorded the name of the Council as "The Kingdom of God and its Laws and Justice and Judgment in my hands." [55] This genuine though somewhat lengthy name was considered to be ineffable, except on special occasions in council meetings.[56] Initially, Smith himself merely called it a "special council." Later he preferred the name "general council." Other designations identifying the group were "Council of the Kingdom," "Council of the Gods," and "Living Constitution." But the most popular and most frequently used name of the organization was simply "Council of Fifty," an appellation that had its origin in the approximate number of men comprising the body.[57]

The Council of Fifty, according to charter member Benjamin F. Johnson, consisted of "a select circle of the prophet's most trusted friends, including the twelve [apostles] but not all the constituted authorities of the Church." [58] Smith failed, as noted above, to initiate Sidney Rigdon and William Law as council members. The Quorum of the Twelve Apostles also served as ex-officio members of the Council. Joseph Smith established the precedent that the president of the church should also be the president of the Council of Fifty, a custom followed both by Brigham Young and John Taylor. That the president of the church should also serve as the first officer in the political kingdom of God was in complete harmony with the theocratic theory of the kingdom. Ultimately, Christ was to be the supreme ruler over both the church and the political kingdom of God.

The concepts of individual rights and separation of church and state required the presence of non-Mormons in the government of the kingdom. Although available membership lists do not reveal any Gentiles among the group, Brigham Young and John D. Lee insisted that these requirements were realized.[59] Such assertions may be based on the fact that Colonel Thomas L. Kane, whose unselfish services in behalf of the Mormons are a matter of record, may have been initiated into the secrets of the Council. Whatever Kane's formal relationship to the group, he actively participated in Council of Fifty deliberations during the Mormon exodus at Winter Quarters, Iowa.[60]

Still another Gentile who may have been a member of the Council was Daniel H. Wells. As Justice of the Peace in Nauvoo, Wells actively aided the Mormon cause. He frequently served as intermediary between the Mormons and the Illinois state government. He also held a commission as Brevet Brigadier General in the Nauvoo Legion. During the expulsion of the Mormons from Nauvoo the Saints bestowed upon him the title "Defender of Nauvoo" in recognition of his steadfast and fearless support of their cause. In 1846 he joined the Mormons on their trek to the Great Basin and was baptized into the faith in Iowa. It is quite probable that Wells, whose actions in Nauvoo reveal him as a Mormon in all but name, may have forgone baptism temporarily in order to maintain the requirement that a Gentile serve on the Council, and for the more practical reason of presenting to the world the image of a Gentile sympathetic to the Mormon cause. Theoretically the Saints considered membership of non-Mormons in the Council of Fifty to be a benevolent concession to the Gentile world. In 1844, however, with the Mormon-Gentile ratio hardly reflective of the anticipated future strength of Mormonism, membership of a Gentile in the Council of Fifty, while hardly advantageous to non-Mormons, may have been of some benefit to the persecuted Saints.[61]

Despite the concept of the separation of church and state, ecclesiastical rank was a powerful source of prestige in the Council. The Twelve Apostles, for example, had special responsibilities both in the church and the political kingdom of God. Benjamin F. Johnson recalled in 1903 one of the last sermons Smith gave before the group:

> With great feeling and animation he graphically reviewed his life of persecution, labor and sacrifice for the church and the Kingdom of God, both of which he declared now organized upon the earth, the burden of which had become too great for him longer to carry, that he was weary and tired with the weight he had so long borne, and he then said, with great vehemence: "And in the name of the Lord, I now shake from my shoulders the responsibility of bearing off the Kingdom of God to all the world, and here and now I place that responsibility, with all the keys, powers and privileges pertaining thereto, upon the shoulders of you the Twelve Apostles, in connection with this council: and if you will accept this, to do it, God shall bless you mightily and shall open your way, and if you do it not you will be damned." [62]

According to Wilford Woodruff, this so-called "last charge" of the prophet represented the climax of several months of intensive instruction to the Council:

> It was not merely a few hours ministering to them the ordinances of the Gospel; but he spent day after day, week after week and month after month, teaching . . . the things of the Kingdom of God. Said he, during that period, "I now rejoice. I have lived until I have seen this burden, which has rested on my shoulders, rolled on to the shoulders of other men; now the keys of the kingdom are planted on the earth to be taken away no more for ever." [63]

What Smith taught in these meetings is largely a matter of conjecture, because the deliberations and actions of the Council of Fifty were then and still remain for the most part shrouded in secrecy. Even half a century after these original meetings had taken place, Patriarch Benjamin F. Johnson, who was present at every session of the Council in the Nauvoo period, did not feel free to divulge the private teachings imparted to the Council by the prophet in 1844. Johnson made it clear that secrecy was a protective measure undertaken to avoid the possibility of misunderstanding by both Gentiles and Saints. Only after attending the Council of Fifty, Johnson affirmed, did he and his associates begin "in a degree to understand the meaning of what he [Joseph Smith] had so often publicly said, that should he teach and practice the principles that the Lord had revealed to him, and now requested of him, that those then nearest to him in the stand would become his enemies and the first to seek his life." [64]

According to John D. Lee, the Council considered guarding the confidential nature of its administrative and governmental activities of vital importance. He told of a council meeting in the early Utah period which concerned itself almost exclusively with impressing upon members the importance of guarding council secrets. Brigham Young, after investigating certain public breaches of confidential council matters, warned his associates in no uncertain terms that "Members of this council should be men of [such] firmness and integrity, that when they leave this council Room that the things that belong to this council should be as safe as though it was locked up on the silent vaults of Eternity but such things must be overcome or the men who indulge in them will be dropped from this council." [65] The fear of such consequences is illustrated by the reaction of John Pack, one of the offenders. He "pled for Forgiveness, Said try me a little longer. Then, if I don't prove true, deal with me as you think proper, if it is to cut my head off, & wept bitterly like a child. His request was granted." [66] Secrecy at times went so far that papers accumulated during a meeting were burned at the close of the session.[67] In what appears as a rather crude attempt to protect the identity of the organization, John D. Lee spelled its name backwards as YTFIF in his diary entries. The first clerk of the Council of Fifty, William Clayton, also tried to veil references to it in his diary by calling it "K. of G." [68]

The haunting question arises how the Mormons could reconcile strong denunciations of secret organizations in the *Book of Mormon* with the existence of the highly secret Council of Fifty. In the thinking of council leaders, this seeming contradiction was most likely resolved as follows: Unlike the secret combinations mentioned in the *Book of Mormon,* and unlike Freemasonry, the Council of Fifty held secrecy to be a merely temporary expedient because the world at large and certain church members in particular had not yet progressed to the degree where they could accept without protest all the doctrines of Mormonism. Brigham Young once indicated that certain doctrines regarding the kingdom of God were not to be revealed before church members were willing and able to keep them secret.[69] In a revelation in *Doctrine and Covenants,* Smith warned his followers to "keep these things from going abroad unto the world until it is expedient in me that ye may accomplish this work in the eyes of the people, and in the eyes of your enemies, that they may not know your works until ye have accomplished the thing which I have commanded you." [70] Ultimately, therefore, the whole world would be aware of the existence of the Council of Fifty. In fact, it is difficult to see how it could have been otherwise, since world government was to be one of the Council's primary missions.

What, then, were these doctrines, discussed and acted upon in the Council of Fifty, which its leaders considered to be too advanced not only for the world but even for most members of the church? Although much of this information is still unavailable, council members occasionally set down some of the purposes and functions of the organization in their private diaries and journals.

That the Council of Fifty was to be the government of the political kingdom of God was made clear by John D. Lee:

"This council aluded to is the Municipal department of the Kingdom of God set up on the Earth, from which all law eminates, for the rule, government & controle of all Nations Kingdoms & toungs and People under the whole Heavens but not to controle the Priesthood but to council, deliberate & plan for the general good & upbuilding of the Kingdom of God on the earth." [71] This function of the Council is also suggested by its name, "the Kingdom of God and His Laws with the keys and powers thereof and judgment in the hands of his servants," and by a passage from the revelation of April 7, 1842: "Ye are my Constitution and I am your God and ye are my Spokesmen." [72] The language of these lines suggests that the governmental powers and duties of the Council were to be executive, legislative, and judicial. This interpretation in fact corresponds with the actual political power exercised by the Council both in Nauvoo and the Great Basin. However, there is a paucity of information as to how these powers were to be divided among the members. It is known that the president of the church also served as president of the Council. As such he presumably was head of state of the political kingdom of God after it had achieved independence, at least until Christ would be able to assume that position.

The scriptures indicated that Christ would rule as king over the kingdom of God. Smith took this idea quite literally and thought it only logical that he, as predecessor of the Saviour, should enjoy certain prerogatives of royalty. Consequently, shortly before his death, the prophet apparently had himself ordained as "King on earth." [73] Brigham Young, upon his arrival in the Salt Lake Valley, likewise reportedly had this ceremony performed in the Council of Fifty.[74] Interpreted literally, this "coronation" is in direct violation of the *Book of Mormon*, which emphatically predicted that no kings were to rule America in the period of the "restoration of the Gospel." [75] But it is quite likely that the ceremony had an essentially symbolic significance. This view is supported by the fact that the vocabulary of royalty, in the nineteenth century, was in great vogue as a mere "fossilized figure of speech" among Americans in general, who could certainly not be accused of favoring monarchy. Two centuries earlier, even as eloquent a writer as John Milton had not been able to find adequate substitutes for the "royal fossils" although he despised kings and helped one lose his head.[76]

The title of king may have been a metaphor, but the power deriving from the office was not. In this respect it is especially important to recall that Smith held his political office by divine right and not by popular sovereignty. However metaphorical these royal pretensions may have been, Smith apparently knew that they were so potentially dangerous as to be entrusted only to the initiated.

The same was true of certain of "His Laws" which the Council of Fifty was enjoined to administer. The idea that the law of the kingdom of God was to be separate from the laws of the world had been introduced as early as 1831, when the Saints were commanded to gather in Ohio: ". . . there I will give unto you my law; and there you shall be endowed with power from on high." [77] Three years later, after the unsuccessful expedition of Zion's Camp, the prophet received a revelation to counteract the discouragement resulting from the failure to "take the Kingdom." The Saints were given the assurance that, eventually, the kingdoms of the world would be "constrained to acknowledge that the kingdom of Zion is in very deed the kingdom of our God and his Christ; therefore, let us become subject unto her laws." [78]

These laws were to be both spiritual and temporal. They comprised the ecclesiastical laws to be administered by the church, and the temporal, political laws to be administered by the Council of Fifty. The discussions on political theory in that organization leave no doubt that the temporal laws of the kingdom of God were to be based on a modified version of the Constitution of the United States.[79]

Unfortunately, the constitution of the kingdom of God is not available for perusal. By examining the constitution of the

State of Deseret, which embodied certain political theories of the political kingdom of God and the Council of Fifty, some slight inferences about the nature of the secret document can possibly be made. Indeed, the constitution of Deseret deviates very little from most western state constitutions, or that of the United States. Undoubtedly, the Council did not yet feel safe to publish the revealed version. One of the most striking features of the constitution of Deseret was an explicit guarantee of religious freedom in its bill of rights; another required that office holders serve without remuneration. As will be demonstrated in the case of Deseret, however, the constitution was at times little more than a piece of paper that could conveniently be disregarded by the Council of Fifty if circumstances required.[80]

It was not that the Council had a cynical attitude toward the law, but, rather, it believed that circumstances might arise which would require the substitution of a higher law for the existing temporal one. The Council of Fifty was the "highest court on earth."[81] As such, it considered itself superior to any codifications of the law, even that of a constitution. While claiming to be guided by divine revelation, the Council was in theory the expression of a fundamental law, as illustrated in the revelation authorizing its organization: "Ye are my Constitution."[82] Accordingly, the Council was occasionally referred to as the "Living Constitution."[83] This was in keeping with Joseph Smith's belief that man-made law could not "meet every case, or attain the ends of justice in all respects."[84] The Council of Fifty, therefore, set an important precedent, according to which justice, in the kingdom of God, was administered in regard to the merits of each case.[85]

As administered by the Council of Fifty, the law itself comprised the entire criminal and civil code of the kingdom of God. Understandably, it had a strong Old Testament flavor, quite in keeping with one of its important functions, namely, that of providing a congenial environment for the practice of that Old Testament institution, plural marriage. This was precisely one of the important reasons why the Council of Fifty was charged with administering "My Laws." As long as the Saints were subject to the civil and criminal codes of the Gentiles, polygamy would be illegal or at best extra-legal. Hence, the Mormons thought it wise to wait until 1852 before they publicly announced the doctrine of polygamy. By that time the laws of the political kingdom of God, at least in a rudimentary fashion, had been established in their new Zion.[86]

The law of blood atonement was still another law revealed from heaven which was difficult to enforce even in the kingdom of God. If, according to this doctrine, a member of the kingdom committed the crimes of murder and adultery, or if he betrayed one of his fellow Mormons to the enemies of the church, or revealed the secrets of the kingdom, he could save his soul only if he expiated for the crime by the shedding of his blood.[87] Blood atonement was, of course, a form of capital punishment. Yet because of its theological implications, and because the Council of Fifty was to administer it, the doctrine was surrounded with an aura of mystery, terror, and holy murder. The Council of Fifty heightened the atmosphere of fear and secrecy associated with this practice by conducting cases involving the possibility of blood atonement in utmost secrecy for fear of public repercussions. The strictures regarding secrecy noted above, which Brigham Young had urged on fellow council members, were in fact directly connected with a case of blood atonement: "The meeting having been called to order by the Press; [he] arose & Said that a member of the council had been guilty of divulging the secrets of this council & that John Pack was charged with it & related that Jackson Reding had been to H. C. Kimble, O. P. Rockwell, & others & told that John Pack had warned him to leave this place fourth with or he would not have the liberty, intimating that his life was in danger."[88]

Whether or not the Council of Fifty ever pronounced the death penalty according to the principles of blood atonement cannot be ascertained. If Smith practiced it in Nauvoo, there is no record of it. Even in Utah the doctrine was theoretical, with the exception of a few attempts by the Council of Fifty to enforce it. In 1888, apostle Charles W. Penrose observed that "Because of the laws of the land and the prejudices of the nation, and the ignorance of the world, this law can not be carried out, but when the time comes that the law of God shall be in full force upon the earth, then this penalty will be inflicted for those crimes committed by persons under covenant not to commit them." [89] However, shortly after the Mormons established the government of God in Utah on what they believed to be a permanent basis, they attempted to enforce the doctrine. Brigham Young insisted that there were "plenty of instances where men have been righteously slain in order to atone for their sins." Gustive O. Larson related "a verbally reported case" of a man found guilty of having committed adultery with his stepdaughter. "According to the report of the reputable eyewitnesses, judgment was executed with the consent of the offender who went to his unconsecrated grave in full confidence of salvation through the shedding of his blood." [90]

John D. Lee reported several deliberations of the Council of Fifty pertaining to blood atonement. On March 3, 1849, the Council discussed the cases of Ira West and Thomas Byres, whose offenses remain unknown. Their crimes, however, were severe enough for Young to have exclaimed: "I want their cursed heads to be cut off that they may atone for their Sins, that mercy may have her claims upon them in the day of redemption." [91] On the following day, the Ira West case was again discussed. All

. . . agreed that he had forfeited his Head, but the difficulty was how he should be disposed of. Some were of the oppinion that to execute him Publickly, under the traditions of the People, would not be safe; but to dispose of him privately would be the most practible, & would result in the greatest good. The People would know that he was gone, in some strange manner, & that would be all they could suggest, but fear would take hold of them & they would tremble for fear it would be their time next.[92]

In the end, neither Byres nor West were put to death, by blood atonement or other means. It is a tragic footnote to history that the recorder of these proceedings, John D. Lee, died before a firing squad for his complicity in the Mountain Meadows massacre. Few official hangings occurred in Utah Territory. And to this day, a condemned criminal in Utah may take the option of the firing squad over the hangman's noose.

The theories upon which the Council of Fifty based such deliberations were spun out by the prophet in the secret meetings of that organization in the spring of 1844. It is obvious that they could be put into effect in Nauvoo only under the greatest secrecy and then only in a limited way. If the laws of God were to be implemented among the Saints, it was plain to Mormon leaders that the kingdom of God would either have to be removed from the world of the Gentiles, or else rise triumphantly over its adversaries.

Quest For Empire:
Joseph Smith and the Council
of Fifty in the Spring of 1844

IV

Nauvoo, in 1844, was one of the most spectacular cities on the western frontier. Among the numerous visitors attracted to the kingdom on the Mississippi two of the most notable were Josiah Quincy—to become mayor of Boston in 1845—and his cousin Charles Francis Adams. Neither stayed to worship, but both were impressed. And to this day, Mormons understandably take pride in quoting Quincy's remark, that "It is by no means improbable that some future textbook, for the use of generations yet unborn, will contain a question something like this: What historical American of the nineteenth century has exerted the most powerful influence upon the destinies of his countrymen? And it is by no means impossible that the answer to that interrogatory may be thus written: *Joseph Smith, the Mormon Prophet*." [1] The Mormon prophet undoubtedly would have agreed with Quincy's verdict. Rarely did he feel any uncertainty about his place in history.

About the future of Nauvoo, however, he became increasingly less confident, as the activities of the Council of Fifty in the spring of 1844 bear out. More and more, the prophet seems to have realized that the rock of revelation—particularly the rock pertaining to the political kingdom of God—proved a more shifty foundation for Nauvoo than the sands of the Mississippi swamps upon which the Saints had built their settlement. For it was in direct response to the political kingdom of God that the Gentile flood threatened to engulf the city.

When Smith organized the Council of Fifty in the spring of 1844, it became quickly apparent that an overt political kingdom of God in the state of Illinois would only intensify the conflict between Mormons and Gentiles and might well lead to the destruction of all the prophet had lived and worked to accomplish. The grand visions of the kingdom of God, which had quickened his imagination from the very beginning of his career, simply could not be realized as long as he and his followers had to mingle with hostile Gentiles. By 1844, moreover, it had become all too obvious that Mormonism, by its very nature, would come into conflict with its environment no matter how sincere the initial overtures of good behavior might be on both sides. The religious, social, and political beliefs of the Saints were simply incompatible with those of their neighbors. A full-fledged political kingdom of God in Nauvoo, or anywhere else east of the Mississippi, inevitably would have resulted in the failure of Mormonism. Viewed from the vantage point of historical hindsight, it is therefore clear that, with the formation of the Council of Fifty as the nucleus government of the kingdom of God, Smith had crossed the Rubicon. That the Saints would sooner or later cross the Mississippi had thus almost become inevitable. Hence, 1844 was the year of decision for the Mormons.[2]

To Joseph Smith, in 1844, this was of course not so obvious. True, as already indicated, he seems to have realized that a temporal kingdom of God in an area surrounded by Gentiles faced at best a precarious future. And, as early as 1842, he had predicted the exodus of the Saints to the Rocky Mountains.[3] Nevertheless, it was with a considerable degree of hesitation that he would seriously consider such a move. The heady atmosphere of power and accomplishment which stirred the Mormons in Nauvoo was much to the prophet's liking. "Excitement has almost become the essence of my life," he once exclaimed. "When that dies away, I feel almost lost. When a man is reined up continually by excitement, he becomes strong and gains power and knowledge."[4] Therefore, when the difficulties with the Gentiles in Illinois began to increase, the Council of Fifty, while seriously contemplating the possibility of emigration, also considered a rather spectacular alternative, namely, to run its leader for the presidency of the United States in the campaign of 1844. During their visit in Nauvoo, Quincy and Adams were told by the Mormon prophet "that he might one day so hold the balance between the parties as to render his election [as president of the United States] . . . by no means unlikely."[5] In fact, Smith and the Council of Fifty seem to have taken the election quite seriously, much more so, indeed, than both Mormons and anti-Mormons have heretofore suspected.

There is reason to believe that the prophet's candidacy may have been proposed as early as September 28, 1843, in the special council meeting described above.[6] On October 1, 1843, the *Times and Seasons,* in an editorial titled "Who shall be our next President?," announced "that we may fix upon the man who will be the most likely to render us assistance in obtaining redress for our grievances."[7] Although Smith held out little hope that such a man might be found among the Gentiles, he wrote identical letters to five possible candidates: John C. Calhoun, Lewis Cass, Henry Clay, Richard M. Johnson, and Martin Van Buren. In these letters, Smith enumerated briefly the persecutions suffered by the Mormons, requesting a "candid reply to 'What will be your rule of action relative to us as a people,' should fortune favor your ascension to the chief magistracy?" [8] Only Calhoun and Clay answered, both evasively. Calhoun, with greater candor than Clay, informed the prophet that the "case of Missouri . . . does not come within the jurisdiction of the Federal Government, which is one of limited and specific powers." [9] Smith sent stinging replies to both candidates. "The glory of America has departed," he wrote to Clay, "and God will set a flaming sword to guard the tree of liberty, while such mint-tithing Herods as Van Buren, Boggs, Benton, Calhoun, and Clay are thrust out of the realms of virtue as fit subjects for the kingdom of fallen greatness." [10] Yet even before Smith received Clay's answer, he had already decided, at a meeting of the Quorum of the Twelve Apostles held on January 29, 1844, to become a candidate for the presidency of the United States.[11]

Why did Smith decide to run for President? Among the enemies of Mormonism, it has been popular to assume that the prophet's power in Nauvoo had gone to his head. In a fit of megalomania, he deluded himself into thinking that he was a kind of superman to whom nothing was impossible. Mormon apologists have pointed out that this interpretation overlooks the fact that Smith was forced into his position out of sheer political necessity. Voting as a bloc, Mormons understandably supported that candidate from whom they could expect most favorable treatment. As a result, they held the political balance of power in Illinois. In currying the favor of the Mormons, both Democrats and Whigs had vied with each other in striving to grant the demands of the Saints. Consequently, the Mormons had achieved a status of almost complete autonomy in Nauvoo.

This seemingly enviable position, however, soon placed them in a difficult situation. Those on the losing side would inevitably blame the Mormons for their defeat. As long as the dominant party supported the followers of Smith there would be no trouble. But the sincerity of such aid, in any case, was at best dubious. In 1843, for example, the Saints had reason to believe that Cyrus Walker, the Whig candidate for Congress, had resorted to trickery in order to secure the Mormon vote. As a result, the Mormons switched to the Democratic ticket at the last moment.[12] By the winter of 1843–44, the Saints had thus alienated both Democrats and Whigs in Illinois. On September 6, 1843, citizens of Hancock County held a mass meeting at Carthage and passed the following resolution: "That as it has been too common for several years past for politicians of both political parties, not only of this county, but likewise of the state, to go to Nauvoo and truckle to the heads of the Mormon clan for their influence, we pledge ourselves that we will not support any man of either party in the future who shall thus debase himself." [13] In the election of 1844, the Mormons, as a result of this situation, decided to vote for their own candidate so as not to repeat the same mistake on a national level. Moreover, it was apparent that they could expect no help from either Whigs or Democrats.

The position of the Mormon apologists is most succinctly summarized by B. H. Roberts:

> Of course there could be no hope seriously entertained that . . . [Smith] would be elected; but, . . . if the Saints could not succeed in electing their candidate, they would have the satisfaction of knowing that they had acted conscientiously; they had used their best judgment, under the circumstances, and if they had to throw away their votes, it was better to do so upon a worthy than upon an unworthy individual who might use the weapon they put into his hand to destroy them.[14]

Such apologists further maintained that a political campaign would give the Mormons an opportunity to dramatize their cause before the nation. Finally, campaign speeches could be used effectively to propagate Mormonism.[15]

B. H. Roberts' contention that Smith was not serious about his candidacy is not without factual support. If Smith had serious hopes of getting elected, why, asked Roberts, was he "pushing vigorously his project of a western movement for the Church" at the same time? [16] Smith, moreover, occasionally referred to his candidacy with some levity. Once he facetiously remarked that "there is oratory enough in the Church to carry me into the presidential chair first slide." [17] He opined on still another occasion that "when I get hold of eastern papers, and see how popular I am; I am afraid myself that I shall be elected." [18]

If the problem is viewed superficially, debunkers and apologists have a case. However, both have divorced Smith's candidacy from its historical context and interpreted it in the light of what seems reasonable according to hindsight and their particular opinion of the prophet's character. If, as the debunkers believe, the Mormon leader was indeed an egomaniac suffering from delusions of grandeur, then he may have in fact entertained the hope of being elected President of the United States in 1844. If, however, he was an intelligent and reasonable man acting on the realities of particular situation, as the apologists insist, then his candidacy was preposterous if he took it seriously; hence he cannot possibly have hoped to win the election. Debunkers and apologists, then, agree on one point: to dignify Smith's 1844 venture as a rational involvement is at the same time to imply that Smith himself acted irrationally.

But in the light of the aspirations of the Council of Fifty, both views must be modified. It was not easy for the prophet and his followers to consider giving up Nauvoo. Reason had compelled them to look westward for the establishment of the kingdom of God. But was it unreasonable for a man who knew that he was carrying out the will of the Lord to believe that God could establish the kingdom in Nauvoo, if He wished, by causing Joseph Smith to be elected President of the United States? Viewed from hindsight, this seems a desperate alternative. But to the Mormons in 1844 the situation looked somewhat different. George Miller wrote hopefully: "If we succeeded in making a majority of the voters converts to our faith, and elected Joseph president, in such an event the dominion of the kingdom would be forever established in the United States." [19]

As a result, the Council of Fifty decided to send all available elders on missions to campaign for Joseph Smith and to preach Mormonism at the same time. "If God goes with them," remarked apostle Willard Richards, "who can withstand their influence?" [20] To anyone who believed with the faith of a Willard Richards, the prophet's presidential aspirations were not at all irrational. In the privacy of the Council of Fifty, Smith clearly viewed his candidacy more seriously than in public. This discrepancy suggests, as do the denials of polygamy, that the prophet's public statements must be taken with caution. Smith's own care in keeping the true purposes of his candidacy secret indicates that he knew that the public at large would treat him as demented if it learned of his actual hopes; but this realization also reveals that he at least knew what he was doing.

It is indicative of Smith's caution that in spite of the presidential campaign he gave specific instructions to the Council of Fifty for searching out a possible new location for the kingdom of God. To B. H. Roberts, the prophet's project of settling the Mormons in the West was evidence that he "did not regard his candidacy as likely to be successful." [21] Such syllogistic reasoning, however, can just as well be reversed. Thus it might be argued that Smith's presence in the presidential race was evidence that he did not contemplate a western movement for the church as seriously as before the campaign of 1844. Yet, neither point is valid. Rather, it is much more reasonable to argue that in an effort to be able to take his cue from the Lord through the natural events of history, the Mormon prophet prepared for all eventualities with equal intensity. Perhaps the kingdom would be established in the United States, or perhaps the Saints would have to look elsewhere for the realization of their dreams. Only time could reveal the will of the Lord.

If Smith had not believed his election in 1844 to be a

possibility, why did he enlist the entire manpower of the church in a quixotic venture? To prevent the Mormon vote from going either to the Whigs or Democrats required no great effort. The vigor with which the prophet threw himself and the entire church into the campaign belies his own casual remarks disavowing any serious political intentions. The logic behind Smith's actions in 1844 may have been a desperate one; yet, in view of his sense of mission and in view of the destiny which he believed God had in store for him and for the kingdom of God, this logic was also inevitable. When the prophet wrote to Henry Clay that the "glory of America has departed, and God will set a flaming sword to guard the tree of liberty," his words were more than idle rhetoric. He considered them as a fulfillment of prophecy, and a promise. The glory of America, Smith had taught, was to be restored through the efforts of the Mormon elders. Ultimately, "the dominion of the kingdom would be forever established in the United States." Perhaps he thought the election of 1844 was the time to accomplish this. The only alternative for establishing the kingdom was removal from the United States. In that event, however, it would be a long time before God could "set a flaming sword to guard the tree of liberty."

Such a move, fraught with enormous expense, would require new sacrifices of the Saints. Reimbursement for the losses sustained in Missouri would help to ease the burden. Believing that their constitutional rights under the Fifth Amendment had been violated, the Saints had taken their case to Washington immediately after their expulsion from Missouri, where both Congress and the President had dismissed their pleas for lack of jurisdiction. The problem lay in the Constitution itself. A strong nationalist and defender of property, John Marshall, in *Barron v. Baltimore,* had made it quite clear that the Fifth Amendment was "intended solely as a limitation on the exercise of power by the government of the United States; and is not applicable to the legislation of the States." [22]

Smith had denounced President Martin Van Buren in the harshest terms for failing to give the Saints their due. His own dog, he once declared, was more fit for the presidency than the "Red Fox of Kinderhook." But the prophet was rapidly learning the intricacies of relations between the states and the federal government. The real culprit for the troubles besetting the Mormons was not Van Buren but the doctrine of states' rights. "States' rights," Smith declared, "are what feed moles. They are a dead carcass—a stink, and they shall ascend up as a stink offering in the nose of the Almighty." [23] The prophet believed that the Mormons might escape the heavy hand of state government and possibly obtain sufficient freedom to establish the political kingdom on firmer ground through a proposal he presented to Congress in December, 1843, under which Nauvoo was to gain recognition as a completely independent federal district.[24] Congress understandably rejected the plan. Ironically, after the Fourteenth Amendment to the Constitution limited the powers of the states and increased those of the federal government, the Mormons jumped from the frying pan into the fire, as demonstrated by the strained relations of the Saints with the federal government in Utah. To Brigham Young, ironically, the "stink" had become incense.

By 1844 the Mormons had not received as much as a penny for their losses of property in Missouri, and their hopes of getting justice in the courts were as remote as ever. They felt, however, that they should exhaust all possibilities. Smith had received a revelation that instructed the Saints to "importune at the feet of the judge; And if he heed them not, let them importune at the feet of the governor; And if the governor heed them not, let them importune at the feet of the president; And if the president heed them not, then will the Lord arise and come forth out of his hiding place and in his fury vex the nation." [25]

According to Brigham Young, one of the first instructions Smith gave to the Council of Fifty was to take "the necessary steps to obtain redress for the wrongs which had been inflicted upon us by our persecutors." [26] In following these instructions, a number of emissaries of the Council travelled to Washington "to present memorials to Congress, for redress of wrongs sustained by the Saints while in Missouri." [27] Although individual members of Congress expressed sympathy for the plight of the Saints, they repeated Van Buren's argument that the matter was beyond federal jurisdiction. In the end, members of the Council of Fifty were as unsuccessful in their attempt to obtain justice for the Saints as were earlier emissaries.

Such experiences in Washington confirmed the Council of Fifty in its suspicions of democratic government. Orson Hyde observed that members of Congress, attempting to serve two masters, were often caught between two stools: "If they would benefit their constituency, they must maintain their influence and popularity in Congress: but if they urge forward a just, but unpopular petition, they lose their influence in Congress; and when that is lost, they have no power to benefit their constituency." [28] This dilemma, Hyde felt, was the real reason why the Mormons were unable to obtain compensation for their losses. In Hyde's opinion, the only ultimate hope for the Saints lay with the kingdom of God. Even in the spring of 1844, he insisted, there was "more wisdom manifest in one of our councils at Nauvoo, than you would ever see here [Washington]. Man's wisdom is folly—his strength is weakness, and a Republican form of Government is as unwieldy in the hands of the people, as a 'Long Tom' in the hands of a school boy." [29]

If only the United States could accept the Mormon version of democracy, all would be well. But before the Council of Fifty could convince a reluctant America that the Mormons were to take over the reins of the government, the political kingdom of God might have to attain a degree of independence from the United States. In Nauvoo, the possibility of achieving this was indeed slight. According to Brigham Young, Smith in fact expressly charged the Council of Fifty with determining "the best manner to settle our people in some distant and unoccupied territory; where we could enjoy our civil and religious rights, without being subject to constant oppression and mobocracy, under the protection of our own laws, subject to the Constitution." [30] Significantly, he left unclear whether he meant the Constitution of the United States, or that of the kingdom of God.

The prophet's tentative desire to remove the Saints from Illinois was thus inextricably bound up with the immediate circumstances leading to the organization of the Council of Fifty. In early March of 1844, Bishop George Miller, one of the leaders of a group of Mormons who had been sent to the Wisconsin pine lands to cut lumber for the construction of the Nauvoo temple, returned to Nauvoo bearing two letters, addressed, respectively, to the First Presidency and to Smith. In these letters, Miller and apostle Lyman Wight petitioned church leaders for permission to lead the Wisconsin Mormons to the tablelands of Texas in order to establish a Mormon colony.[31] In his personal history, Joseph Smith recorded that on March 11, 1844, he commenced with the organization of the Council of Fifty for the purpose of taking "into consideration the subject matter contained in the above letters, and also the best policy for this people to adopt to obtain their rights from the nation and insure protection for themselves and children; and to secure a resting place in the mountains, or some uninhabited region, where we can enjoy the liberty of conscience guaranteed to us by the Constitution of our country." [32] The Council of Fifty acted on the matter at once. On March 14, it sent Lucien Woodworth, architect of the Nauvoo House, to Texas to negotiate with Sam Houston and the Texas Congress for the acquisition of a tract of territory in the Nueces River region large enough to settle not only the Wisconsin Saints but also the entire church.[33]

Smith and the Council had a number of reasons for choosing Texas as a possible site for establishing the kingdom. Shortly before the organization of the Council, the prophet had contemplated Oregon or California as locations "where we can remove to after the temple is completed, and where we can build a city in a day, and have a government of our own, get up into the mountains, where the devil cannot dig us out, and live in a healthful climate, where we can live as old as we have to mind to." [34] Stephen A. Douglas and Henry Clay both advised the Saints to choose Oregon. But Smith had heard that his old enemies, the Missourians, were already moving there in large numbers. California was still in the hands of Mexico, and the Mexican government was not favorably disposed toward North American immigration after the loss of Texas. In 1844, migration to Texas was one of the few alternatives open to the Mormons. The political situation in Texas at the time, moreover, augured well for the establishment of a Mormon state in that area.

The lands on which the Mormons wanted to settle were in the region extending from the Nueces River south to the Rio Grande, which had been disputed between Mexico and Texas since the treaty of Velasco in 1836. In this treaty, the Texans forced the captive Santa Anna to recognize their independence, and to acquiesce in territorial claims extending the boundary of the new republic to the Rio Grande. Santa Anna, after his release, refused to recognize these treaty terms and engaged in numerous border raids in an attempt to bring the Texans to terms. The region between the Rio Grande and the Nueces was largely uninhabited. The Mexicans could cross into Texan territory without difficulty, causing considerable anxiety to the Texas government. Texans, therefore, were eager to have large groups of settlers move into the area in order to establish a bulwark against both Mexican and Indian depradations. Sale of public lands, furthermore, was one of the principal sources of revenue for the financially embarrassed republic. The Mormons thus had good reason to believe that they would be welcome in Texas.[35]

Mormon plans, of course, were based on the assumption that Texas would remain independent. In the spring of 1844, this supposition was not unreasonable. Annexation fever in the United States had subsided considerably after an armistice in June, 1843, had ended the bloody border warfare. The political situation in the United States, moreover, gave the Mormons hopes that annexation would never take place. Both Henry Clay and Martin Van Buren thought it politically expedient to oppose annexation. Anti-slavery Democrats and Whigs, therefore, worried President Sam Houston and southern expansionists considerably. Nevertheless, Houston submitted the annexation question to the Texas Congress in January, 1844. The Texan minister to Washington received instructions to negotiate for annexation and had all but completed the draft treaty when the American Secretary of State, Abel P. Upshur, in February, 1844, was killed by a gun explosion on the U.S.S. *Princeton*. To the Mormons, who saw in all disasters and catastrophes the movements of divine providence, Upshur's death, in retrospect, was a fulfillment of prophecy and omen favorable to their aspirations. When Brigham Young learned of the disaster, he remarked: "The Lord is cutting off the bitterest branches. Look at the explosion of the big gun on board of the *Princeton* war-steamer at Washington. God will deliver his faithful Saints." [36]

The Council of Fifty, however, did not feel that it could leave the matter entirely to God. It had sent an emissary to Washington in order to keep abreast of the latest developments on the Texas situation. Orson Hyde's letters to Joseph Smith reveal that he was well informed of developments in the capital. Hyde predicted that as a result of strong opposition by Whigs and anti-slavery Democrats an annexation treaty would be turned down by Congress: "She [the United States] is afraid of England, afraid of Mexico, afraid the Presidential election will be twisted by it." [37] Finally, annexation would of course not take place if God willed it so: "There are many powerful checks upon our government, preventing her from moving in any of these important matters; and for aught I know these checks are permitted to prevent our government from extending her jurisdiction over the territory which God designs to give to His Saints." [38] The optimism with which church leaders regarded the Texas plans, as well as their magnitude, is revealed in Brigham Young's letter to Reuben Hedlock, encouraging the emigration of British Saints: "You may send a hundred thousand there if you can, in eighteen months." [39]

Hyde also noted that England and France appeared to be instruments in the hand of God, for both powers vigorously supported Texan independence. Lord Aberdeen, in fact, had developed a "carefully constructed plan for joint action with France." Britain and France were to mediate between Mexico and Texas for a Mexican guarantee of the Rio Grande boundary, and for a Texan guarantee, given to the mediators, that she would remain independent. Under these seemingly auspicious circumstances the Council of Fifty sent its emissary to Texas.[40]

The negotiations between the Council and the Texas government reveal that the Mormon leaders, somewhat too optimistically and prematurely, acted as if the kingdom of God were already a political state, or at least a quasi-independent government. George Miller referred to the negotiations as if they were conducted on a diplomatic level between two independent states. He insisted that Lucien Woodworth was sent as "minister to the then Republic of Texas to make a treaty with the cabinet of Texas for all that country north of a west line from the falls of the Colorado River to the Nueces, thence down the same to the Gulf of Mexico, and along the same to the Rio Grande, and up the same to the United States Territory." [41] The Republic of Texas was to recognize the Mormon kingdom of God as an independent nation. In return, the Saints were to help the Texans "defend themselves against Mexico, standing as a go-between [sic] the belligerent powers." [42] Miller's language is in keeping with that of an address by George Q. Cannon, made to a group of Mormon missionaries, in which Cannon said the kingdom of God was "to become a political power, known and recognized by the powers of the earth; and you, my brethren, may have to be sent forth to represent that power as its accredited agents . . . at the courts of foreign nations." [43]

It seems doubtful, however, that the Texas government formally "received" Woodworth, thereby recognizing the diplomatic pretensions of the "minister." Recognition of the esoteric Mormon government would have placed the Texans in a most embarrassing position *vis-à-vis* the United States. According to Miller, however, Woodworth returned from Texas with the preliminary draft of a "treaty," although it is unlikely that the Texans saw the negotiations in that light.[44]

Woodworth arrived back in Illinois on May 2, 1844. On the following day, the Council of Fifty convened and received the report of its emissary. Miller reported that "it was altogether as we could wish it. On the part of the church there were commissioners appointed to meet the Texan Congress to sanction or ratify the said treaty, partly entered into by our minister and the Texan cabinet. A. W. Brown, Lucien Woodworth and myself were the commissioners appointed to meet the Texan Congress." [45]

On May 3, the Council of Fifty also "voted to send Almon W. Babbitt on a mission to France." [46] The nature and purpose of Babbitt's mission cannot be fully determined. Since the Council of Fifty had no ecclesiastical authority, it could not have sent Babbit on a church mission. The circumstances of the venture suggest that, like Woodworth's mission to Texas, it had an essentially political purpose. It is significant that Babbitt received his commission after the Council of Fifty had deliberated on the Texas question for the better part of a day. It is also noteworthy that Babbitt would later undertake a number of political missions for the Council of Fifty under Brigham Young and that Babbitt would also serve as territorial delegate of the Mormons in Washington. He was, therefore, an important Mormon diplomat.[47] It is highly probable that Babbitt was sent to France as a representative of the kingdom of God to determine the reaction of the French government to the establishment of a Mormon state in Texas.[48]

The question arises as to why the Council left no record of sending a special emissary to Great Britain. A likely explanation is that Mormon leaders were already in England on church business. One of these leaders quite possibly may have been designated as "diplomatic" agent of the kingdom of God. In a letter to the president of the British mission of the church, Brigham Young stated that the Council was "in hopes of sending a special messenger to France in a few days," again implying that the messenger was not on church business.[49] It is also possible that the Council of Fifty preferred initial diplomatic contact to be with the French rather than the English. Joseph Smith thought of himself as a Jeffersonian Republican, and he shared the anti-British bias of his times. Although his attitude toward the French is conjectural, he did speak in glowing terms of the Marquis de Lafayette. The French had helped establish American independence and they were the first European power to recognize the Republic of Texas; perhaps the Mormons hoped they would do as much for the kingdom of God.[50]

The Council of Fifty, however, did not stake its entire plans on Texas, but also explored other potential habitats for the kingdom of God. Orson Hyde, emissary of the Council of Fifty in Washington, had instructions to negotiate with the federal government to secure its aid in settling the Saints in some unoccupied region of the trans-Mississippi West. It was in connection with this mission that Willard Richards was appointed by the Council on March 21, 1844, to draw up a memorial to Congress, requesting the federal government to give Joseph Smith authority to raise an army of 100,000 men that would thereby extend the authority of the United States over Oregon and possibly Texas.[51] On March 26, this memorial was approved by the Council of Fifty. The emissary of the Council reported from Washington that the Saints could expect little federal support for their plan, and advised Smith and his associates that "if the Saints [are to] possess the kingdom I think they will have to take it; and the sooner it is done, the more easily it is accomplished." [52] To the Mormon prophet, this was gratuitous advice. The problem was not *that* the Saints had to "take the kingdom," but *how* this could be accomplished. Having transferred the task of establishing the kingdom to the "twelve" and the Council of Fifty, Smith was soon tragically absolved of any further responsibility to accomplish this Herculean mission. For on the evening of June 27, 1844, a mob, with blackened faces, stormed the Carthage jail, where Smith and his brother Hyrum were imprisoned on charges of treason. After the assault, the prophet and his brother were dead.

The stunned Saints had to forget their hopes of establishing the kingdom of God in the United States with their prophet. But, if they could not revive Smith, some members of the Council of Fifty felt, they could revive the plan of setting up the kingdom in Texas. The United States Senate had rejected the annexation treaty shortly before the prophet's death. The earlier calculations of the Council had thus proved correct. Lucien Woodworth and George Miller therefore urged Brigham Young to send them to Texas "with the necessary papers, and proceed to meet the Texas Congress as before Joseph's death agreed upon." [53]

To their surprise, Young was implacably opposed to the plan, and for good reasons. Under the date of April 30, 1844, Orson Hyde had written Joseph Smith from Washington that a projected buffer state between Texas and Mexico would place the Mormons in a most precarious situation. Mormon independence, Hyde warned, would require the support of a strong army and navy; the necessary requirements for manpower and financial resources would easily prove more than the new government could bear.[54] Moreover, the Senate's rejection of the Texas treaty had done little to stabilize relations between Texas and Mexico. The armistice between the two countries was terminated in June. The establishment of a Mormon buffer state under such conditions would have led the Saints into a situation from which they were trying to escape—interference in their internal affairs. "Thus," lamented Miller, "all hopes were cut off of establishing a dominion of the kingdom . . . when . . . I verily believed that all that we had concocted in council might so easily be accomplished. I was really cast down and dejected." [55] In 1846, therefore, Young realistically moved the main body of the Saints west and established the Mormon kingdom in the Rocky Mountains the following year.

The Mantle of the Prophet

V

"A Church without a Prophet is not the Church for me;
It has no head to guide it; in it I would not be;" [1]

Of all the Mormon hymns, this hymn the Saints had always sung with special fervor and conviction, for it summed up one of the central doctrines of Mormonism—one that perhaps more than any other doctrine set it apart from the majority of Protestant sects of the time. After the Saints had buried their beloved prophet, the song took on an almost tragic poignancy, reminding them of a loss that most of them felt was all but unbearable. The song was also a pointed reminder of the *raison d'être* for Mormonism. That a new leader had to be found was axiomatic—but who should it be?

That question, undoubtedly, went through the minds of many Saints as they listened to Sidney Rigdon, who, as sole remaining member of the First Presidency, pleaded before an assembly in Nauvoo that he should be the new oracle or at least the "guardian" of the church until "Young Joseph," Smith's twelve-year-old son, could assume his rightful position in the church, to which he presumably had been appointed by his father.[2] Most of the Saints, however, turned a deaf ear to the strident voice of the former Campbellite minister whose prestige and popularity with the rank and file had been declining for some time before the death of the prophet—in fact Smith had all but repudiated Rigdon in the spring of 1844. For the future of Mormonism it was fortunate indeed that the cards were thus stacked against Rigdon. It was true that as an orator he could lift up the hearts of his listeners, but as a leader of men he lacked judgment and could not curb a certain reckless arrogance that had brought the church into difficulty more than once. What the Saints needed was a strong leader who could keep his wits in times of extreme pressure. They needed this kind of leader desperately if they were not to fall apart and become a prey to the "wolves" of Hancock County, or those in sheep clothes, the numerous "false" prophets attempting to lead the Saints astray. But where could they find another Joseph? Surely, if any man had been able to engender undying, even fanatical, loyalty, it was he. How many men would have followed anyone else from one disaster to the next—from Kirtland to Zion, from Far West to Nauvoo? There was no one, it seemed, who could take the place of Joseph.

It was, then, with questions and doubts in their hearts that the Saints of Nauvoo, on August 8, 1844, listened to Brigham Young's carefully reasoned but impassioned plea that the Quorum of the Twelve (of which Young was president) should lead the church.[3] Did this mean that Young was the new prophet, seer, and revelator? That explosive question the new leader avoided for the time being. An uncomfortably large number of Mormons, nevertheless, responded to Young's claims with a resounding *No*. But many of those who listened to Young's speech suddenly thought that they heard the voice of Joseph and saw the face of the prophet instead. It was a miracle—or so it seemed! Joseph had personally placed his mantle on Brigham.[4] Those who had the vision became as loyal to Young as they had been to Smith—or almost so. And they never doubted that the Lord's choice had been the right one. For if Young lacked the tact and sophistication or the introspection and gentleness of Joseph, he was a leader second only to the murdered prophet.

Young possessed both the humility and the shrewdness to acknowledge Joseph's primacy as leader all of his life. If he had not, it is doubtful that the charisma of that afternoon in August of 1844 would have carried him far. Yet with that acknowledgment Young also inherited some very serious problems—indeed, problems which had played a major role in the death of his predecessor. Would it be wise to continue doctrines such as plural marriage, baptism for the dead and other temple ordinances, and, most crucially, the political kingdom of God and the Council of Fifty—doctrines and practices which influential Mormons close to Joseph Smith had violently opposed? [5] Young's answer was unequivocal. Not only would he accept these doctrines but he would also expand and institutionalize them to such a degree that might have amazed even Smith. In view of the explosive situation prevailing in Nauvoo, however, he kept most of these ideas secret until removal of his followers to the new Zion permitted their open acknowledgment and practice.

The confusion prevailing even among members of the Council of Fifty suggests that Young's secrecy was well advised. Perhaps Joseph Smith had taught so many things at the meetings of the Council in the spring of 1844 that it may have been difficult for some to remember exactly what the prophet had said on each occasion. Perhaps some members may have been lax in attendance. Perhaps, also, the grand visions which Joseph apparently painted in the imagination of these men, unlettered and literal-minded as many of them were, caused havoc with their aspirations. It was, after all, a heady prospect for a tinsmith or a farmer to be told that he would be one of the governing princes in the kingdom of God with authority to rule the nations of the earth.

The amazing thing about the Council of Fifty, therefore, is

not that several of its influential members defected, either starting schismatic movements of their own or giving their loyalty to one of the lesser claimants to the mantle of the prophet, but that the majority accepted the leadership of Brigham Young. This, undoubtedly, was one of the major trumps in his cards, although most of his followers obviously had never heard of that group of men. In fact, the secrecy of the organization must have been one of its major assets to Young. Although he unquestionably dominated the Council, one may wonder if without it the kingdom would have survived.

Yet, if the Council of Fifty were an asset to Young, it was also a liability, not as an organization but because of the resistance of some of its most influential and erstwhile members to his policies. Several of these members, for example, believed that the Council of Fifty held the keys not only to the leadership of the political kingdom of God but to the church as well. Thus, on July 30, 1844, George Miller and Alexander Badlam proposed to "call together the Council of Fifty and organize the Church." Apostles George A. Smith and Willard Richards, themselves members of the Council, reminded the petitioners of what they should have known, namely, "that the Council of Fifty was not a Church organization." Membership in that group was irrespective of religious belief; "the organization of the church belonged to the Priesthood alone." [6]

Several members of the Council of Fifty refused to accept this distinction, considering their authority to be equal to that of Brigham Young. In the spring of 1844, for example, James Emmett had received instructions from Joseph Smith to take an expedition to the Missouri River in order to help determine a possible future location for the kingdom of God. Acting on these original instructions after the death of the prophet, Emmett led a company of Saints into Iowa, against the explicit counsel of Young, who in fact ordered his return. Emmett believed that he could disobey such orders because he belonged to the Council of Fifty, and because his commission had proceeded from "the highest court on the earth." [7] Thus, he refused to listen to the pleas of two emissaries who found his company at the Iowa River "in a deplorable condition." As a final resort, Young had him disfellowshipped, and only then did the recalcitrant member of the Council of Fifty return to Nauvoo. Yet the reconciliation that followed was short-lived. A year later, at Winter Quarters, further difficulties led to Emmett's excommunication, this time permanently. [8]

Even more reluctant to accept Young's leadership was the proud and headstrong Lyman Wight. W. W. Phelps, whose pastime was the invention of colorful nicknames for prominent church leaders, had once appropriately called him the "Wild Ram of the Mountains" because of his independent spirit. The name remained with him for life. Young, the "Lion of the Lord," lacked the art of taming the ram. The only man to whom Wight had deferred in his life was Joseph Smith. After the prophet's death, there was no one to whom the apostle would listen, partly because like Miller and Badlam he considered the authority of the Council of Fifty to be superior to that of the Quorum of the Twelve, even though he belonged to the latter group as well. He reasoned that, upon the death of Smith, "the first thing to have been done would have been to have called the fifties together from the four quarters of the earth, which contained all the highest authorities of the church . . . that had not the fifty constituted the highest authorities, it would have been a species of weakness to have ordained all the highest authorities into that number." [9] After their return, the Council of Fifty should have organized the leadership of the church, recognizing "Young Joseph" as the rightful heir to the succession. [10]

Unable to prevent the appointment of Young, Wight sought to establish the kingdom in Texas in an attempt to follow up the earlier negotiations with Sam Houston, which, it will be remembered, were carried out by the Council of Fifty on

Smith's instructions. Young, as mentioned previously, adamantly refused. Wight, nevertheless, decided to move. Yet, in self-control and diplomatic skill he clearly was no match for Young. Only the Wisconsin Saints, whom the Council of Fifty had originally singled out as the first to move to Texas, followed Wight's leadership. Wisely avoiding a direct confrontation at one of the most critical times in Mormon history, Young finally allowed Wight and his followers to depart for Texas, albeit without his blessings.[11]

After the main body of the Saints arrived in Salt Lake Valley, the Quorum of the Twelve summoned Wight as one of their members to the new Zion. The leader of the Texas Mormons, however, still insisted on the superior authority of the Council of Fifty and at the same time refused to accept Young's leadership of that body. In answer to his reply that "nobody under the light of the heavens except Joseph Smith or John Smith, the president of the Fifty, could call him from Texas to come to Salt Lake City," the Twelve imposed the extreme penalty of excommunication.[12]

George Miller, who had been presiding bishop of the church in Nauvoo, was another member of the Council of Fifty reluctant to give up the Texas plans. As late as April, 1847, while the Saints were already well on their way to the Rocky Mountains, Miller still hoped to convince Young to move to Texas. Although "a very few words from different ones on the subject caused him to confess the impracticability of his plans," Miller continued to chafe under Young's leadership.[13] In fact, had it not been for Miller's previous great prestige among the Saints, it is doubtful that Young would have put up with him as long as he did. The Mormon leader, however, apparently feared that Miller might divide the leadership of the church even more when already too many Saints, even among those who had migrated to Winter Quarters, needed further convincing that Young was the legitimate successor to the prophet. These considerations undoubtedly had much to do with cooling Brigham's temper toward the bishop. The latter, however, was not easily placated. Adding to his irritation were those new members of the Council of Fifty who had only recently been appointed by Young and whose obvious support of their leader clearly had had much to do with the fact that they were called to such eminent positions. Disdainfully, Miller remarked that "this Council . . . was now swelled to a great crowd under Brigham's reign. . . . I was greatly disgusted . . . that I from this time determined to go with him no longer." [14] The bishop thereupon made his way to Texas and joined Lyman Wight and his Wisconsin colony. One need not be a prophet, however, to predict that two individuals as ambitious and headstrong as Miller and Wight would soon come to a parting of ways. In 1849, Miller wrote a letter to James J. Strang—one of the rising stars in a galaxy of aspiring Mormon prophets—and found him eager to use his many talents. Thus, Miller made his way to Michigan, becoming one of Strang's chief lieutenants in the Beaver Island kingdom.[15]

Of all those who attempted to emulate Joseph Smith's temporal kingdom of God, James J. Strang was undoubtedly the most ambitious and colorful. Alpheus Cutler, a prominent member of the Council of Fifty who presided over the temporary settlement at Winter Quarters, finally broke with Brigham Young and established a political kingdom of God of his own. Charles B. Thompson, another aspirant to the mantle of the prophet, made himself king of a theocratic settlement in Iowa; and Gladden Bishop, who attracted a group of Wisconsin Saints to his cause, organized, in the words of one observer, "what he calls the Kingdom of God, and it was the queerest performance I ever saw." [16] Yet none could compete with Strang, who in the late 1840's and early 1850's posed the most serious of all threats to Young's claim for leadership of the Saints.

For Strang, Smith's martyrdom seemed to have opened the way for fulfillment of youthful dreams of royalty and power.[17] He produced a letter, purportedly written by the prophet himself, appointing him Smith's successor. Many of the leaderless Saints, at this point, were ready to grasp at any straw; the will to believe became a ready substitute for evidence, and, for those who were desperately seeking a prophet, the letter was quite enough, also considering the added demeanor and bearing of Strang. That the letter could have been a forgery never seems to have occurred to most of his followers.

It is true that Smith could not always remember what he had promised to whom as well as whom he had ordained or commissioned to what office or task. Visitors moved in and out of his Nauvoo mansion house in a steady stream. In his bustling and pragmatic energy the prophet was willing to try any suggested idea that seemed at all reasonable at least once. Strang, whose imagination continually worked overtime, undoubtedly struck a responsive chord in the restless prophet, who personally baptized the new admirer after only a brief acquaintance. That the ambitious Strang, under the circumstances, may have received a commission to establish a gathering place for Mormons in Wisconsin seems entirely possible, and even probable, particularly since Smith was beginning to modify his views on the gathering, declaring the entire North and South American continents to be Zion in the spring of 1844.[18] But that Smith could have been serious in appointing Strang his successor would seem doubtful even if the authenticity of the letter could be verified. I concur with Dale Morgan that its authorship is open to the most serious questions.[19]

Whatever the origins of the letter, Strang clearly must have felt that it was not enough. A revelation from God, designating him as the divinely appointed new head of the Church of Jesus Christ of Latter Day Saints, and the discovery of supposedly ancient metal plates containing additional revelation concerning the kingdom of God were intended to enhance his prestige among the faithful. Brigham Young and his followers were excommunicated and delivered over to the "buffetings of Satan." [20]

Under the alleged personal commission from Joseph Smith,

Strang declared Voree, Wisconsin, as the gathering place—the heart of the new Zion. But the expected influx of Saints to the "Garden of Peace" never amounted to more than a trickle. Among those who came, however, were a number of prominent followers of Joseph Smith, such as William Smith, patriarch of the church and brother of Joseph; John E. Page, one of the apostles; William E. Marks, former president of the Nauvoo Stake; and none other than John C. Bennett, former mayor of Nauvoo and major general in the Nauvoo Legion, who had been excommunicated in 1842. Significantly, the first three had been members of the Council of Fifty, although Marks himself had serious doubts about that organization. Bennett had been forced to leave Nauvoo before the establishment of the Council of Fifty; nevertheless, there is reason to believe that some of his own ideas may have contributed to the formation of that group.[21]

As mentioned in Chapter III, it was Bennett who first suggested to Strang the organization of a secret society called the Halcyon Order of the Illuminati, a para-monarchical organization with an imperial primate, a grand council, viceroys, and noblemen, which was to be the governing body of the Strangite kingdom of God on earth. Bennett maintained that the idea had come from a revelation given to Smith on April 7, 1841, with instructions that he, Bennett, was to establish the Order of the Illuminati after the prophet's death as a means of perpetuating the kingdom. Whether or not Bennett told Strang the truth about the organization is difficult to determine. Nevertheless, it is not improbable that Bennett did obtain some information from one of Smith's unpublished revelations.[22]

Whether or not Strang had heard of the Council of Fifty before the arrival of Bennett and the three Mormon dignitaries who had been charter members is a matter of conjecture, but it seems unlikely that he could have missed the rumors. His baptism under the hands of Smith took place only two weeks before the organization of the Council of

Fifty. But, even if no information of its existence should have leaked to Strang at the time, it seems only reasonable to assume that he should have heard as much about the secret activities of the Council as Governor Ford, especially with three of its former members joining him at Voree. At any rate, Strang's administration of an oath of allegiance, sworn to him personally by members of the Order of the Illuminati, is a striking parallel to Ford's account of the oath of allegiance administered by Smith to his secret council.[23]

But the position of Strang's embryonic kingdom of God was at best a tenuous one in an area where most of the land had been pre-empted by previous settlers. Yet land was clearly one of the primary prerequisites of an earthly kingdom. Its lack at Voree caused considerable dissension among the Saints. Disharmony was further fanned by the personal ambitions of William Smith and Bennett, both of whom found themselves excommunicated from Strang's church in 1847. To place his kingdom on firmer ground, Strang decided to remove it to Beaver Island on Lake Michigan. It was thence that the first group of Saints migrated in 1847, to be followed by the majority of Strang's followers between 1848 and 1850. Soon the kingdom was in a flourishing condition and Strang in firmer control than ever. As a result, he took his final and formal steps toward the inauguration of a theocratic kingdom.

Precisely what proportion of the theocratic ideas and practices in Strang's kingdom derived from his youthful dreams of royalty and power and what proportion from Joseph Smith and his followers in the Council of Fifty will most likely forever remain undetermined. Yet the notion that "his faith was as far from the Mormonism of Utah as it was from his boyhood baptism" will bear revision.[24] For a comparison with Smith's theocratic ideas and practices reveals that Strang's kingdom on Beaver Island resembled that of the Mormons in Nauvoo much more closely—if in a garbled way —than has heretofore been suspected. Although many significant differences exist, a number of striking resemblances are not explained satisfactorily if they are dismissed as being coincidental, particularly because at least six persons who had held leading positions in Strang's kingdom at one time or another had been privy to important secret ideas and practices initiated by Smith in connection with the temporal kingdom of God on earth.[25]

When the full and final organization of the kingdom on Beaver Island took place in the summer of 1850, Strang thus had ample precedent on which to build his ambitious pretensions of royalty. On July 8, he convened a conference of the church which culminated in an announcement that according to divine revelation the kingdom of God was to be re-established on earth, headed by James Strang as king. God had revealed the details of the organization of His kingdom on the "Plates of Laban," to be translated as the *Book of the Law of the Lord*.[26] As Milo Quaife, Strang's biographer, has pointed out, this record contained "a surprisingly comprehensive framework of theocratic government . . . ample in scope to serve the needs of a kingdom of whatever size." [27] In keeping with the new revelation, Strang was crowned king that very day. Clad in a bright red robe, he received the crown from his second in command, George J. Adams, attended by some four hundred of his followers.

Although Strang's coronation was less metaphorical and more theatrical than Smith's, the *Book of the Law of the Lord* revealed that a number of fundamental ideas behind Strang's theocracy were similar to those behind Smith's kingdom of God. Both rested their claims in part on the prophetic vision of Daniel. The following passage, for example, is a typical one from the *Book of the Law of the Lord*:

As clearly as the Scriptures show that God established the Kingdom of Israel, so clearly do they show that he will establish a universal Kingdom in the last days; for Daniel, after prophetically tracing the great national events down to the division of the Roman Empire into the modern European nations, says, "In the days of these Kings shall the God of heaven set up a Kingdom, which shall never be destroyed; but it shall break in pieces all these Kingdoms, and it shall stand forever." [28]

Like Joseph Smith, Strang believed in the ultimate temporal sovereignty of the kingdom of God: "By the first Commandment God establishes a government among men, which he makes supreme in all things . . . every form of government among men, which was not instituted of God, is a usurpation, and that every exercise of the proper functions of government under it, is a taking of the name of God in vain, as every exercise of functions not proper to government, is tyranny." [29] Orson Pratt expressed analogous ideas when he proclaimed that "the Kingdom of God . . . is the only legal government that can exist in any part of the universe. All other governments are illegal and unauthorized. . . . Any people attempting to govern themselves by laws of their own making, and by officers of their own appointment, are in direct rebellion against the kingdom of God." [30] Such claims, inevitably, aroused the hostility of Gentiles. Like Joseph Smith before him, Strang was murdered partly because he taught and practiced such principles.

Strang's violent death probably saved his movement, which was racked by dissension from within. The number of converts to the religion by 1855 (the year of Strang's death) had been very small indeed. Particularly disappointing to Strang must have been the small number of erstwhile disciples of Joseph Smith who continued to sustain the kingdom at Beaver Island.

These difficulties were mostly of Strang's own making. To a large degree, his is the story of a lost opportunity. Of all the claimants to the mantle of the prophet, Strang clearly posed the most serious threat to Young's leadership in the late 1840's. While Young concentrated on consolidating his power in Nauvoo, Strang sent his missionaries throughout the eastern United States, convincing many congregations of his claims to leadership. If he had been able to hold on to these Saints, the story of Mormonism today might be a different one. If Strang failed, it was partly because of his immense ambition, and partly because he did not understand the nature of the dissension which had contributed to Smith's assassination, and which divided the Mormons more and more as the rumors concerning plural marriage, the political kingdom of God, and other doctrines and practices could no longer be suppressed.

As Robert Flanders has pointed out so perceptively:

> the Nauvoo experience caused a permanent division in the Mormon Church. . . . Although the numerous Mormon sects which arose in the ensuing generation were divided by complex controversies over doctrine, there was also in the separation a simple dichotomy. On the one hand were those who favored or at least acquiesced in the vision of a corporate or "political" Mormonism as it had been expressed in the building of Nauvoo. On the other hand were those who came to oppose what Nauvoo stood for and who wished for a simpler, more orthodox manifestation of the faith.[31]

It was one of Young's luckiest breaks that so few of his rivals, Strang among them, understood this. Too many of "those who would be leaders" provided what was often nothing but a bizarre caricature of the kingdom in Nauvoo. Too often, as in the case of Strang, their opposition to Young was merely the expression of a power struggle—a struggle in which they simply were no match for the "Lion of the Lord." As the bewildered Saints who refused to follow Young flitted from one leader to the next, they soon learned that many of these leaders struck a posture which, consciously or unconsciously, imitated Brigham and his kingdom.

Strang should have been able to discern the sentiments among many of his early followers more accurately. Shortly after news about his Order of the Illuminati leaked out, the Boston branch sent a strong letter of protest:

Resolved that this Branch do hereby in the most decided and unequivocal manner, firmly and solemnly protest against the introduction of any, and every, Secret Society, or Combination; especially in connection with the Church of Jesus Christ: And we look upon them with the greatest aversion, and abhorrence, believing with the Book of Mormon *"That the Lord worketh not in secret combinations"* Also That *"They are built up of the devil who is the Father of lies"* And if preserved [sic] in "will lead to the utter destruction of the nations of the earth" and therefore we *cannot* nor *will* not fellowship or sustain any man, or body of men, engaged in propagating any such secret communications.[32]

This attitude was shared by William Marks, although he had witnessed Smith's coronation as a member of the Council of Fifty. After the death of Joseph Smith he maintained that "I could not conceive [the kingly government] to be in accordance with the laws of the Church, but I did not oppose this move, thinking it to be none of my business." [33] His unquestioning loyalty to Smith undoubtedly overrode any reservations. Obviously, Marks would be equally opposed to Strang's kingdom, with the exception that no ties of personal fealty would prevent him from making that kingdom very much his business.

Another dissenter from Brigham Young who could not accept the claims of Strang for the same reasons was Stephen Post, whose brother Warren had settled in the Beaver Island kingdom:

> . . . calling himself as successor to Joseph and these officers the officers of the church is rather too much. Now readest thou in the Doc. and Cov. "Ye shall have no king or ruler." We can consistently support no king in the church but Jesus. Whilst living under the laws of the U.S. we are bound to obey the laws.—No man can serve two masters. You cannot have a temporal king and a Republican government at the same time. The thing is preposterous.[34]

One wonders what would have happened to Strang if he

had been more sensitive to such feelings and assumed the spiritual leadership of all those who were disillusioned with corporate, political Mormonism. As it was, Young had successfully transplanted the political kingdom of God to the Great Basin. Unity proved a great advantage in missionary work. Brigham's emissaries clearly had an advantage over dissension-racked competitors from the "churches of the dispersion." Soon a steady stream of converts from the East and Europe flowed to the Rocky Mountain kingdom.

Young's opponents thus had lost their chance. When the Reorganized Church of Jesus Christ of Latter Day Saints, by 1860, was finally able to provide a roof for most of those whose chief objection to Young was his insistence on continuing polygamy and the Nauvoo kingdom, Utah Mormonism had far outdistanced all its competitors. Smith's vision clearly had prevailed. By the middle 1850's, the major threat to Young's kingdom came from the United States, not internal dissenters.

Exodus

VI

WHEN JAMES GORDON BENNETT, editor of the *New York Herald*, learned of the murder of Joseph Smith, he could not refrain from announcing in an extra edition on July 8 that "the 'latter day saints' have indeed come to the latter day." [1] But if Bennett, at times, became intoxicated with his own rhetoric, he quickly recovered. Only two days later he observed more realistically that "Instead of sealing the fate of Mormonism, we are now rather inclined to believe that this revolting transaction may give additional and increased strength to that sect. Joe and his brother will be regarded as martyrs to their faith, and but little knowledge of human nature and the history of the past is necessary to inform us of the fact that violence, oppression, and bloodshed strengthen instead of subduing fanaticism." [2] The Gentile inhabitants of Illinois soon came to the same conclusion. As a result they followed the example of the Missourians and hounded the Mormons until, in 1845, Brigham Young promised that he and his followers would leave the state of Illinois in the spring of 1846. [3]

The Council of Fifty assumed major governmental responsibilities during this time of conflict. According to Hosea Stout and John D. Lee, its function was "to bring a semblance of order into the civil affairs" of Nauvoo. "Whenever anything of importance was on foot this Council was called to deliberate upon it." [4] Under a system of interlocking chairmanships and directorships the Council controlled the city government (the mayor was a council member), the school board, and the Mercantile and Mechanical Association. After the repeal of the city charter of Nauvoo, which had been a major cause of contention between Mormons and Gentiles, the Council of Fifty corresponded with Governor Thomas Ford on the best method of organizing the city. Through a new act of incorporation, five trustees governed Nauvoo, three of whom were members of the Council of Fifty.[5]

The Council also played a leading role in defending the Saints against the mob violence which was threatening to break into open civil war in 1845. Terrorism had begun soon after Smith's death. In the fall of 1844, the enemies of the Saints in Hancock County sent out invitations for a "wolf hunt" designed to drive Mormons off their land and burn their homes in a systematic manner. Small bands of ruffians pillaged and burned Mormon homes and ran off their livestock. Courts and law enforcement officers proved powerless. In desperation, the Saints took the law into their own hands and repaid their enemies in kind. The Council of Fifty urged moderation upon the Saints, but, understandably, defended those for whom arrest warrants had been issued; "It was considered best for those who are hunted with writs to go on missions." [6]

Tension, nevertheless, increased. Reprisals brought new retaliations. In the fall of 1845, rumors began to circulate among the Gentiles that they were about to be massacred by the Mormons. Consequently, anti-Mormons requested military aid from the state to subdue the Saints. The latter, in response, prepared for defense under the leadership of the Council of Fifty. The Council's earlier policy "to pursue a

medium course avoiding extremes that might raise an excitement in the country" had failed utterly.[7] Gentile depredations
in Hancock County increased at an alarming rate.

On October 4, the Council of Fifty met to consider correspondence received from Governor Ford, General John J.
Hardin, commander of the state militia, and a committee of
citizens from Quincy, all to the effect that the Mormons
could expect no protection in Illinois. Unless the Saints left
the state the following spring, warned the citizens of Quincy,
"violent measures will be resorted to, to compel your removal,
which will result in most disastrous consequences to yourselves and your opponents." [8]

These warnings, however, came some time after Young
had made up his mind to remove the Mormons from Illinois.
The policies he pursued between 1844 and 1846 suggest that
he knew that the kingdom of God could not remain in peace
in Nauvoo. Yet before Young could transplant the kingdom
he had to be sure that it was sufficiently strong to survive the
strain of removal. The remaining part of the year 1844,
therefore, was spent in consolidating his power. Had he announced his decision to remove the church from Illinois in
1844, it is quite probable that he would have met considerable
opposition from the Saints. Nauvoo, for many of them, was
the third location of the anticipated Zion. To give up their
land and homes once more would be a severe test of faith
even for the most stalwart. Furthermore, the migration of a
people numbering approximately twelve thousand souls
required extensive preparation. A hasty, ill-organized exodus
could easily be disastrous. Young recorded in his personal
history that in 1845 he saw Joseph Smith in a dream, saying:
" 'Brother Brigham, don't be in a hurry,' which was repeated
the second and third times with a degree of sharpness." [9]

To the Gentiles, such delay indicated that the Mormons
had chosen to remain permanently in Nauvoo. This mistaken
belief contributed considerably to the persecutions visited
upon the Saints. When, in the fall of 1845, Young finally

publicized the decision of the Mormons to leave Illinois, he had been forced to reveal his plans as a result of the threats of the Gentiles. By that time, however, feelings ran so high that the impending departure of the Mormons failed to pacify the enemies of the Saints. In fact, the increased furor of the mob suggests that Young may have been wise in keeping his plans confidential as long as he had. Now that the Mormons were definitely leaving, Gentiles saw a final chance to settle old scores and, most important, an opportunity to make a profit. Systematically, they made a potential buyers' market more favorable by crowding the seller for time, by putting to the torch the homes of those Mormons who would not sell at the ridiculously low prices offered, and by creating a general atmosphere of fear. That chaos and hysteria did not ensue was largely the result of the effective leadership of Brigham Young and the Council of Fifty.[10]

The most important task facing the Council of Fifty in 1845 was the preparation for the exodus of the Mormons from Illinois.[11] On March 1, the Council decided to "send nine brethren westward, to search out a location for the Saints." [12] Many subsequent meetings of the Council dealt with the problem of emigration. One of the reasons why Young hesitated to leave Nauvoo was that he had to have a place where the Saints could settle permanently. It is of course a moot question to speculate whether or not Mormonism could have survived another migration after the exodus from Nauvoo. Young, at any rate, did not want to risk such a possibility.

But where could the Mormons find lands not coveted by the Gentiles and still sufficiently fertile to sustain a people that numbered about twelve thousand with the ambitious plan of establishing an earthly kingdom of God that would hold many times that number? Texas was out of the question, in spite of the pleadings of George Miller and Lucien Woodworth. The prospects of establishing the kingdom in California also seemed dim. Too many adventurers were already on their way to California, raising before Young's eyes the specter of renewed conflict. The same was true of Oregon. Vancouver Island was another possibility, suggested, like Oregon, by Stephen A. Douglas, who seemed to have believed that in this manner he could accomplish two purposes at the same time: removal of the obnoxious Mormons from Illinois, and establishment of a counterweight against British power in the Pacific Northwest. Young, however, seems not to have considered this possibility seriously, although he did initiate negotiations with the British Crown for the settlement of converts from Great Britain on the island.[13]

In fact, about the only possible region open to Mormon colonization was the area of the Great Basin. Throughout the spring and summer of 1845, the Council of Fifty discussed the future site of the kingdom of God, making careful studies of as much of the western travel literature as was available at the time, especially of the reports of John C. Fremont. On September 9, 1845, the Council of Fifty "resolved that a company of 1,500 men be selected to go to the Great Salt Lake valley and that a committee of five be appointed to gather information relative to emigration, and report the same to the council." [14] On October 4, the committee made a full and detailed report of the necessary requirements for outfitting the Saints on their projected journey.[15]

During the winter of 1845–46, depredations against the Mormons became so violent that the Council of Fifty had to alter its original plans of starting the exodus from Nauvoo in the spring of 1846. As a result, the Council worked feverishly through the winter to perfect the quasi-military organization under which the migration was to be directed. On January 13, 1846, the Council of Fifty met in the almost completed Nauvoo temple: "The captains of fifties and tens made reports of the number in their respective companies, who were prepared to start immediately, should the persecutions of our enemies compel us to do so: one hundred and forty horses and seventy wagons were reported ready for immediate service."[16] On January 19, the Council decided that the captains of the different companies should prepare as many of their men as possible to start westward. On February 4, flatboats and skiffs took the first company of Saints through the floating ice of the Mississippi to the Iowa shore. It may have been mere coincidence that Charles Shumway, a member of the Council of Fifty, was the first to cross the river, but it was also fittingly symbolic.[17]

The first encampment was set up at Sugar Creek, Iowa, on the west side of the Mississippi River. It was from here that, on March 1, the first wagons rumbled westward across the frozen plains. As Benjamin F. Johnson noted, the Council of Fifty continued to direct "all general movements relating to our exodus as a people from Nauvoo."[18] John D. Lee and William Clayton have recorded frequent council meetings in the tents and temporary shelters along the way.[19] Most of these gatherings, however, were attended only by a fraction of the total membership of the Council because of the considerable distance between various camps set up to facilitate emigration. Only at Winter Quarters, on the east bank of the Missouri River, did the Council convene in a number of meetings with a majority of its members present to discuss and implement the final plans for the trek to the valley of the Great Salt Lake.

Winter Quarters became the major way station for the Mormon emigrants. The longest part of the journey, across the plains of Nebraska and of Wyoming, lay still ahead. It was here that Brigham Young gave his only revelation to be published in the *Doctrine and Covenants*. On January 14, 1847, he made known "The Word and Will of the Lord concerning the Camp of Israel in their journeyings to the West."[20] It merely confirmed the para-military organization already effected by the Council of Fifty in Nauvoo, and largely patterned after Zion's Camp of 1834 in Missouri. The revelation also gave some practical advice on how the Saints should conduct themselves on the trip. According to John D. Lee, the "Word and Will of the Lord" was "first laid before the Council as a revelation to the church and acknowledged by the Council of Fifty. It was then presented to the First Presidency of the seventies and so on down and acknowledged." [21]

On April 16, a pioneer company of one hundred and forty-three men, three women, and two children, left Winter Quarters under the leadership of Brigham Young to locate the precise area in the Rocky Mountains where the kingdom should be established. Eighteen members of the Council of Fifty accompanied this advance group. Of considerable interest is a meeting of the Council held on Sunday, May 30. William Clayton, clerk of the Council, recorded in his diary that

> . . . all the members of the council of the K. of G. in the camp except brother Thomas Bullock, went unto the bluffs and selecting a small, circular, level spot surrounded by bluffs and out of sight, we clothed ourselves in the priestly garments and offered up prayer to god for ourselves, this camp and all pertaining to it, the brethren in the army, our families and all the Saints, President Young mouth. We all felt well and glad for this privilege. . . . Albert Carrington and Porter Rockwell . . . having no clothing with them, stood guard at a little distance from us to prevent interruption.[22]

On July 19, ill with fever, Brigham Young sent a small party ahead to seek the best route through the canyons into the Great Basin of the Wasatch. On July 21, two members of the Council of Fifty, Orson Pratt and Erastus Snow, were the first to set foot on the territory of the future kingdom of God, over which they hoped to rule.

A question much debated by historians is whether the Mormons, upon leaving Nauvoo, intended to establish a separate government beyond the territorial limits of the United States, or whether they anticipated becoming part of the Federal Union. Nineteenth-century writers such as Benjamin G. Ferris assumed that the Mormons had attempted permanently to remove themselves from the United States. When the Mexican War resulted in their homesite becoming federal territory, they had to make the best of a bad situation: "The next best thing to becoming a state independent of the Union, was to become an independent state of the Union." [23] Frederick Logan Paxson came essentially to the same conclusion. In his opinion, the Mormons did not look favorably upon the treaty of Guadalupe Hidalgo. After its ratification, however, there was nothing they could do "but make the best of these facts and to seek from the United States the same sort of autonomy they had received from Illinois." [24]

Yet these writers have ignored considerable evidence which suggests that the Mormons may have intended all the while to associate their new land and future with that of the United States. Hubert Howe Bancroft, for example, who wrote his *History of Utah* in cooperation with Mormon church officials, insisted that "the Mormons did not, however, hope to remain an independent republic, nor did they probably wish to do so." [25] But Bancroft's statement is ambiguous, to say the least. More to the point is Leonard Arrington, who called attention to "continuous Mormon pleas for civil aid and federal recognition" and to "repeated Mormon assertions, if they are worth anything, that all the troubles they had been through had not alienated them from 'the institutions of our country.' " [26]

To assess the worth of these assertions is one of the more difficult aspects of the problem. Therald N. Jensen attempted to answer this question in 1938. His investigation contradicted the assertion of Leland Creer, who found "no evidence that the Mormons had ever contemplated withdrawing from the American Union. Nothing is more clearly established from the sources than their continued loyalty and patriotism." [27] Jensen cited considerable evidence casting doubt about the Mormons' loyalty to the United States. But he considered the evidence to the contrary far stronger, so that, in balancing Mormon sentiments of disloyalty against their professed love for the Union, the scales tipped heavily in favor of loyalty to the United States. Expressions of Mormon disloyalty were mere "back eddies," a natural result of resentment against persecution.[28] Jensen urged that it "is helpful to constantly bear in mind that the Mormon Pioneer was also an American pioneer." [29] This sentence is the key to understanding Jensen's position, and that of several other Mormon historians, on the topic of Mormon loyalty. In writing of the Mormons as if they were typical frontiersmen, these historians, in the tradition of Frederick Jackson Turner, have emphasized that part of Mormon history which is part of the mainstream of American civilization and of the westward course of empire.[30]

But in 1846 the Mormons, or at any rate the members of the Council of Fifty, hardly saw their move in this light. The apologists failed to perceive that Mormonism was part of manifest destiny only in a very peculiar way. It is true that Joseph Smith, in the campaign of 1844, had portrayed himself as an expansionist: "Oregon belongs to this government honorably; and when we have the red man's consent, let the Union spread from the east to the west sea; and if Texas petitions Congress to be adopted among the sons of liberty, give her the right hand of fellowship, and refuse not the same friendly grip to Canada and Mexico." [31] Such ideas, however, must not be separated from Smith's hope that the time would come when the kingdom of God would be master over the United States. Should this mastery not occur in the immediate future, Smith was not at all adverse to having Texas remain an independent state, as revealed through the negotiations of the Council of Fifty.

The error in the work of apologist historians is that they have written Mormon history from hindsight. The image of Mormons leaving the United States in order to set up an independent kingdom of God conflicts with the subsequent self-conscious Mormon view of themselves as loyal citizens of the pluralistic twentieth century. What these writers fail to acknowledge, simply, is that a transformation has taken place in the attitude of Mormons toward the United States. This shift, while patently apparent, has in fact served to obscure Mormon understanding of their own past. Of course, such distorting influences upon historiography have been ever present in the reconstruction of the national pattern of American history.

Jensen solved the problem of Mormon loyalty toward the United States with the bland assumption that the "Mormon pioneer was also an American pioneer," as if this fact would automatically take care of a potential conflict of loyalties.[32] In the nineteenth century, it was of equal if not more significance that this American pioneer was also a Mormon pioneer. Since both, to the apologist, were the same thing, conflict of loyalties was eliminated. That is why to Jensen the political kingdom of God could not figure prominently in the immediate aspirations of the Mormons. The *raison d'être* of Mormonism, said Jensen, was not to set up a political kingdom of God, but to wait for Christ.[33]

As anti-Mormon writers have ignored the genuine, democratic, and patriotic motives inspiring the Mormons, the apologists have ignored the equally authentic separatist tendencies that found expression in the political kingdom of God. Since it seemed almost impossible to reconcile the contradictory evidence, each side either ignored or explained away those sources that did not fit the image they wanted to portray. A notable exception was Franklin D. Daines, whose conclusion that separatist and patriotic tendencies in Mormonism were equally genuine and capable of existing side by side is confirmed by Thomas F. O'Dea, who argues that the Mormons could do this because they "never worked out consistently the political implications of their religious philosophy." [34]

The negotiations between the Council of Fifty and the Texas government reveal beyond doubt that the Mormons had at least contemplated the possibility of leaving the territorial limits of the United States. Likewise, there can have been no question that, in the fall of 1845, Brigham Young knew that the area to which he hoped to move the Saints was not part of the United States. In an "Epistle to the Brethren of the Church of Jesus Christ of Latter-day Saints, Scattered Abroad Through the United States of America," Young admonished his followers that removal beyond the boundaries of the United States was a test of orthodoxy:

> If the authorities of this church cannot abide in peace within the pale of this nation, neither can those who implicitly hearken to their wholesome counsel. A word to the wise is sufficient. You all know and have doubtless felt for years the necessity of a removal provided the government should not be sufficiently protective to allow us to worship God according to the dictates of our own consciences, and of the omnipotent voice of eternal truth. Two cannot walk together except they be agreed. Jacob must be expatriated while Esau held dominion.[35]

This letter indicates that Young had not contemplated the possibility that the United States would take over in the near future the region where the Saints hoped to establish the kingdom of God. The Mexican War, however, changed these calculations. Young undoubtedly knew in the spring of 1846 that it was highly probable that the kingdom of God would come under the jurisdiction of the United States.

In the fact that the Saints readily offered the federal government a battalion for service in the war Mormon apologists believed they have found proof that Young desired affiliation with the United States.[36] Indeed, to several generations of Mormons, the epic march of the Mormon battalion from Fort Leavenworth, Kansas, to San Diego, California, has become shining proof of Mormon loyalty to flag and country, a supreme example of a people harassed by a government serving its persecutors in time of crisis. Contrary to popular belief among Latter-day Saints, however, the battalion was not requested by the United States government. Rather, as even Mormon historian B. H. Roberts pointed out, a contingent of two thousand men was actually offered to the government by the Mormons, "and the service was almost piteously pleaded for" by Jesse C. Little, representative of the Saints in Washington.[37] Young and the Council of Fifty had offered the service of Mormon men in order to obtain badly needed cash for the Saints through the military pay to be earned by the Mormon soldiers. President James K. Polk was somewhat apprehensive of so large a Mormon army moving west and only authorized a contingent of five hundred men. In his diary he recorded ". . . that when Colonel Kearney reached that country, he was authorized to receive five hundred of the Mormons into the service so as to conciliate them and prevent them from becoming the enemies of the United States, but if the Mormons reached the country, I did not desire them the only forces in the country." [38]

The motives of the Council of Fifty in sending out the Mormon Battalion, then, were primarily economic. Furthermore, the men who answered the call did so out of loyalty to the kingdom of God and not to the United States. Hosea Stout recorded in his diary that he was "uncommonly wrought up" about the request. He was "glad to learn of war against the United States and was in hopes that it might never end until they were entirely destroyed for they had driven us into the wilderness & was now laughing at our calamities." [39]

Such feelings were a result of the persecutions which the Saints had suffered almost constantly during the brief history of the church. Although the United States had not been responsible for these outrages, the Mormons charged the government with failure to secure justice for them. Irene Haskall Pomeroy wrote from Nauvoo in the summer of 1845: "The fourth of July is just past. I suppose there were balls, tea parties and the like in the east, but here there were nothing of this kind. The Mormons think the liberty and independence of the United States has been too long trampled upon to be celebrated." [40] Ursulia B. Hascall, in 1849, expressed the opinion that "the destruction of the states as a nation is just as sure as the sun will ever rise and set. It is near at hand. It is all ready to burst upon it." [41] Such sentiments were not isolated expressions by members of the Mormon rank and file. Rather, they were inculcated by the leaders. Brigham Young predicted: "God Almighty will give the United States a pill that will put them to death, and that is worse than lobelia. I am prophet enough to prophesy the downfall of the government that has driven us out. . . . Wo [sic] to the United States: I see them going to Death and destruction." [42]

In the light of these observations, it is necessary to re-examine the circular letter by church leaders addressed to the non-Mormon world in 1846, which asserted: "Our patriotism has not been overcome by fire, by sword, by daylight or by midnight assassinations which we have endured; neither have they alienated us from the institutions of our country." [43] This document, of course, was directed to the Gentiles, who were all too eager to suspect the Mormons of disloyalty and treason. Still, the language of the circular did not entirely contradict the private sentiments of the Mormons toward the United States, for Brigham Young drew a significant distinction between the Constitution and the "damned rascals who administer the government." [44]

To the Mormons, therefore, it was quite possible to leave the United States and still remain loyal to its *institutions*. For they were transferring the latter with them in what they believed to be an uncorrupted form in the political institutions of the kingdom of God. In fact, if the United States was to be destroyed, removal of the Saints beyond its boundaries was necessary for the preservation of the kingdom of God. Upon arriving in Salt Lake City, one of Young's followers wrote: "The Lord has provided this place for us and if we are faithful the troubles and calamities of the Gentile nation will not harm. When all is past, we will step forth from our hiding place the secret chambers spoken of in the bible." [45] Presumably, the Saints would thereafter continue the American political tradition through the political kingdom of God. In this sense, Mormons considered themselves superior to Gentiles as upholders of basic American institutions and values. Gentiles had perverted the American concept of liberty by allowing the persecution of a minority group. The Mormons, on the other hand, wanted to preserve liberty for minorities through the political kingdom of God. On July 28, 1858, Brigham Young proclaimed in a sermon:

> It is published from East to West, and from North to South, that the Mormons are opposed to the government of the United States. That is not true, and never was. But many of the officers and people of the United States are too much opposed to their own institutions, and are taking a course to destroy the best form of government instituted by man. They lay the ax at the root of the tree, and it will fall and be as though it had not been.[46]

Young's statement, however, reveals the difficulty of reconciling two conflicting loyalties. In fact, the Mormons have always pretended that the conflict did not exist. Joseph Smith had given a revelation in 1831 admonishing the Saints that he who "keepeth the laws of God hath no need to break the laws of the land." [47] Although the Mormon leaders, throughout the nineteenth century, were to cling to this position without deviation, the realities of conflict between the United States and the political kingdom of God revealed that the Mormons could maintain their position only with some rather strange semantic somersaults, as exemplified by a pronouncement of Apostle John Taylor: "What does it mean, then, where it says if we keep the laws of God, we need not break the laws of the land? Because the laws of God are so much more pure and elevated, so much more adapted to the wants and situation of humanity, that we walk right over everything of that sort; and it is nothing comparatively for us to do; what is required we can easily do it, and a great deal on the back of it." [48]

At best, this pronouncement is confused, an indication of its author's own ambivalence toward the problem. Contradictions between the political theories of the kingdom of God and those of the United States, and conflicts of loyalty posed by the two institutions, were such that the Mormons could not safely afford rationally to examine their varied attitudes. By proclaiming a sincerely felt patriotism in Fourth of July orations, claiming undying allegiance to the Constitution and to the institutions of the United States, and proudly pointing to the courageous deeds of their revolutionary forefathers, the Mormons glossed over the separatist tendencies of the political kingdom of God.

The Gentiles considered such expressions of patriotism to be the height of hypocrisy. Judge Thomas J. Anderson questioned the honorable intentions of the Mormons in the following words: "Will men become attached to the principles of the Constitution of the United States when they hear the government constantly denounced as tyrannical and oppressive? It would be as unreasonable to expect to gather grapes from thorns, or figs from thistles." [49] What Anderson failed to understand was that men do not always think and do what appears reasonable. Brigham Young was quite sincere when he claimed that "to accuse us of being unfriendly to the Government is to accuse us of hostility to our religion." [50] One of the major difficulties was that Mormons and Gentiles were using the same words in totally different contexts and with conflicting connotations.

Nevertheless, the problem of Mormon loyalty to the United States needs to be examined as more than a semantic problem. In their vigorous proclamations of loyalty the Saints apparently were attempting to convince not only the Gentiles but also themselves that their patriotism was burning as bright as ever. This was a difficult demand, indeed, not only because of Gentile persecution, but also because the political kingdom of God required of its citizens a separate loyalty that was difficult to harmonize with loyalty to the United States.

John D. Lee gave a moving illustration of this conflict in an entry in his journal made on January 5, 1851. Lee had been sent to Southern Utah on the so-called Iron County Mission for the purpose of establishing an iron industry. Among the colonists was a large group of converts from the British Isles. During the journey, Lee recorded: "We have had first rate feelings generally. Still I was accused of causing National feelings by speaking of great battles that have been fought by the Americans. I hope never again to excite that kind of National Feelings. All governments on earth but one are corrupt & that is the government of God that is my National Interest." [51] As a member of the Council of Fifty, Lee knew more about this "National Interest" than those who were traveling with him. He knew that one of the main reasons for the exodus was to achieve the ultimate independence of the kingdom of God, so that it could send its accredited ambassadors to the nations of the earth.

"Exalted Above The Hills":
The Rocky Mountain Kingdom

VII

THE CONCEPT OF the migration of a people as a symbolic act, as a rite of passage, is almost as old as history itself. The people of ancient Israel wandered in the wilderness for forty years. Hence not even the gas chambers of Auschwitz could cremate Jewish nationalism. The Puritans insisted that their migration be that of a community rather than the transplantation of disparate individuals to the wilderness of America. And even for those who followed, in groups or alone, the voyage became a ceremony of initiation into a community that was distinct from the rest of the world. The Atlantic Ocean thus became an infathomable well nurturing American nationalism. For the Mormons, the hegira to the Great Basin, just as the Moslem's to Mecca, served the same purpose. It was during the trek to the promised land that apostle Ezra T. Benson, a member of the Council of Fifty, exulted that Israel, at last, had become a "distinct nation." [1]

If Benson was referring to the hearts and minds of the Mormon people, he was undoubtedly right. About the stature and prospects of the political kingdom of God, however, he was clearly too optimistic; but so were nearly all of his fellow council members. As they unfurled the "Ensign to the Nations" in their Rocky Mountain kingdom—whether figuratively or literally cannot be ascertained—little did they know that their first steps toward the ultimate goal of establishing the kingdom of God as an independent nation would come closer to that hope than all subsequent efforts.[2] Little did they know that the State of Deseret, lasting less than two years, would become a symbol of Mormon nationalism in the Rocky Mountains, not its fulfillment. But it is just as well that their prophetic powers did not extend that far.

Eric Hoffer observed in *The True Believer* that modern utopian movements will succeed only if they tap an indigenous nationalistic fervor, a fervor which is of little use unless the participants are "ignorant of the difficulties involved in their vast undertaking." Only under such circumstances will the movement be capable of engendering the kind of "extravagant hope" necessary "to generate a most reckless daring."[3] Without such daring, the Council of Fifty clearly would have failed in transforming a hostile desert environment into a Mormon commonwealth that proved to be the most successful colonization experiment of nineteenth-century America. As it was, the Council of Fifty never ceased striving to transform its vision of Mormon nationalism into reality—at least as long as it controlled the temporal affairs of the "Great Basin Kingdom."

The protective walls of the "everlasting mountains" provided the Council with a singular opportunity for organizing the government of God without Gentile interference. Biblical prophecy, moreover, augured well for the establishment of the kingdom. Joseph Smith had interpreted Isaiah's prediction "that the mountain of the Lord's house shall be established in the top of the mountains" metaphorically, insisting that "it should be in the center of the land."[4] With the organization of the kingdom of God in the Rocky Mountains,

Isaiah's prophecy—and that of Daniel, which referred to the kingdom of God as a stone "cut out of the mountain"—could now be interpreted literally.[5] According to an editorial in the *Millennial Star,* "the nucleus of the mightiest nation that ever occupied the earth is at length established in the very place where the prophets, wrapt in sacred vision, have long since foreseen it." [6] Orson Pratt, applying himself to the task of exegesis, insisted that the government of God would have to originate "in a high place or mountainous region." [7] As a member of the Council of Fifty, Pratt had in fact done his part to insure the validity of this interpretation by participating in the organization of the government of the kingdom of God in the Rocky Mountains shortly after the Council had completed its task of directing the search for the promised land. Brigham Young had boasted that if the Saints had ten years in the Rocky Mountains to set up the kingdom, they would not be rooted out. Yet even before that time was up, the "Lion of the Lord" had grown confident. In a sermon given in July, 1855, he boldly announced to his audience: "The Kingdom of God is actually organized and the inhabitants of the earth do not know it." [8] The prophet, of course, was referring to the political, not the ecclesiastical, kingdom of God.

As a result of the researches into the Council of Fifty and the kingdom of God, it is now possible to arrive at a more adequate understanding of the origins of government among the Mormons in Utah.[9] Franklin Daines' assertion that "for two years after the advent of the pioneers in the Great Basin, they had no need to consider any problem connected with the establishment of civil government" and Leland Creer's opinion that the church met all governmental requirement, clearly, are outmoded.[10] For even the first government in the Salt Lake Valley, established on October 3, 1847, reflected the political theory of the political kingdom of God, as the members of the Council of Fifty understood it. John Smith, who became president of the "municipal high council" in the valley, was a prominent member of that council. So were Charles C. Rich, the military commander, and Albert Carrington, clerk, historian, and deputy postmaster. These men, in accordance with the political theory of the kingdom, derived their temporal authority from the Council of Fifty. Nevertheless, at a meeting held on October 10, 1847, Parley P. Pratt pointed out that the laws made by the High Council were only temporary: "No one quorum has power to give eternal laws for this people but a greater council . . . may do this. . . . The council above named will regulate this matter as soon as they come up and sit." [11] Thus, even in the early colonial period, the Mormons kept up at least a theoretical separation of church and state.

The High Council functioned as an executive, judicial, and legislative body until the autumn of 1848, although it was not formally relieved of municipal duties until January 6, 1849.[12] By that time, Brigham Young and a majority of Council of Fifty members had settled permanently in the valley of the Great Salt Lake. Sometime during that second winter in the valley, the Council of Fifty assumed the reins of government. The first record of a council meeting of the government of God in the promised land, entered in the diary of John D. Lee under December 9, 1848, states that "the Council of Y T F I F *again* met at the House of H. C. Kimball," indicating earlier meetings in Salt Lake City.[13]

In his study of the State of Deseret, Dale Morgan observed that a "council" organized itself into a legislature even before the formal establishment of the State of Deseret.[14] There can be no doubt that this was the Council of Fifty. Many years later, Benjamin F. Johnson recalled that "the Colonial Council or Legislature of Deseret, I think was organized in December, 1848, to which I was elected and held membership through the colonial period." [15]

The activities of the Council of Fifty during the winter of 1848–49, though far removed from ideas of world government, were crucial for the survival of the Saints in a hostile environment. The Council regulated the distribution of land, determined water rights, granted mill privileges, discussed the appropriateness of price control measures in the face of inflation, and legislated stray pen laws to control the cattle. The Council dispatched members to operate ferries and selected plots for a cemetery. It levied taxes for the construction of roads, bridges, and other public works. Concerned with defending the Saints against possible intruders, the Council reorganized the Nauvoo Legion and appropriated funds for the construction of an arsenal. When, during the winter, food became scarce, the leaders of the kingdom ascertained the amount of victuals available in the valley and assured their equitable distribution, threatening those unwilling to cooperate with the death penalty. John D. Lee recorded that "if those that have do not sell to those that have not, we will Just take it & distribute among the Poor and those that have and will not divide willingly may be thankful that their Heads are not found wallowing in the snow." [16]

More important than all these measures, however, were the Council's deliberations on the political status of the kingdom of God and its relation to the United States. On June 28, 1848, George A. Smith and Ezra T. Benson, both members of the Council of Fifty, discussed the alternatives open to the Mormons in a letter to Brigham Young. If the region should be annexed by the United States, they considered the possibility of either becoming a state in the Union, or a territory.

> But as we are in possession of the soil our destiny would be independence should Mexico maintain her old lines. We are not particularly in favor of either plan, but are willing to abide your better judgment, and are willing to use our humble endeavors to the utmost in carrying out any project you may desire for the establishing of the "kingdom of God and his Laws." [17]

Smith and Benson considered possible affiliation with the United States an expedient that would facilitate the transaction of business with the federal government through Mormon agents "and thus save great expense and loss; but we go in, for once in all our life, if possible, to enjoy a breath of sweet liberty and independence." [18] In a letter dated October 10, 1848, the two Saints called the disadvantages of an affiliation with the United States to Young's attention. They pointed to Oregon as an example of how the government treated its territories, sending "a set of starved office seekers, hungry for a loaf from some quarter to be governor, judges and big men, irrespective of the feelings or rights of the hardy emigrants who had opened the country, made the roads, killed the snakes, etc., etc." [19] Liberty for the kingdom of God, however, was possible only if the Mexicans could obtain modifications of the treaty of Guadalupe Hidalgo, which, indeed, they had refused to ratify in February, 1848. But this refusal was little more than a heroic gesture, and by the autumn of 1848 the Mormons knew that their territory had been annexed to the United States. As a result the establishment of the "Kingdom of God and His Laws" in an independent government had become unfeasible if not impossible. The Saints had little choice but to seek affiliation with the United States.

On December 9, 1848, the Council of Fifty met at the house of Heber C. Kimball to deliberate on the advisability of petitioning Congress for a territorial government. It was agreed upon that such a government should only be requested with the understanding that the Mormons could choose their own officers. "Should they send such men as Lilburn Boggs, Neal, Gilliam Benton, King, William & others [who were enemies of the Mormons]," recorded John D. Lee, "we should send them Cross Lotts to Hell, that dark & dreary Road where no traveler ever returns." [20] Not surprisingly, all the officers of the proposed government were members of the Council of Fifty, with Brigham Young as governor. The Council then drafted a petition to be signed by all the Mormons in the Great Salt Lake Valley. John M. Bernhisel was appointed to go to Washington and present the petition to Congress. When the emissary of the Council of Fifty finally left for the national capital on May 3, 1849, the document had grown twenty-two feet long, bearing 2,270 signatures.[21]

In the meantime, however, the Council of Fifty proceeded to establish a civil government without the blessings of Congress. Contrary to Leland H. Creer, however, the Mormons were not "following well established precedents of frontier impatience and restlessness" in organizing the State of Deseret.[22] The fact is that the Saints had migrated to the West precisely for the purpose of setting up their own government. This government, then, was only incidentally an adaptation to frontier conditions. Moreover, as the political theory of the kingdom of God indicates, Mormon separatism was more than "the tendency to emphasize strongly the American principle of local self-government." [23] A commonly held opinion is that the State of Deseret was created by default, because the United States had not yet provided a government for the region, or because gold-seekers and other Gentiles required it.[24] This is not the case. Had a government already existed in the area, the Mormons most likely would not have migrated there. Even if gold-seekers and other Gentiles had not come to the region, the Council of Fifty still would have set up a formal government.

The Council of Fifty apparently established the State of Deseret in order to realize as many of the ideals of the political kingdom of God as possible before affiliation with the United States. Only in this way could the kingdom attain a degree of independence, and independence was one of the main goals of the Mormons. Shortly after the arrival of the first pioneer company in 1847, Norton Jacob quoted Brigham Young as saying:

A man may live here with us and worship what God he pleases or none at all, but he must not blaspheme the God of Israel or damn old Joe Smith or his religion, for we will salt him down in the lake. We do not intend to have any trade or commerce with the gentile world. For so long as we buy of them, we are in a degree dependent on them. The Kingdom of God cannot rise independent of the gentile nations until we produce, manufacture and make every article of use, convenience or necessity among our own people. . . . I am determined to cut every thread of this kind and live free and independent, untrammeled by any of their detestable customs and practices.[25]

In 1849, Young, however, obviously realized that it would be impossible to cut the political threads with the United States; yet he did his best to make those threads as thin and weak as possible. As a result he established the State of Deseret at a time when the Council of Fifty was in absolute political control of the Great Basin, so as to present the federal government with the accomplished fact of a kingdom of God before Gentiles could hamper its development.

The Council of Fifty, in creating the State of Deseret, paid lip service to the doctrine of the sovereignty of the people and the democratic practices of a constitutional convention and free elections. Actually, the new government was formed through the highly centralized and autocratic control of its own organization. Significantly, all officers of the constitutional convention and all members of the various committees drafting the constitution were members of the Council. The fact that the constitution was read to the convention on March 8, 1849, only three days after the convention had opened its session on March 5, suggests that the document was framed after an already existing pattern, undoubtedly the constitution of the kingdom of God. On March 10, the constitution was unanimously adopted by the convention.[26] This move was synonymous with ratification.

The constitution of the State of Deseret was either *prima facie* evidence of the disingenuousness of the Council of Fifty or of its inability to recognize the inherent contradiction of this democratic document with the manner in which it had been created and the conditions under which it would operate. It is quite possible that the framers of the document honestly believed that "all political power is inherent in the People," as stated in the preamble.[27] However, they may also have been aware of the favorable impression such a statement would create in Congress. Perhaps, most important of all, this clause, expressing a doctrine highly respectable in the American tradition, could provide much needed support for political autonomy in the face of potential Gentile interference. Section two of the "Declaration of Rights" affirmed:

> All political power is inherent in the people; and all free Governments are founded in their authority, and instituted for their benefit; Therefore, they have an inalienable and indefeazible [sic] right to institute Government; and to alter, reform, and totally change the same, when their safety, happiness, and the public good shall require it.[28]

But this passage was hardly intended to encourage the principle of popular democracy, for, according to the political theory of the kingdom of God, sovereignty rested not with the people but in the hands of God. And the repository of this sovereignty on earth was not the people but the Council of Fifty.

It is therefore not surprising that the constitution of Deseret had hardly been adopted when the Council of Fifty saw fit to set it aside. Since the Council conceived of itself as the "Living Constitution," such disregard for a constitution merely established on paper was apparently no serious infraction. Article five of the new document provided for an election of a general assembly and state officers on May 7, 1849.[29] This date, however, conflicted strangely with a decision of the Council of Fifty made on March 4, one day before the opening of the constitutional convention, providing for an election to be held on March 12, 1849, "for the purpose of Electing the following men to fill the different Stations in office": Brigham Young, governor; Heber C. Kimball, chief justice; Willard Richards, secretary of state; Newel K. Whitney and John Taylor, associate justices; Horace S. Eldredge, marshal; Newel K. Whitney, treasurer; Albert Carrington, assessor and collector.[30] The election was held on March 12, as planned by the Council of Fifty. Utah historian Andrew L. Neff remarked: "Everything had been cut and dried; . . . How to account for the duplicate procedure, and the inharmonious results is difficult to fathom, so slight is the record." [31] One possible explanation for the irregular procedure is that the Council wanted to establish itself as a formal government as soon as possible, before its position could be weakened by outsiders. But why then did the Council incorporate another election date in the constitution of Deseret? The most logical explanation seems to be that it was done so as not to arouse the suspicions of the federal government. The election of March 12 was obviously too close to the ratification date of the constitution (March 10) to have allowed ample operation of the democratic process. After the admission of Deseret either as a territory or state into the Union, the Mormons hopefully believed that they themselves would be in complete control. According to the preamble of its constitution, the government of Deseret was "Free and Independent." [32] The Mormons saw no reason why, in fact if not in theory, it should not continue to be so. Once the formalities of affiliation with the United States had been taken care of, the irregularities under which the Mormon government had been created needed no explanation.

The general assembly of the State of Deseret, consisting of a senate and a house of representatives, convened for the first time on July 2, 1849. It is difficult to determine, however, how the legislators received their mandate. At the election on March 12, 655 votes were cast for state officers, but no record of an election for the legislature has so far been found. Indeed, it is quite likely that no election occurred. Hosea Stout recorded in his diary that he was mystified by what procedure he had received his mandate.[33] In view of the circumstances, the most likely explanation is that the Council of Fifty simply hand-picked the assembly. The executive and judicial branches of the new government were filled entirely by members of the

Council of Fifty. Of the forty-five members constituting the general assembly, however, only twenty-seven belonged to the Council; yet in the politically more powerful senate, thirteen of the sixteen members held seats on the Council of Fifty. Although only fourteen members of the house out of a total of twenty-nine representatives belonged to the Council of Fifty, they held key positions on all important legislative committees, in keeping with a rule requiring members of the Council to serve as chairmen of all committees to which they belonged.[34] As far as the exercise of political control was concerned, the establishment of the State of Deseret was little more than a *de jure* confirmation of a *de facto* situation.

The general assembly passed no legislation in its July session. This lack of urgency for providing civil laws and institutions is evidence that the Council of Fifty, as the living embodiment of the Law of God, effectively could control the temporal affairs of the kingdom of God without the trappings of democracy. Not until its second session in December, 1849, did the assembly conduct its first legislative business. Interestingly enough, these sessions, like those of the Council of Fifty, were held in Heber C. Kimball's school room.

Dale Morgan has studied the legislation of the general assembly in detail; hence there is no need to recount it, with the exception of two ordinances that reveal the role of the Council of Fifty in a particular light.[35] One of these was the establishment of probate courts. The exact relationship of these courts to the Council of Fifty cannot be determined, but a combination of facts seems to indicate that the probate courts acted as the extended arm of the Council, administering the laws of the kingdom of God on a local level. The probate judge himself had the greatest direct influence on county government in Deseret. It was his duty to choose the first officers of the county. In many ways, the functions of a probate judge in Deseret were comparable to those of a county commissioner. His position was non-elective, subject to appointment by the governor and the legislature. Since the Council of Fifty controlled both the executive and legislative branches of government, the leaders of the political kingdom of God, through the probate courts, could influence the administration of the counties. After the establishment of Utah Territory, the probate courts also assumed criminal jurisdiction to fill a temporary void created by the departure of the Gentile "runaway judges" in 1852. However, even after these unfriendly non-Mormons had been replaced by more sympathetic judges, the probate courts refused to yield their position of power to the district courts. Not until 1874, with the passing of the Poland Act, did the Council of Fifty lose this significant tool for controlling the political kingdom of God.[36]

Another act of the general assembly of Deseret of special significance to the political kingdom of God was an ordinance passed on September 14, 1850, which granted legal status to the Perpetual Emigrating Company. As mentioned previously, the doctrine of the gathering was of special importance for the establishment of the kingdom of God. If the State of Deseret was to become a viable nation-state, its population would have to expand at a rate considerably faster than natural increase would provide, even with the supposed benefit of polygamy. Immigration, therefore, was one of the principal means for increasing the population of the kingdom of God. As a result, the doctrine of the gathering was more strongly emphasized after the Saints had reached the Rocky Mountains than at any previous period in Mormon history.

Since the Council of Fifty had directed the exodus it was only logical that it should continue its role of transplanting the elect to the new Zion. In September, 1849, Brigham Young "proposed the creation of a revolving fund for the purpose of helping the poor to reach Salt Lake." [37] The committee established to raise the necessary sum consisted entirely of members of the Council of Fifty. On September 7, 1850, Willard Snow, Edward Hunter, and Daniel Spencer of the Council of Fifty were appointed to direct the operations of the rotating fund, now named Perpetual Emigrating Fund. It was further decided to organize the fund into a company, chartered by the state. Consequently, Daniel H. Wells introduced a bill to this effect on September 11. On September 14, the general assembly of Deseret approved the charter. The following day, officers of the company were elected at a special conference of the church. The six candidates for the directorship were all members of the Council of Fifty; needless to say, all six were elected.[38]

Activities of this nature suggest that the separation of church and state in Deseret was more theoretical than real, confirming the observations made by Captain Howard Stansbury of the United States Topographical Engineers:

> While there are all the external evidences of a government strictly temporal, it cannot be concealed that it is so intimately blended with the Church that it would be impossible to separate one from the other. This intimate connection of the church and state seems to pervade everything that is done. The supreme power in both being lodged in the hands of the same individuals, it is difficult to separate their two official characters and to determine whether in any one instance they act as spiritual or merely temporal officers.[39]

The free and independent state of Deseret lasted for only two years. At the time the Mormons did not know this, but Deseret was to be the closest they would ever come to achieving an autonomous government of their own. A monument to the national aspirations of the Latter-day Saints, the geographic area covered by Deseret was truly vast, including within its ambitious boundaries all of Utah, most of Nevada and Arizona, substantial portions of Wyoming, Colorado, and New Mexico, sections of Idaho and Oregon, and almost half of California, with San Diego as a seaport.[40] A region of such dimensions was quite beyond the ability of the Mormons to police and settle within a reasonable time unless they expected a rapid influx of converts. Seen in this light, Mormon missionaries who extolled the virtues of the promised land to the working classes of Europe, especially in England, Scandinavia, and Germany, were serving not only as agents of the church but also of the political kingdom of God. Although Deseret never achieved the independent status of a nation-state, and the Mormons soon learned that their freedom would not last, they made the most of it while they had it. For two years, no strangers interfered in Deseret's internal affairs. In 1849, the state printed its own currency. In 1849 and 1850, it also coined its own money. The revived Nauvoo Legion served as its army of defense.[41]

When Brigham Young and the Council of Fifty initiated steps to gain either territorial status or become a state of the Union they did so not because they loved the United States, but because they had no choice. Failure to initiate the move undoubtedly would have aroused the suspicion of Washington. It is only reasonable to assume that the federal government would have taken all necessary measures to ensure that a territory comprising about two-thirds of the Mexican cession remained in the Union. The Council of Fifty, through its actions, revealed that it hoped to maintain as much control as possible while giving the appearance of fully cooperating with the government of the United States. The Council had already taken steps to gain territorial recognition for the new settlement in December, 1848. In May of 1849, John M. Bernhisel left for Washington to carry out the instructions of the Council.

In the meantime, however, the Council of Fifty organized the State of Deseret and decided to press for its recognition as a state in the Union. In a letter dated July 19, 1849, Brigham Young informed Orson Hyde at Kanesville, Iowa, of the creation of the State of Deseret, stating somewhat disingenuously that "we could not well await the tardy operations of the Federal Government without adopting some form suited to our present necessities." [42] Hyde was expected to cooperate with a new delegate sent by the Council to obtain "our admission as a sovereign and Independent state into the Union upon an

equal footing with the original states."[43] This letter reveals
that Young apparently realized that the doctrine of states'
rights, which had worked to the detriment of the Saints in
Missouri and Illinois, could be used to great advantage in
maintaining a considerable degree of independence for the
political kingdom of God in the Rocky Mountains. The
clauses "sovereign and independent" had much greater significance before the ratification of the Fourteenth Amendment.
Had Deseret achieved statehood, the political control of the
Council of Fifty quite likely would have continued with little
outside interference. With such hopes in mind, Almon Babbitt
was sent to Washington to reverse Bernhisel's policy and direct
every effort toward the recognition of statehood for Deseret.[44]
Frank Cannon's assertion that the Mormons attempted to
gain admission to the Union in order to escape its authority,
as paradoxical as this may sound, is thus basically correct.[45]

Babbitt's mission, however, was not to be successful, although anti-Mormon sentiment in Congress at this time was
negligible. But the sectional controversy over slavery worked
just as effectively to frustrate Mormon hopes of obtaining
statehood for Deseret. The southern block in Congress combined with northern advocates of popular sovereignty to
relegate the Mormon kingdom to territorial status under the
Compromise of 1850.[46]

In a special message to the general assembly on March 8,
1851, Governor Young summarized the achievements of the
State of Deseret: "We can ever carry with us the proud satis-
faction of having erected . . . a peaceful, quiet, yet energetic
government, under the benign auspices of which, unparalleled
prosperity has showered her blessings upon every interest."[47]
A month later, on April 5, the legislature of Deseret voted its
own dissolution.

The Council of Fifty, of course, was disappointed over the
failure of Deseret to obtain statehood. Still, if the Council
could place its own officers into key territorial positions, "the
Kingdom of God and His Laws" would be in operation just as

they had been in the State of Deseret. After President Millard Fillmore signed the Organic Act creating the new territory on September 9, 1850, John M. Bernhisel exerted all his efforts to secure appointment of his proposed list of territorial officers. The original instructions had called for suggesting Brigham Young as governor, Willard Richards as secretary, John Taylor as chief justice, Heber C. Kimball and Newel K. Whitney as associate justices, Daniel H. Wells as attorney general, and Joseph Heywood as marshal. All these men belonged to the Council of Fifty.[48] When Bernhisel, however, learned that legal training was required for the positions of chief justice and attorney general, he substituted the names of Zerubbabel Snow and Seth Blair, who were properly qualified but did not belong to the Council.[49] Bernhisel's influence with President Fillmore, however, did not prove sufficient. When news of the approval of the Organic Act reached Salt Lake City on January 27, 1851, the Mormons were disappointed to find that the chief justice, one of the two associate justices, and the secretary of the territory were to be Gentiles.[50]

The Council of Fifty, apparently to forestall interference in its operation by the Gentiles, organized the territorial government of Utah without the assistance of the newly appointed federal officers, who were shortly to arrive from the East. On February 3, 1851, Daniel H. Wells, Chief Justice of the State of Deseret and member of the Council of Fifty, administered the oath of office to Brigham Young. When the eastern officials arrived in the summer of 1851, the Mormons had already held a census. On August 4, they elected their legislature without the benefit of eastern supervision. In this way they could assure that, of the thirty-nine legislators elected from the various counties, at least twenty and possibly more would be members of the Council of Fifty.[51] Incensed over these irregularities, alleged Mormon disloyalty to the United States, priesthood dominance, and polygamy, the Gentile officials left their posts and returned east, eagerly spreading highly distorted stories of Mormon immorality, disloyalty, and treason.[52]

Benjamin G. Ferris, a Gentile who served as secretary of Utah Territory shortly after these incidents, recorded that from 1851 on "the laws of the United States have been *nominally* in operation" but that the facts were quite otherwise.[53] Of the details, however, even Ferris remained ignorant. Although he observed that the Mormon hierarchy exercised complete political control, he did not know how this was achieved. In fact, even at the present time the evidence on how the Council of Fifty ruled the kingdom of God is largely circumstantial.

An examination of Utah territorial legislatures from 1851 to 1896 reveals that not until the 1880's, when the influx of Gentiles into the territory in large numbers began to crack Mormon political hegemony, did the Council of Fifty lose its political influence. Throughout this period it controlled key legislative committees. Council members, of course, frequently went abroad on church missions so that there was considerable fluctuation in the personnel controlling the government. Significantly, whenever a key member of the Council of Fifty returned from abroad, he immediately resumed an important position in the territorial government.[54]

Since church members followed the advice of the hierarchy in matters both spiritual and temporal, the Council never had any difficulty in assuring election of its candidates. Nominations were made by leading church authorities; absence of the secret ballot assured that only the most recalcitrant would dare oppose the official slate. Stanley S. Ivins, in a study of eighteen annual elections from 1852 to 1870, observed that "of the 96,107 votes cast, over this 18 year period, 96 per cent went to the regular candidate. And if the known Gentile ballots are eliminated, the percentage rises to 97.4." [55]

Casting a vote in opposition to approved candidates was severely frowned upon, but was not in and of itself grounds for disciplinary action. Running for political office without church approval, however, was a much more serious matter. In the Mormon colony of San Bernardino, California, B. F. Grouard and F. M. Van Leuven were disfellowshipped simply because they ran for political office against other church members nominated by the authorities, who, incidentally, also happened to be members of the Council of Fifty.[56] Another case of wilful opposition to the political counsel of church leaders occurred in 1854. One of the candidates nominated as representative for Salt Lake County in the legislature, Albert P. Rockwood, had incurred the dislike of a group of voters, who nominated a candidate of their own, Stephen H. Hales, in opposition. According to John Hyde, Jr., a Mormon apostate, Hales obtained the majority; "Stephen Hales was accordingly sent for by Brigham, who gave him a severe reprimand for *daring* to allow his name to be used as an opponent of 'the church nomination.'" Hales was compelled to resign, and Rockwood seated instead.[57] The most important fact of this incident, apparently unknown to Hales and his supporters, and to Hyde, was that Rockwood belonged to the Council of Fifty.

At times, the general Mormon populace, in ignorance of the desires of the hierarchy, put up their own candidate in good faith. Hosea Stout recorded in his diary on August 2, 1855, that he

> . . . took stage and went to Davis County. The annual Election coming on next Monday the good people of Davis had brought their nominee for the Legislature. . . . My business to Davis was to have one of the nominees withdrawn and John D. Parker put on the track in his Place. Accordingly, I called the Bishop and other leading men together and laid the matter before them. The plan was adopted and A. Call withdrawn and Parker in his place, all to the most perfect satisfaction of all parties.[58]

What Stout did not record was that although both Call and

Parker were faithful church members, Call was most likely the more popular man, indicated by the fact of his nomination. But John D. Parker was a member of the Council of Fifty, having been personally ordained under the hands of Joseph Smith.

In view of these circumstances it is not surprising that voters were quite apathetic about exercising their franchise. When Elias Smith, member of the Council of Fifty and editor of the *Deseret News*, chastised his readers for their laxity in going to the polls, claiming ignorance of "how to account for the apathetic feeling that exists in Great Salt Lake County in regard to elections, as few of those having the right of franchise seldom exercise that privilege by going to the polls and voting for those they prefer for official stations within their gift," he was either hypocritical or utterly naive.[59]

As a member of the elite that controlled the kingdom of God, Elias Smith should have known better, although it is quite possible that he clung to the notion that Mormonism was the expression of an equalitarian political tradition.[60] Although both Mormon theology and social institutions were inimical to a society structured along rigid class distinctions, the idea of an elite, openly proclaimed by Joseph Smith and sanctioned by Mormon scriptures, was clearly supported by Brigham Young. The notion of a spiritual aristocracy is expressed in the *Pearl of Great Price*. Abraham allegedly had a vision in which God had shown him ". . . the intelligences that were organized before the world was; and among all these there were many of the noble and great ones; And God saw these souls that they were good, and he stood in the midst of them, and he said: These I will make my rulers; . . . and he said unto me: Abraham, thou art one of them; thou wast chosen before thou wast born." [61] Smith declared in a sermon that "every man who has a calling to minister to the inhabitants of the world was ordained to that purpose in the Grand Council of heaven before this world was. I suppose that I was ordained to this very office in that Grand Council." [62] So, presumably, were the members of the Council of Fifty. Since the latter possessed the priesthood, the idea of a spiritual aristocracy could easily be transformed into the concept of a political elite.

According to what criteria were members of this elite selected? Leadership ability was one of the most important qualifications. The outstanding man in this category, after the death of Joseph Smith, was Brigham Young. Others, such as Reynolds Cahoon, William Clayton, Benjamin F. Johnson, Orrin Porter Rockwell, and John D. Lee, owed their membership in the Council primarily to their unquestioned loyalty to Smith and Young. Almon Babbitt, though lacking in character and fortitude, provided the Council with the special services of a trained lawyer and an able diplomat. A few men were college graduates. Lorenzo Snow had received his training at Oberlin College, Union College was the alma mater of Orson Spencer, and John Bernhisel was an honor graduate of the University of Pennsylvania. In the latter part of the nineteenth century, family connection was of some importance, possibly signifying a decline in the vigor of the organization. Four vacancies in 1867 were filled by sons whose fathers belonged to the hierarchy; this was also true of several new members chosen in 1880. Success in business may have influenced the selection of Horace Eldredge, the wealthiest Mormon merchant in Utah Territory before the coming of the railroad. Angus M. Cannon and John W. Young were mining and railroad entrepreneurs. Both Abraham O. Smoot and Feramorz Little served as mayor of Salt Lake City at the time of their initiation. On the other hand, John D. Lee, prominent in the Council, was a farmer. Philip B. Lewis worked as a tinsmith. In fact, Brigham Young as well as Joseph Smith before him tried to obtain as wide a variety of skills and trades in the Council as necessary to direct the economic development of the kingdom of God. It can be deduced that the nine Mormons with an annual income of one thousand dollars or more tabulated for the years 1862–72 belonged to the Council of Fifty.[63] It is significant, however, that all others averaged incomes of less than a thousand dollars per year. According to Leonard Arrington, the "distribution of income in pre-1869 Utah was much more equal than that of the nation as a whole." [64]

Of considerable interest is the ethnic origin of council members. It has been possible to assemble a list of the names of one hundred and two men belonging to the Council of Fifty between 1844 and 1880. On this list only one name, that of John M. Bernhisel, suggests origins outside of the British Isles and Ireland. Bernhisel, born in Pennsylvania, was of Swiss ancestry. Of the others, eighty-two can be traced positively to England, Wales, Scotland, and Northern Ireland. At least eleven were foreign-born: seven in England, three in Canada, and one in Scotland. Thirty-three came from New England, eleven listed New York as their birthplace; three were born in Pennsylvania and Kentucky, two in Ohio, and one each in Maryland, New Jersey, and Virginia. Seventeen were second-generation Mormons born in Ohio, Missouri, Illinois, or Utah. It may be of significance that in spite of a strong influx of Scandinavian converts to Utah, and a lesser immigration of German and Swiss Mormons, none of these groups achieved important positions of leadership in this period. On the other hand, some of the most forceful leaders in the Council, such as George Q. Cannon and John Taylor, were born in the British Isles.

Precisely how many members of the Council of Fifty were polygamists could not be determined. In Nauvoo the percentage was relatively small. But there is no question that the majority practiced plural marriage in Utah. Of eighty-seven men identified as belonging to the Council of Fifty between 1847 and 1880, at least fifty-six practiced polygamy. Of the others, it is highly probable that only very few remained monogamous. The high percentage of polygamists among council members supports the fact, openly admitted by Mormons, that plural marriage was a practice reserved primarily for the elite. The ratio of married males practicing polygamy in Mormon society as a whole was only around ten per cent between 1846 and 1890.[65]

Since membership in the Council was for life (subject to good behavior), turnover of personnel was slow. Of the fifty-two men comprising the Council of Fifty in 1880, twenty-one had served since 1847 or earlier. Access to the seats of power, impossible to Gentiles without special dispensation by the Council, was thus severely restricted, even for Mormons. When Joseph Smith organized the Council of Fifty in 1844, it was essentially composed of bright, adventurous young men. By 1880, with few exceptions, the Council had turned into an assembly of patriarchs. In 1844, the average age of the Council was forty-two, with the median being around thirty-eight. In 1880, the average age was fifty-eight, the median being sixty-two. Among the numerous factors contributing to the decline of the Council toward the turn of the century, old age may have been an important one.

Active and vigorous men controlled the destinies of the Council during the formative years of the kingdom of God in the Rocky Mountains. Not only did they dominate territorial government, but they also supervised the colonization of the kingdom, the development of its economic resources, and the establishment of schools and a university. When Brigham Young, for example, sent a group of colonists to southern Utah in 1851 to establish an iron industry, John D. Lee, apostle George A. Smith, and Philip B. Lewis began construction of the new settlement in their authority as members of the Council of Fifty.[66] In the 1860's, the Council supervised the construction of telegraph lines and railroads.[67] The Deseret Express and Road Company, the Deseret Agricultural and Manufacturing Society, and the Deseret Iron Company are only representative examples of organizations that had members of the Council of Fifty on their boards of directors.[68] The editor of the *Deseret News* belonged to the Council of Fifty. So did four territorial superintendents of schools.[69]

Council members Orson Spencer and Orson Pratt lectured at the University of Deseret.

The paucity of information available on the Council of Fifty during the 1860's suggested to one historian that the organization, having "played an important role in shaping Mormon economic policy during the first decade in Utah," lost much of its influence thereafter, with the role of economic leadership devolving upon the School of the Prophets, organized in 1867 as a means of economic defense against the influx of Gentiles.[70] The discovery of further documentary evidence, however, suggests strongly that the Council of Fifty continued as a shaper of policy during the decade of the 1860's.

On January 25, 1867, Brigham Young initiated eleven new members into the Council at a meeting held in the city hall at Salt Lake City.[71] The School of the Prophets, however, was not organized until December, 1867, almost a year after the Council of Fifty had been invigorated by the addition of its new members. Although membership in the School of the Prophets was restricted to faithful holders of the Mormon priesthood, and admission to meetings was by card only, the very size of the new organization precluded its being a successor to the Council of Fifty. According to an authoritative estimate, "approximately 5,000 priesthood members belonged to various branch schools." [72] Not a school in the ordinary sense, the School of the Prophets was an assembly of community leaders holding the Mormon priesthood "in which theology, church government, and problems of church and community were discussed and appropriate action taken. . . . So far as its secular phase was concerned, the School of the Prophets resembled an economic planning conference." [73]

Leonard Arrington has summarized the "economic policies of the School of the Prophets—and the programs initiated for the purpose of bringing those policies into effect" as follows: The School sponsored a contract in the name of Brigham Young for construction of the Union Pacific Railroad through Utah Territory in order to prevent "5,000 or 6,000 Irish,

German, and other laborers crowding through our peaceful vales." [74] In order to make the Mormon community more self-sufficient, local cooperative enterprises were established, such as the Provo Woolen Mills and the Utah Manufacturing Company, the latter to produce agricultural machinery, carriages, and wagons. To render prices of these products competitive with those of the East, the School decided on a substantial reduction in local wages. Success of Mormon industry depended largely on an effective transportation system. The financing of interior branch roads was handled largely by members of the School of the Prophets. Sales of products were to be channelled effectively through mercantile cooperatives buying their products from a wholesale house, Zion's Cooperative Mercantile Institution, also established by the School. In order to prevent Gentile merchants from wrecking the cooperative system the School voted "that those who dealt with outsiders should be cut off from the Church." [75] A serious problem confronting the church after the completion of the transcontinental railroad in 1869 was the question of land titles. Mormon property rights were not confirmed by Congress until after the completion of the railroad. In order to prevent Gentiles from acquiring title to land on which Mormons had settled the School of the Prophets appointed a committee to gather information on the legal rights of the Mormons and to "report to the people what steps were necessary to take to preserve their homesteads being claimed by the railroad companies." [76] Finally, the School played a prominent part in a drive to raise money for the Perpetual Emigrating Fund by enjoining its members to observe the "Word of Wisdom" (a revelation by Joseph Smith indicating that tobacco, alcoholic drinks, tea, and coffee were detrimental to the health of man) and to donate the money saved to the Fund.[77]

Although the School of the Prophets unquestionably played the major role in carrying out these various policies and programs, there is strong evidence that the policies themselves actually originated in the Council of Fifty. Council member

Abraham O. Smoot reported to the Provo School of the Prophets that ". . . after conference the council of 50 met and while at the meeting it was proposed that we organize a Mercantile Cooperative Association—in the first place to start a wholesale store so that the necessities of the people may be supplied and not do as our merchants have in bringing such things that our people want and not necessities." [78] Speaking at a priesthood meeting two days later, Smoot instructed his audience in the same manner: "Give the Co'operative system your influence and support, it is a measure concocted by the Council of Fifty as suggested by the President." [79] The construction of railroads, likewise, was decided upon in the Council of Fifty.[80] Whether or not the Council had a hand in planning the other enterprises mentioned above cannot be determined. But, in view of the supervisory capacity of the Council of Fifty, it may safely be assumed that all these activities had the sanction of that organization; in fact, it is highly probable that the Council of Fifty organized the School of the Prophets in order to carry out a vast economic program that could not depend for its immediate supervision on a mere fifty men. The existence of other organizations, implementing the orders of the Council, seems only a logical assumption.

All these measures had one thing in common. They were designed to bring about economic independence for the kingdom of God. The Council of Fifty furthermore believed material self-sufficiency to be one steppingstone to political independence, the ultimate goal for which its members worked so incessantly throughout the territorial period. Dissatisfied with territorial status, the Council repeatedly petitioned Congress for the admission of Deseret as a state into the Federal Union as an alternative to independence. As late as 1874, Young gave some of his reasons for wanting statehood for the kingdom of God: "We regret that we are not in a capacity to make our own laws pertaining to our domestic affairs as we choose; if we were in a State capacity we could do so. . . . But we can not do this now, we are not a State—We are in the capacity of servants now." [81]

With the influx of Gentiles into Utah Territory after the completion of the railroad it became doubtful, however, that statehood would give the Council of Fifty the opportunity to enact the laws of the kingdom of God. At a constitutional convention held in 1872, Gentiles were able to exert their influence for the first time. Significantly, the draft of the new constitution departed extensively from its earlier models. The same was true of the constitutional drafts of 1882 and 1887, neither of which Congress accepted as evidence that the Mormons were giving up polygamy and political control of the territory, these being the chief obstacles for Utah's admission to the Union as a state. When Congress granted statehood to Utah in 1896 it was with the explicit understanding that the Saints had not only ceased the practice of polygamy, but that the Mormon hierarchy had also relinquished its control over the temporal affairs of the kingdom of God. If Zion was still "exalted above the Hills," it was so only in the hearts of the faithful. The banner of the political kingdom of God on Zion's Mount—so at least the Gentiles hoped initially—had ceased to wave to all the world.

That the radical transformation of Mormon society implied in such measures could not have been effected without a major struggle seems self-evident. The political kingdom of God had been one of the chief targets of Gentiles for over half a century. The Saints had suffered immensely in behalf of its defense. Only by demonstrating that the political kingdom of God was a major cause for Mormon-Gentile conflict will it be possible to understand why the Saints struggled so fiercely in behalf of its preservation and why at least the younger generation was at the same time greatly relieved when the Saints were no longer called upon to defend an institution which, by the early twentieth century, had outlived its usefulness.

The Kingdom of God vs.
The Kingdoms of the World

VIII

O N THE AFTERNOON of October 30, 1838, one of the most
brutal butcheries of men and children in the annals of
the state of Missouri occurred. According to one of the survivors, Joseph Young, "a large company of armed men, on
horses," advanced toward the flour mill of Jacob Haun on
Shoal Creek, where about thirty Mormon families had gathered for refuge. Defenseless, the Saints scattered, some into
the woods, others into a blacksmith shop. Overtaken by the
mob, seventeen men and two boys were killed and a dozen
were wounded. Nine-year-old Sardius Smith, who had sought
refuge under a bellows, was dispatched with a blast in the
head. The butcher boasted afterwards: "Nits will make lice,
and if he had lived he would have become a Mormon." [1]

The shots of the Haun's Mill massacre were to keep echo-
ing in the ears of the Saints, reminding them that Satan was
fighting with real bullets against the kingdom of God. The
Mormons knew that Christ's kingdom was not to be of this
world, but they believed fervently that it was to be very much

in it. They also knew that as a result they would have to expect persecution. Yet, understandably, it was difficult to accept and to bear. The massacre at Haun's Mill became a symbol seared indelibly into the memory of the immediate participants, and, vicariously, into the minds of all the Saints. It came to stand for the persecutions that began shortly after Joseph Smith announced his first revelation to the world, which led to the death of the Mormon prophet at the hands of assassins, and which pursued the Saints relentlessly even into the recesses of the "everlasting mountains."

Why did the Mormons, throughout the nineteenth century, experience such harrowing persecutions? This question is one of the most frequently asked about Mormon history.

The Saints themselves found a simple and straightforward answer. Smith had made it clear that "the influence of the devil and his servants will be used against the Kingdom of God." [2] In fact, if Mormonism were the work of God, then Satan had no choice but to oppose it with all the means at his disposal. Persecution, therefore, became one of the touchstones for the divinity of Mormonism; the blood of the martyrs was the seed of the church.

Satan might for a time impede the progress of the kingdom of God but, in the end, the Saints would triumph. The temporary success of the forces of evil was an indication that the Saints had not sufficiently purified themselves: "I, the Lord, have suffered the affliction to come upon them, wherewith they have been afflicted, in consequence of their transgressions; . . . because they did not hearken altogether unto the precepts and commandments which I gave unto thee." [3] Another reason why the Saints were "being driven and smitten by the hands of . . . [their] enemies" was that God had "suffered them thus far, that they might fill up the measure of their iniquities, that their cup might be full," justifying the Lord in pouring out over the enemies of the kingdom of God "my wrath without measure in mine own time." [4]

Although Mormon apologists have searched for more objective reasons to explain the persecutions suffered by the Saints, their ultimate conclusions are not too far removed from those of the early Mormons. Apologists generally agree that the persecutions were primarily a result of Gentile prejudice against Mormonism as a *religion*.[5] The Mormon-Gentile conflict presumably revealed more about the persecutors than about those being persecuted. There is no question that Gentile hatred of the Mormons is a fruitful area for an investigation of aberrations of mass psychology; it is true that intolerance of Mormons can be compared with instances of the mass hysteria and persecution that marked American social history in other eras.[6]

Yet the burden of responsibility must not be placed, in the fashion of the defenders of Mormonism, entirely on the Gentiles. What the apologists have done is to project twentieth-century Mormon values and practices into the nineteenth century. They, understandably, can see no reason why anybody would want to persecute *them*. Neither can they concede this possibility to their ancestors. Consequently, in the eyes of the apologists, the cessation of conflict is primarily evidence of a matured American society willing to accept the religious peculiarities of Mormonism. What the apologists do not want to admit is that Mormonism itself had to undergo fundamental changes in order to make possible its acceptance by society at large.

Even the apologists, however, cannot ignore the fact that polygamy was abolished, if not in 1890, then in 1904. But they portray this change as being superficial, in no way affecting the fundamental values of Mormonism. Yet polygamy became the primary target through which Gentiles could strike at one of the most fundamental institutions of nineteenth-century Mormonism, the political kingdom of God. It was the final decision of church leaders to postpone attempts to establish this kingdom to an undetermined future that marked the extensive underlying change which has affected Mormon society since the turn of the century, and which has made it not only acceptable but also eminently respectable in twentieth-century America.

As long as the Saints, however, exerted all their efforts toward the realization of a temporal kingdom of God on earth, conflict with their environment was inevitable. One enemy of the Saints asked the pointed question, if the Mormons were entirely the victims of the ill will of their neighbors, "why have they come into violent conflict with the people in all their seven places of settlement? For they have tried every different kind of people, from New York, through Ohio, Illinois, and Missouri, to Salt Lake. Are *all* the people of *all* those places incurably vicious, mobbers and trespassers on religious right?" 7

Anti-Mormon writer J. H. Beadle thought he had an obvious answer. He believed the Mormons had brought about the persecutions themselves by incorporating their economic, social, and political ideas and practices within their religion. The Saints, on the other hand, insisted that the First Amendment gave them the right to worship God according to the dictates of their own conscience, and claimed that their enemies were depriving them of their freedom of *religion*, thus returning one of the chief arguments of the Gentiles, that is, Mormonism was un-American, with the retort that violation of the First Amendment was certainly equally as unbecoming of Americans. The Gentiles, therefore, tried to argue that Mormonism was more than a religion. Mormon apostate John Hyde, for instance, declared that "as a religion, Mormonism cannot be meddled with; as a civil policy it may." 8

The Saints of course disagreed with this interpretation, but they did occasionally admit that building of a kingdom was a major cause for persecution. Edward W. Tullidge wrote in the *Millennial Star* as follows:

It is because there has, day after day, and year after year, grown up and fast spread in America a realization, and with it a fear of the empire-founding character of "Mormonism" and the "Mormons," that this Church has such heartrending pages in its history. It is because of the growth of this presentiment and fear that a Joseph, a Hyrum, a Parley, a David Patten, and many others of the chief Elders and Saints have been directly or indirectly Martyred.[9]

Even before the temporal claims of the Mormons had caused disturbances with the Gentiles, Smith's insistence on leadership in both spiritual and temporal matters provoked some internal difficulties in the church. T. B. H. Stenhouse claims that "as early as the second year of the Church some of the leading elders of Zion (in Missouri) were accusing Brother Joseph in rather an indirect way of seeking after monarchial power and authority." [10]

Refusal to acknowledge the authorities of the church in temporal matters played an important role in the excommunication of Oliver Cowdery, who had been Smith's closest associate in the most formative period of Mormonism and who had been designated as "Second Elder" in the church. While answering charges "for virtually denying the faith by declaring that he would not be governed by any ecclesiastical authority or revelations whatever in his temporal affairs," [11] Cowdery asserted:

> The very principle of . . . [ecclesiastical authority in temporal affairs] I conceive to be couched in an attempt to set up a kind of petty government, controlled and dictated by ecclesiastical influence, in the midst of this national and state government. You will, no doubt, say this is not correct; but the bare notice of these charges, over which you assume a right to decide is, in my opinion, a direct attempt to make the secular power subservient to church direction—to the correctness of which I cannot in conscience subscribe—I believe that the principle never did fail to produce anarchy and confusion.[12]

Cowdery was promptly excommunicated.

It is reasonable that the Gentiles objected even more vigorously to Smith's temporal authority. As early as 1833, a resident of Missouri charged that

> Their prophet also induced his followers to believe that he would form a temporal kingdom or government, and they would not be subject to the laws of the state, but should make their own laws, have their own civil officers to execute them, Joseph, the prophet, being dictator, aided by revelation and his cabinet or council; and when their edicts were sent forth they were obeyed without a murmur by his followers.[13]

Such sentiments, clearly, were at least as important as strictly religious matters for inflaming the passions of the Gentile mob, thus leading to the expulsion of the Saints from Jackson County.

If the quest for peace in western Missouri, likewise, proved illusory, it was again because the Gentiles, among other reasons, resented the fact that Mormonism extended its claims into the temporal affairs of man. By the autumn of 1838, increasing resentment between Saints and Gentiles erupted into open warfare. On October 25, about seventy-five Saints and a mob of Missourians engaged in a skirmish known in the annals of Mormon history as the battle of Crooked River. Five days later the massacre at Haun's Mill occurred.

Shortly after these outrages, Joseph Smith and his associates were brought to trial, while the Missourians went free. Judge Austin A. King, moreover, conducted the trial in a very biased manner. Any Mormon witness sought by the defense in behalf of Smith was immediately hunted down and arrested. As a result, the testimony given at the trial was offered by enemies of the Mormons or personal enemies of Smith, including a number of apostates. But, although such testimony has to be viewed with considerable caution, it cannot be discounted entirely, especially in view of Smith's subsequent endeavors in behalf of the political kingdom of God. The evidence of the apostates, in fact, reveals how far Smith had attempted to go in establishing that kingdom. Thomas

B. Marsh, a former apostle who was reinstated in the church in Utah, testified: "The plan of said Smith, the prophet, is to take this State; and he professes to his people to intend taking the United States, and ultimately the whole world. This is the belief of the church, and my own opinion of the prophet's plans and intentions." [14] George M. Hinckle asserted that

> . . . the general teachings of the presidency were, that the kingdom they were setting up was a *temporal* as well as a spiritual kingdom; that it was the little stone spoken of by Daniel. Until lately, the teachings of the church appeared to be peaceable, and that the kingdom was to be set up peaceably; but lately a different idea has been advanced—that the time had come when this kingdom was to be set up by forcible means, if necessary.[15]

Such statements grossly distorted the means by which Smith hoped to establish the kingdom of God. But the fact that he did, indeed, dream of setting up a political kingdom he could not deny. In his personal history, Smith recorded that "our Church organization was converted, by the testimony of the apostates, into a temporal kingdom, which was to fill the whole earth, and subdue all other kingdoms." [16] The prophet implied that this testimony was false, and so, technically, it was. But what Smith failed to confide to his history —which he was very much aware he was writing as a public record for posterity—was that he believed in a distinction between the church and the political kingdom of God, and that it was the latter which was "to fill the whole earth, and subdue all other kingdoms."

Whatever the official teachings of the leaders of the church, there can be no question that the faithful thought in terms of a temporal kingdom of God that would triumph over its enemies not only spiritually but physically as well. Albert P. Rockwood wrote to his father: "Far West is headquarters of the Mormon War, the Armies of Israel that were established by Revelation from God are seen from my door every day.

. . . the companies are called Dan because the Prophet Daniel has said the Saints shall take the Kingdom and possess it forever." [17] Rockwood, one of these Danites, became a member of the Council of Fifty in 1844, and continued to serve the kingdom in the Rocky Mountains. His zeal in attempting to set up the political kingdom of God as taught by his prophet clearly contributed to his expulsion, and that of his fellow Mormons, from the state of Missouri.

The attempt to build a political kingdom of God was also the primary reason why the Mormons were forced to leave Illinois, and why Smith was murdered in 1844. When the Mormon prophet organized the Council of Fifty in Nauvoo under strictest secrecy, he must have been rather too optimistic a judge of human nature to expect all of the members to have sealed lips at a time when close associates were becoming enemies overnight. It was thus only to be expected that rumors of the secret council and its doings would soon circulate in Nauvoo and spread among friend and foe alike. These rumors and half-truths gave to the political kingdom of God, in the eyes of Gentiles and apostates, the aspect of the sinister and the subversive. The opposition that led directly to the assassination of the prophet was partly caused by rumors that the Mormons were planning to overthrow the government when they got strong enough, and to take possession of the country—rumors that seemed to confirm John C. Bennett's revelations that Smith planned to establish a Mormon empire in the Middle West. Thomas Gregg, in his *History of Hancock County*, observed that the Gentile residents of the area feared the Mormon doctrine of a political kingdom, observing that "It is not to be wondered at, . . . that the sober and reflecting citizens of the County should become alarmed." [18] Governor Thomas Ford, who claimed that he had spies both among the Mormons and their enemies, reveals in his *History of Illinois* that he had learned some of the important secrets connected with the political kingdom of God, albeit in distorted form:

It seems, from the best information that could be got from the best men who had seceded from the Mormon Church, that Joe Smith about this time conceived the idea of making himself a temporal prince as well as spiritual leader of his people. He instituted a new and select order of the priesthood, the members of which were to be priests and kings temporally and spiritually. These were to be his nobility, who were to be the upholders of his throne. He caused himself to be crowned and anointed king and priest, far above the rest; and he prescribed the form of an oath of allegiance to himself, which he administered to his principal followers. To uphold his pretensions to royalty, he deduced his descent by an unbroken chain from Joseph the son of Jacob, and that of his wife from some other renowned personage of Old Testament history. The Mormons openly denounced the government of the United States as utterly corrupt, and as being about to pass away, and to be replaced by the government of God, to be administered by his servant Joseph.[19]

Even more detailed is the account by George Davis, who claims for his source of information none other than defected members of the Council of Fifty:

That the authority with which God had clothed him [Smith], being *"Jure Divino,"* extended over all mankind, and was paramount and superior to any human authority. Joe further stated, that God had revealed to him, that the Indians and Latter Day-Saints, under Joe as their King and Ruler, were to conquer the Gentiles, and that their subjection to this authority was to be obtained *by the sword!* From this revelation, he enforced upon them that it was necessary he should be crowned King, and they, believing in the gross imposition, yielded to his edict. Joe was accordingly crowned KING under God, over the immediate house of Israel. This ceremony was performed in 1842, by a council of fifty in number denominated the "ANCIENT OF DAYS." . . . He further impressed upon the council crowning him, that God's desire was, as revealed to him (Joe), that, for the time being, this was to remain *a perfect secret* until God should reveal to the contrary. And accordingly Joe swore them all to present secrecy, *under the penalty of death!* [20]

If such accounts implied that Smith had engaged in treasonable activities, some of his enemies came right out and said so. In an unpublished reply to Smith's famous appeal to the Green Mountain Boys sent to Thomas C. Sharp, anti-Mormon editor of the *Warsaw Signal,* the writers accused Smith "That you and your clan did consider yourselves a separate nation as much so; as any foreign nation. . . . you and your followers cast off all allegiance to the General or states government and assumed a new one for yourselves, and that act, we consider no less than high treason—" [21]

The most direct accusations, however, were to be made by Wilson Law, one of the Mormon prophet's closest associates before his excommunication in 1844. In an attempt to obtain a warrant against Smith for treason, Law charged that the prophet, while preaching on the text of Daniel 1:44, declared "that the kingdom referred to was already set up, and that he was king over it." [22] Almost identical charges were levelled against Smith in the Nauvoo *Expositor.*

The *Expositor* allegations and the subsequent reaction triggered the immediate events leading to the death of Joseph Smith and his brother Hyrum. Although the affair has been described many times, none of these accounts takes into consideration the existence of the Council of Fifty in Nauvoo in 1844; yet an examination of its role in the controversy provides a new dimension to understanding the causes of the death of the Smith brothers.

The *Expositor* was a newspaper started by a group of disgruntled Mormons under the leadership of Dr. Robert D. Foster, who put up most of the money for the press, and William Law, second counselor to Joseph Smith for over two years. Law was firmly convinced of the validity of Mormon doctrine. By April of 1844, he was equally certain that Joseph Smith was a fallen prophet. According to Law, the rift with

Smith had its origins in the prophet's authoritarian insistence upon managing all temporal affairs of the Saints, including those of William Law. The second counselor, however, claimed that he avoided an open break with Smith until he learned of the doctrine of polygamy. Dr. Foster, likewise, insisted that he broke with the prophet over this same doctrine. Smith had set April 20 as the date for Foster's church trial. Foster, however, intended to use the trial as a platform to condemn the prophet. To prevent such a possibility, a secret council excommunicated Foster along with William, Wilson, and Jane Law "for unchristianlike conduct." [23] It is of considerable interest that, of the thirty-two persons present at this meeting, twenty-two can be identified as members of the Council of Fifty.

Why should the Council of Fifty take such a special interest in a church trial? That its concern was warranted is indicated by the aims of Law and Foster. Law was more dangerous to church unity than apostates like John C. Bennett because he still professed to believe in Mormonism. Law, in fact, maintained that his major motivation was to reform the church of Joseph Smith. It was with this purpose in mind that he started his newspaper in order to "expose" the alleged malpractices of Smith and his followers. Francis Higbee, one of Law's disciples, wrote a letter to the editor of the *Warsaw Signal* outlining the aims of the forthcoming edition of the *Expositor*. The paper was to be an exposé of Smith's "Mormon *Seraglio* a[nd] *Nauvoo Harem;* and his unparalleled and unheard of attempts at Seduction." [24] Most writers have emphasized this aspect of the affair. Higbee, however, noted that the edition was to be "fraught with Joe's peculiar and particular mode of Legislation—and a dissertation upon his delectable plan of government." [25] Was Higbee referring to the Council of Fifty and its ambition to set up a political kingdom of God? Had the apostates learned important secrets concerning that organization? It seems that they had.

A number of reasons support this assumption. In a prospectus the publishers proclaimed it their "sacred duty . . . to advocate unmitigated DISOBEDIENCE TO POLITICAL REVELATIONS, and to censure and decry gross moral imperfections wherever found, either in the plebeian, patrician or SELF-CONSTITUTED MONARCH." [26] When the first and only issue of the *Expositor* was published on June 7, 1844, it contained the significant passage: "We will not acknowledge any man as king or lawgiver to the church." These allusions suggest that the apostates must have had at least some knowledge of ideas and practices connected with the Council of Fifty. If the spectacular news of Smith's kingship could reach Governor Ford, it seems likely that it could also reach those who were even closer to the scene. The objection to Smith as lawgiver suggests that Law, Foster, and their associates must have had at least a rudimentary knowledge of "The Kingdom of God and His Laws": their objection to Smith as lawgiver in an ecclesiastical sense would not have been logical as long as they accepted the revelations providing the foundation for the church; these revelations Law and Foster professed not to reject.

The publication of the *Expositor* put Smith in a dilemma. If he did not stop its publication, exposure of the secrets of polygamy and the political kingdom of God might well rend the church asunder and leave it a prey to the Gentiles. If he closed the paper, he faced charges of flaunting one of the most sacred of American liberties, the freedom of the press. The attempt to obtain an injunction against the publishers on grounds of libel—difficult to get in any case—might have backfired if Law and Foster had endeavored to prove the veracity of their charges in court hearing.

If the Mormon prophet could not afford to tolerate an apostate newspaper dedicated to the exposure of practices and principles which—at least for the present—had to remain secret at all cost, he had no recourse but to silence the press by force. When Smith convinced his rubber-stamp city council, in a trial without lawyers, witnesses, or jury, that the paper should be declared a public nuisance, its press smashed, and the remaining copies of its first and only issue burned, he may not have been prepared to pay for such a course of action with his life; but there can be no question that he was prepared to pay a high price for the preservation of the kingdom. As an experienced leader of his people, Smith must have known that his action in the *Expositor* affair would not remain without far-reaching consequences. He had been forced to weigh in his own mind what would be worse for the kingdom, the disease or the remedy; and he had made his decision.

In destroying the press Smith had overstepped both his authority and the bounds of propriety. Yet in the eyes of faithful Mormons the public indignation was out of all proportion to the outrage committed. The Saints could not help but remember the lack of public concern over their own tribulations in Missouri. In fact, Gentile indignation was not only caused by a somewhat hypocritical concern for free speech. The destruction of the press provided them with an opportunity to vent their hatred for the Mormons, which had built up for some time. On June 12, 1844, the Warsaw *Signal* wrote: "We have only to state that this is sufficient! War and extermination is inevitable! CITIZENS ARISE, ONE and ALL!!! Can you *stand* by, and suffer such INFERNAL DEVILS! to ROB men of their property rights, without avenging them? We have no time for comment! Every man will make his own. LET IT BE WITH POWDER AND BALL!! [27]

For Joseph and Hyrum, it was indeed powder and ball. When Governor Ford learned of the destruction of the *Expositor,* he went to Carthage demanding that Smith and all others involved in the incident stand trial in that town. Although Smith and his brother Hyrum hesitated to submit to Ford's demands, and even crossed into Iowa to escape to the Rocky Mountains, they finally went to Carthage, believing that the Gentiles would otherwise ravage the city of Nauvoo.

They went with the heavy foreboding that they would not live to see Nauvoo again. Their premonitions were tragically accurate. On June 27, 1844, the prophet and his brother became martyrs to the cause of the kingdom of God.

It is the consensus of most historians that if Smith had handled the *Expositor* affair with more caution he and his brother would not have died at Carthage. George Gayler speaks for most historians who have written on the subject: "It cannot be doubted that the destruction of the press of the Nauvoo *Expositor* was the most serious blunder committed by the Mormons since their arrival in Illinois four and a half years previously." [28] B. H. Roberts, however, differs from this interpretation. He admits that the destruction of the press was illegal, but a matter of expediency, and under the circumstances essential for the survival of the Mormons in Illinois.[29]

Roberts, however, bases his evaluation on the assumption that the Gentiles would have believed what he considered to be the *slanderous* statements made in the *Expositor*. But, in the light of the Council of Fifty and the concept of the political kingdom of God, it now appears that many of these charges, however distorted they appeared in the newspaper, had a basis in fact. It seems quite likely, therefore, that the destruction of the press was a greater necessity than even Roberts concedes. The prophet was faced with a kind of Hobson's choice, in which he viewed destruction of the press as perhaps the lesser of two evils. It is, therefore, not unreasonable to affirm that demolition of the *Expositor* was the correct decision, even though it resulted in personal tragedy. Had Smith lived and allowed the apostates to publish their allegations, the pent-up fury of the Gentiles might have precipitated a repetition of the events that drove the Mormons from Missouri in 1839. If this had happened, the exodus to the West would have occurred under possibly disastrous circumstances; the Saints might have been forced to migrate without necessary provisions or equipment. As it was, the death of Joseph and Hyrum Smith temporarily stilled the furor of the bigots of western Illinois. When the conflict between Gentiles and Mormons revived to the point where removal to the Rocky Mountains became a matter of survival for the Saints, Brigham Young and the Council of Fifty had had sufficient time to prepare for an orderly migration. Through his death, Smith may well have become the saviour of his people.

Although the death of Joseph Smith temporarily calmed the tension between the Mormons and their neighbors, the existence of the political kingdom of God and the Council of Fifty continued to be a cause for apprehension on the part of Gentiles and apostates. In a writ issued for the arrest of prominent citizens of Nauvoo for "treasonable designs against the state," mention was made of a private council of which the accused supposedly were members. Whoever originated the complaint must have had some information regarding the Council, for six of the seven persons named in the complaint belonged to the Council of Fifty.[30] And in the summer of 1845, John S. Fullmer, while on a mission for the Council of Fifty, reported: "The apostates are trying to get up an influence with the president of the United States to prevent the Saints emigrating westward, and that they have written to the president informing him of the resolutions of the General Council [Council of Fifty] [sic] to move westward, and representing that Council guilty of treason, etc." [31]

As subjective a term as treason, however, leaves wide room for interpretation. The Polk Administration chose to construe it broadly and even allowed five hundred Mormons to enlist in a battalion under General Stephen Watts Kearny, if with some misgivings. The Mormons vehemently denied such charges by making a semantic distinction in their minds between loyalty to the institutions of the United States and fealty to the government. Words that must have sounded treasonable to Gentile ears might readily have been uttered by Mormons who regarded themselves as exemplary patriots. Understandably, enemies of Mormonism refused to accept

semantic distinctions. Shortly after their arrival in the Salt
Lake Valley, the Saints made the painful discovery that mountains, desert, and vast expanses of sagebrush proved little
more protection than semantics. Consequently, controversy
followed the Saints to their refuge. Only too soon, the halls
of Congress resounded with the echoes of conflict from the
"everlasting mountains" and continued to reverberate until
the political dreams of a Mormon empire were crushed.

The opposition which the kingdom of God was to
encounter in its new Zion was foreshadowed by a petition
referred to the Committee on Territories of the United States
Senate on December 31, 1849. This letter was signed by none
other than William Smith, brother of Joseph and former
member of the Council of Fifty who had joined apostate
James Strang's kingdom on Beaver Island in Lake Michigan.
Protesting "against the admission of the Salt Lake Mormons
into the Union as a State," Smith insisted that

> . . . Salt Lake Mormonism is diametrically in opposition to the
> pure principles of virtue, liberty, and equality, and that the
> rulers of the Salt Lake Church are bitter and inveterate enemies
> of our government. They entertain treasonable designs against
> the liberties of American freeborn sons and daughters of free-
> dom. They have elected Brigham Young (who is the president
> of their church) to be the Governor of the proposed State of
> Deseret. Their intention is to unite church and state and whilst
> the political power of the Roman pontiff is passing away, the
> American tyrant is endeavoring to establish a new order of
> political popery in the recesses of the mountains of America.[32]

Smith and Strang, of course, were less concerned about political popery, a practice of which they themselves were guilty,
than about the competition to their kingdom from that in
the Rocky Mountains. When Congress, at the time, turned a
deaf ear to such demands, being involved in the more important business of hammering out the Compromise of 1850,

Strang hoped that he might be able to route the opposition by receiving the appointment as governor of Utah Territory.[33]

In the light of the "carpetbag" officials, under whom the Mormons suffered somewhat impatiently for over a generation, Strang, who acquitted himself as an able legislator in the state of Michigan, actually might not have been the worst choice. The Mormons, at any rate, were quickly disenchanted with the federal officials who arrived in 1851, providing a foretaste for conflict that was to last until 1890 and longer. Mormon desire for self-rule, under the auspices of the political kingdom of God, understandably was the major bone of contention.

To their amazement and consternation, the first federal officials to arrive in the territory found an organized government already well established. The celerity with which the Saints had created their territorial government caused these officials to suspect that the Mormons considered their presence superfluous. B. D. Harris, territorial secretary, flatly refused to recognize the Mormon legislature, claiming its election to be illegal. The Mormons, however, ignored Harris' protestations. More trouble arose when Judge Perry Brocchus lectured the Saints on their patriotic duties and cast some aspersions on the moral virtue of the women in his audience. The Mormons were understandably enraged; more serious difficulties were avoided only by the rapid departure of the "foreign" officials from the territory. The Mormons, however, had only gained a reprieve, for the "runaway officials" inevitably would call to the government's attention what they considered Mormon obstinacy and disloyalty. Fortunately for the Saints, John M. Bernhisel, territorial delegate, arrived in Washington before the "runaways," and could thus counteract anti-Mormon propaganda. The Fillmore Administration accepted Bernhisel's explanations and sent more amenable representatives. Congress even passed a law under which territorial officials absenting themselves from their post without cause would forfeit their pay. In gratitude, the Saints named their new territorial capital Fillmore, and the county, Millard.[34]

Amicable relations between the Mormons and the federal government, however, lasted but for a short time. Rumors of Mormon disloyalty to the Union kept circulating in Washington, and they were more readily believed because polygamy, now openly avowed by the Saints, seemed a singularly un-American social system to most Americans. When President James Buchanan sent an ill-starred expedition to Utah in 1857, it was as much to suppress polygamy as an alleged Mormon rebellion. As Richard Poll has pointed out, the Democrats were in dire need of stealing some of the thunder from the Republican "twin relics" platform of 1856 to prove to a reform-minded North that they, too, were against at least one relic of barbarism.[35]

The "Utah War," as it turned out, was a rather half-hearted attempt to bring the Mormons to terms. Congressmen might deliver rhetorical cannonades against social and political conditions in Utah, but "votes were cast in terms of national political considerations." [36] Advocates of popular sovereignty were painfully aware that too zealous a crusade might backfire. If one relic of barbarism could be rendered criminal, what about the other one—slavery? [37]

Such sentiments may in part account for the inglorious end of "Buchanan's Blunder." To the Saints, it was a matter of divine providence, even if the directions of this providence were at times difficult to discern. At the outset of the "war," Brigham Young suggested that the Lord might have precipitated the conflict as a means to achieve the political independence of the kingdom of God. In a speech on August 2, 1857, a week after the ominous news of the approaching United States Army had reached the Saints, he declared:

> The time must come when there will be a separation between this kingdom and the kingdoms of this world. Even in every

point of view, the time must come when this kingdom must be free and independent of all other kingdoms.

Are you prepared to have the thread cut today? . . . I shall take it as a witness that God desires to cut the thread between us and the world when an army undertakes to make their appearance in this Territory to chastise me or to destroy my life from the earth. . . . We will wait a little while to see; but I shall take a hostile move by our enemies as an evidence that it is time for the thread to be cut.[38]

According to Norman Furniss, such speeches were merely "propaganda designed for home consumption" and, undoubtedly, that was part of their purpose.[39] Yet Young's private sentiments, confidentially revealed to none other than Thomas L. Kane, cannot be dismissed that easily. "The time is not far distant," he wrote to the staunch friend of the Mormons in 1858, "when Utah shall be able to assume her rights and place among the family of nations."[40] Official documents of the period, no doubt purposefully, are dated "State of Deseret," not "Territory of Utah." One letter, directed to Col. Thomas Ellerbeck of the Nauvoo Legion, was signed by Thomas Tauner [sic] as "Captain of the Royal Artillery, Deseret."[41] Yet hopes for immediate independence were short-lived. The successful mediating efforts of none other than Kane himself saw to it that the kingdom of God would continue its course indefinitely within the boundaries of the United States.

With the outbreak of the Civil War, the Mormon question was temporarily eclipsed by considerations of far greater weight. Yet, if Lincoln had been aware of the extent to which the Mormon hopes for the impending establishment of an independent kingdom of God had been revived, he might have viewed the Saints with more apprehension. As it was, he replied to a question of what he planned to do about the Mormons by saying: "I propose to let them alone." He compared the Mormon question to a knotty green hemlock log on a newly cleared frontier farm. The log being too heavy to remove, too knotty to split, and too wet to burn, he thought it best to "plow around it." [42]

The Saints, for more obvious reasons, did the same with the United States. Confident that the political independence of the kingdom of God would come in the Lord's due time, they did not feel compelled to engage in overt acts of treason. At the opening of the overland telegraph, Young dramatically cabled: "Utah has not seceded." [43] Yet, understandably, the Civil War quickened Mormon expectations for the deliverance of Zion. Joseph Smith himself had predicted that war, beginning in South Carolina, would envelop the earth and lead to the "full end of all nations." [44] The punishment to be meted out to the United States was to be the just reward for her failure to redress the wrongs committed against the Saints. The government would be utterly wasted. "Not so much as a potsherd [would] be left." [45]

Remembering these prophecies, church leaders predicted the inevitability of conflict even before the outbreak of hostilities. In January, Young wrote to William Hooper, territorial delegate in Washington: "True, South Carolina may be permitted to secede peaceably for a time, but as dissolution gains area it will also gain bitterness, until the fierce spirit urging to civil war will whelm fair portions of a once renowned Republic in rapine, flame, and bloodshed." [46] In anticipation of the impending destruction, Young confided to Hooper: "We are very·thankful that Congress has not admitted us into the Union as a State. However, we shall continue to tease them on that point so long as they even pretend to legislate for the past Union...." But, at the height of crisis, he wrote "that people, whom the very great majority have striven to obliterate, will step forward and continue to honor the Heaven-inspired Constitution bequeathed to us so rich a legacy by our forefathers." [47]

Certain enemies of the Mormons, nevertheless, charged the Saints with desiring a confederate victory. What the Mormons, however, really seem to have expected—at least during the beginning of the war—was a mutual destruction of both sides. Such expectations found expression in the diary of Charles Walker who, in 1861, wrote: "The Virginians are preparing to seize the capital at Washington, and where it will end they know not, but the Saints know and understand it all. . . . Bro. Brigham spoke of the things in the East said he hoped they would both gain the victory said he had as much sympathy for them as the Gods and Angels had for the Devils in Hell." [48] But, whatever the rhetorical expressions of the Mormons and their leaders, no openly hostile actions toward the government occurred. The Saints assumed a waiting attitude; they believed if the Lord saw fit to permit the destruction of the United States they would be ready to take over. Declared Heber C. Kimball: "We shall never secede from the *Constitution* of the United States. We shall not stop on the way of progress, but we shall make preparations for future events. . . . God will make the people free as fast as we are able to bear it." [49]

In keeping with this idea of preparedness, the Council of Fifty held itself in readiness to take over when other earthly governments would crumble. After it had failed to obtain statehood for its revived State of Deseret in 1862, the Council nevertheless continued the state organization in the enigmatic meetings of the so-called ghost legislature of Deseret, which convened the day after the close of each session of the territorial legislature during the 1860's. A private message given to this "legislature" by Brigham Young in 1863 reveals its nature and purpose:

Many may not be able to tell why we are in this capacity. I do not think that you see this thing as it is. Our organization will be kept up. We may not do much at present in this capacity, yet what we have done or shall do will have its effect. . . . This body of men will give laws to the nations of the earth. We meet here in our second Annual Legislature, and I do not care whether you pass any laws this session or not, but I do not wish you to lose one inch of ground you have gained in your organi-

zation, but hold fast to it, for this is the Kingdom of God. . . .
We are called the State Legislature, but when the time comes, we
shall be called the Kingdom of God. Our government is going
to pieces and it will be like water that is spilt upon the ground
that cannot be gathered. . . . I do not care whether you sit one
day or not. But I do not want you to lose any part of this
Government which you have organized. For the time will come
when we will give laws to the nations of the earth. Joseph Smith
organized this government before, in Nauvoo, and he said if
we did our duty, we should prevail over all our enemies. We
should get all things ready, and when the time comes, we
should let the water on the wheel and start the machine in
motion.[50]

James Duane Doty, Gentile governor of the territory (1863–
65), revealed his awareness of these political realities in a
letter to Secretary of State William Seward. He said if the
three existing governments in the territory, that is, the church,
the military, and the civil, exercised power only in those
spheres consistent with their function, friction could usually
be avoided. Unfortunately, the church, in 1861 (he pointed
out in his letter), had revived "an Independent government
called the State of Deseret whose boundaries include Utah
and portions of Nevada and Arizona. This form of government is preserved by annual elections of all of the *State*
officers; the Legislature being composed of the same men who
are elected to the Territorial Legislature, and who by resolution, re-enact the same Laws for the 'State,' which have been
enacted for the Territory of Utah. . . . This *fourth* government," concluded Doty, "is now fully inaugurated." [51]

The permanent establishment of this fourth government,
at least in the near future, depended of course on the disintegration of the Union. When Lee surrendered to Grant at
Appomattox, however, it became only too obvious that the
anticipations of the Saints and God's foreknowledge once
again had not coincided. Nevertheless, more than a year
after the cessation of hostilities, Frances P. Dyer could write
to her father that apostle John Taylor "could not finish" an

address to the Saints "without running on to the one string that they all harp on all the time till I get sick of it, that is the *down fall* of the United States government and the building up of *Mormonism.*" [52] It is understandable, therefore, that the leaders of the kingdom of God continued the operations of the "fourth government."

J. Wilson Shaffer, a gubernatorial appointee of the Grant Administration, who arrived in Salt Lake City in 1870 with the boast that "never after me, by God, shall it be said that Brigham Young is Governor of Utah," quickly learned that promises of this kind escaped the lips as easily as they were difficult to fulfill.[53] In a letter to Shelby M. Cullom, the representative from Illinois whose anti-polygamy bill had recently been defeated in the Senate, Shaffer complained that he found his office to be "a mere sinecure. . . . A mockery. A farce. . . . It is hard to be nominally Governor in Utah. Brigham Young is permitted to exercise the power of the law giver. . . ." [54] Even a cursory examination of the correspondence between Mormon territorial delegate William H. Hooper and his ecclesiastical superior reveals that Shaffer's frustrations were not without foundation.[55] These frustrations, moreover, were not alleviated when Brigham Young ceased to convene the ghost legislature of the kingdom of God after 1870. The Gentiles apparently did not attribute this decision to a change of heart among Mormon leaders. For it was in the 1870's that the anti-Mormon crusade slowly gained momentum, bursting upon the Saints with its full force in the following decade. Few Gentiles, clearly, believed that the Mormon hierarchy would suddenly disintegrate like the Puritan oligarchy, as described in Oliver Wendell Holmes' celebrated poem of the wonderful "One-Hoss-Shay."

Dedicated Protestant clergymen therefore decided to organize missions—much as those sent to "darkest Africa," or those to convert the "Heathen Chinese"—to teach the Mormons the errors of their social and political ways and, perhaps, reclaim them for civilization, or, failing this, to save innocent women and children from a corrupt and lecherous

Mormon priesthood.[55] Although the Gentile inhabitants of the territory did not always share the crusading zeal of their spiritual guardians, they quickly perceived that moral indignation could be turned to political advantage. Men like Frederick T. Dubois, who were primarily interested in undermining and destroying the centralized control exerted by the political kingdom of God, outlined some of the important political considerations behind the anti-polygamy forces:

> Those of us who understand the situation were not nearly so much opposed to polygamy as we were to the political domination of the Church. We realized, however, that we could not make those who did not come actually in contact with it, understand what this political domination meant. We made use of polygamy in consequence as our great weapon of offense and to gain recruits to our standard. There was a universal detestation of polygamy, and inasmuch as the Mormons openly defended it we were given a very effective weapon with which to attack.[57]

Consequently, a veritable flood of printer's ink inundated the presses and carried a wave of anti-Mormon sentiment across the country. An examination of this literature reveals that those who saw the political kingdom of God as Mormonism's greatest threat to American liberties could raise their voices in as shrill a tone as those who considered polygamy to be the foulest blot to stain the honor of American womanhood. J. H. Beadle, author of the notorious *Life in Utah,* insisted that it was "the union of Church and State, or rather, the absolute subservience of the State to the Church, the latter merely using the outside organization *to carry into effect decrees already concluded in secret council,* that makes Mormonism our enemy." [58] The following excerpt from one of the numerous anti-Mormon pamphlets of this period further illustrates this position:

> Had Deseret been admitted as a state of the Union, the States would been [sic] confronted not only by polygamy, a foul blot

upon civilization, but by a state dominated by an autocratic hierarchy, whose cardinal principle it is that the so-called "Kingdom of God on Earth," i.e. the Mormon Church-State is the only legitimate government on earth, and that all other states and nations must eventually acknowledge its sway. The expurgation of this incubus upon the nation would undoubtedly have involved a civil war.[59]

Another pamphlet, aptly titled *The Mormon Conspiracy to Establish an Independent Empire to be called the Kingdom of God on Earth;* . . . assessed the role of polygamy in the fight against the kingdom of God as follows:

Congress after Congress has been importuned by the saints for the privilege of coming in [to the Union], but the request has been denied each time, wholly on account of the polygamous practices of Utah's people, which they could not give up. How strange it is, that a matter of comparatively small consequence to the nation as polygamy is, should have served as the sole means of many years to hold in check this diabolical conspiracy for the founding of a theocratic empire in the very heart of the greatest and freest Republic the world has ever known.[60]

Historians have been aware for some time that the popular belief according to which polygamy was the primary reason for the persecutions of the Mormons after the Civil War is incorrect, and that polygamy was largely a convenient excuse to strike at the political influence of the Mormon hierarchy.[61] Some Mormon historians, however, while acknowledging the fact that the Gentiles were attempting to eradicate a political kingdom of God, have denied that such a kingdom ever existed, thus dismissing Gentile accusations as lacking substance. In view of the idea of the political kingdom of God and the activities of the Council of Fifty, this interpretation can no longer be supported. However much the Gentiles exaggerated and distorted Mormon aims to establish a political kingdom of God, the charges are not without a basis in fact. Although this revision provides more understandable motives for Gentile actions against the Mormons, it does not, of course, exonerate the anti-Mormons from unjustly persecuting the Saints. Mormon values, in certain respects, differed significantly from those of American society at large, but this difference was no license for intolerance.

Although it is difficult to document the precise role the Council of Fifty played in this conflict, it stands to reason that it assumed major responsibilities in a struggle involving its very existence. This conjecture is supported by some important circumstantial evidence. When the Gentiles, in 1870, threatened the political hegemony of the kingdom of God by forming the Liberal Party, the Mormons responded by organizing the People's Party, which served as the political arm of the kingdom of God until 1892. It should not be surprising, therefore, that the chairman of the central committee of the People's Party, John Sharp, was a member of the Council of Fifty. Significantly, the Mormon party never failed in obtaining the major political prize—the congressional seat in Washington—as long as the majority of Mormons had the franchise. William H. Hooper, who served the Mormons in Washington until 1872, belonged to the Council of Fifty. So did George Q. Cannon, who replaced Hooper and served until 1882, when he lost his seat under the Edmunds Act. This act not only outlawed polygamy, but also denied all those convicted of "unlawful cohabitation" the right to vote or to hold office. Cannon went to the penitentiary as a polygamist.[62]

By ousting Cannon, the Gentiles believed they had won a major victory. Their triumph, however, was short-lived, for the People's Party returned another candidate, John T. Caine, to Washington. In view of the circumstances it is highly probable that Caine, too, was a member of the Council of Fifty, although the fact cannot be documented. By curtailing the political activities of Cannon, the Gentiles, nevertheless, had struck at the seat of power. After the death of Brigham Young in 1877, George Q. Cannon had more influence in the church than any other man. The non-Mormons, recognizing this fact, had dubbed him the "premier of the Mormon state" or the "Mormon Richelieu." [63] It is highly significant, for instance, that, until the reorganization of the Council of Fifty in April, 1880, it was George Q. Cannon who kept the records, of the Council, and not John Taylor, president of the Quorum of the Twelve and subsequent president of the church.

The reorganization of the Council of Fifty in 1880 suggests that it may have been dormant for a period, possibly since the death of Brigham Young or perhaps even longer. On March 3, 1880, L. John Nuttall, secretary to the Quorum of the Twelve, wrote the following letter to George Q. Cannon in Washington, D.C.:

> Dear Brother: At the last meeting of the Council of the Apostles, the propriety of calling together the Council of Fifty was considered. On enquiry as to the whereabouts of the records and names of the members it was understood that you have the custody thereof upon which I was directed to write to you for such information as will put the Council in possession of said records, preparatory to calling the members together. Please answer at your earliest convenience.[64]

On March 20, 1880, Nuttall acknowledged the receipt of the records: "Dear Brother: Yours enclosing the key of small box came safely to hand: we have also obtained the box and records in good shape." [65] On Monday, March 29, Nuttall recorded in his diary that he "went this morning with Elder Franklin D. Richards at his office and examined the records of the council of 50 or Kingdom of God and made out lists of members now living." [66]

The reorganization of the Council took place immediately after the general conference of the church in April. On Saturday, April 10, the Council of Fifty convened at 10 A.M. in the council house, and at 2 P.M. at the city hall. According to the minutes of these meetings, "some of the first members spoke upon the objectives of the Council etc. and repeated many things that had been said by the Prophets. Elders Taylor, Rich, Woodruff, E. Snow, B. F. Johnson, E. Hunter and Joseph Young." [67] On April 21, the Council again convened at the city hall. At this meeting, Feramorz Little, Mayor of Salt Lake City, was "admitted as a member." [68] The records of the Council indicate that thirty-eight old members were on the lists when the reorganization occurred. During April, fourteen new members were initiated. These fourteen men, with few exceptions, were ecclesiastical, political, and economic leaders of the territory. Two of them were to be ordained apostles in October, 1880.[69]

The reasons for the regathering of the Council, and the matters discussed at its meetings, are conjectural. The records are silent on these points. Several circumstances surrounding the reorganization, however, should be noted. In 1880, the church was half a century old and in commemoration of its founding the Quorum of the Twelve proclaimed a jubilee year. In October of that year, the First Presidency, under the leadership of John Taylor, was reorganized. The new president was the exponent of a very conservative and fundamentalist viewpoint in the church. The Council of Fifty, organized by Joseph Smith himself through revelation, apparently could not simply be pushed aside.

Such considerations, however, most likely were of secondary significance, for the reorganization both of the Council of Fifty and of the First Presidency occurred at a very crucial period in Mormon history. It was in 1880 that the Liberal Party made a special drive to challenge Cannon's seat in Congress. It was in 1880, also, that President Rutherford B. Hayes contemplated a change in policy toward the Mormons. On January 13, Hayes recorded in his diary that he had decided to destroy the temporal power of the Mormon church: "Laws must be enacted which will take from the Mormon Church its temporal power. Mormonism as a sectarian idea is nothing, but as a system of government it is our duty to deal with it as an enemy of our institutions, and its supporters and leaders as criminals." [70] In a message to Congress in December, 1880, Hayes requested the creation of a federal commission to control political affairs in Utah.[71] These circumstances lend credence to the assumption that the Council of Fifty directed the defense of the kingdom against the anti-Mormon onslaught. A somewhat cryptic letter, written by L. John Nuttall in 1881 to Bishop William D. Johnson of Kanab in southern Utah, seems to indicate that, at its October meetings in 1880, the Council of Fifty may have decided either to expand its organization or else to create subsidiaries reminiscent of the School of the Prophets to meet with the new emergency:

> In regard to the admission of more members to the C————l I do not think it would be advisable at present. In a short time we may organize another, then changes and other admissions may be made. What instructions you may have to impart to those two brethren named, can be done in the usual manner.— Do not forget to uphold the authorities of the Church and Bro. Cannon at Washington—I am not surprised at the condition of the Canaan Herd, and look for their dissolution.[72]

This time, however, the Council of Fifty was unequal to its task. Under the watchful eye of the Utah Commission, the courts zealously prosecuted offenders of the Edmunds Law. The Mormons called it legal persecution, and many, including John Taylor, went into hiding rather than submit to the humiliating circumstances under which these trials were conducted. The Edmunds-Tucker Law of 1887 further increased the pressures on the Saints. Under its provisions, witnesses were compelled to testify, including wives against their husbands; voting, holding office, and serving on juries was possible only to those pledging, under a test oath, obedience to the anti-polygamy laws; church property in excess of $50,000 was subject to escheat proceedings; the church itself was disincorporated. Because they considered even these measures insufficient to crush the political influence of the Mormon hierarchy, the anti-Mormons introduced the Cullom-Struble

Bill in Congress in 1889, which threatened complete dis-
franchisement of all Mormons by providing that belief in the
doctrine of polygamy alone was sufficient to bar an individual
from the franchise and from holding office. Realizing the
futility of further resistance church leaders finally decided to
give in to the demands of the government in order to save the
church from destruction. On September 25, 1890, church
president Wilford Woodruff issued a statement denying that
the church still solemnized polygamous marriages; "And I
now publicly declare that my advice to the Latter-day Saints
is to refrain from contracting any marriage forbidden by the
law of the land." On October 6, 1890, this Manifesto was
unanimously sustained at a general church conference.[73]

The Council of Fifty, however, apparently had not given
in without a heroic fight. The details of this struggle are at
present still unknown. But, here and there, windows are
opened into the activities of individual council members in
this period. One of the most important of these insights is
provided in the correspondence of John W. Young with the
hierarchy. Young, who had the advantage of being a mo-
nogamist in dealing with the Gentiles, had far-flung business
connections as a railroad entrepreneur of some stature. Because
of his wide range of acquaintances, he worked incessantly in
Washington in behalf of the kingdom. In fact, Young's business activities, in part, seem to have been a cover up for the
more serious purposes of representing the interests of the
kingdom of God. "The part I am constrained to assume," he
wrote to fellow council member Franklin D. Richards, "is not
for business success nor worldly show, but the good that can
be accomplished, and business is merely the incidental part
and only forms the veil to cover my real objects, which, if left
too open, would scare away those to whom I now apply, and
whose aid I fain would use for the benefit of our beloved
cause." [74] The delicate and confidential nature of Young's
negotiations with members of the Cabinet, senators, and congressmen to secure favorable political appointments for Utah,
to obtain support against anti-polygamy legislation, and to

work for a more favorable climate of opinion toward the Mormons is underscored by "a letter to the Presidency which is of such a private nature it could not be trusted to the mails and must not be entrusted to anyone but the *most secure hands* . . . as it is of the very gravest importance to the Great Cause for which we labor." [75]

In Utah, likewise, Young's activities and influence seem to have been of crucial importance. He reacted to criticism of his financial manipulations and his railroad enterprises by arguing that he was motivated by the desire to prevent "outsiders" from gaining control of the railroads. "Unfortunately, for the success of our plans all these matters have to be kept private." [76] In politics, he supported the participation of certain key Gentiles to the city council of Salt Lake City in hopes that such collaboration would accrue to the benefit of the beleaguered kingdom. The problem was to find the right Gentiles. In a remarkable letter of the First Presidency to Young, the election of such persons, once they would agree to run, was simply taken for granted. As late as 1888, the leaders of the kingdom were apparently quite confident of being able to deliver the votes. [77]

In fact, as more evidence begins to accrue, it now appears that, contrary to popular opinion, political control did not cease with the Manifesto—at least not immediately. It is, indeed, all too easy to fall into the old *post hoc ergo propter hoc* fallacy, that is, simply because Mormon political hegemony did in fact cease some time *after* the Manifesto, the Manifesto heralded the beginning of the end for polygamy. But this is not to say that polygamy ceased *because* of Woodruff's famous declaration. On the contrary, it is doubtful that John Taylor's successor foresaw at all the full consequences of his actions. Quite possibly, he may have considered the Manifesto merely a tactical maneuver in order to protect the kingdom as well as the church. The preservation of the church alone, as a religious institution, would have made the restitution of polygamy almost impossible in a social environment hostile to its practice—as demonstrated, indeed, by the history of Mormonism in the twentieth century. But, if the kingdom of God could have been preserved, perhaps it might have been possible to continue polygamy publicly once the Gentile onslaught had spent itself.

With the advantage of hindsight, this argument may appear as a mere begging of the question. But, to Woodruff, continuation of the political kingdom of God seems to have been a real alternative. True, in 1889, the First Presidency publicly declared "that this Church does not claim to be an independent, temporal kingdom of God, or to be an *imperium in imperio* aiming to overthrow the United States or any other civil government," and once again affirmed its traditional public position that "Church government and civil government are distinct and separate in our theory and practice. . . ." [78] To those who understood the political theory of the kingdom of God, however, this declaration was in complete harmony with the one issued four years later, at the completion of the Salt Lake Temple in 1893, by a convocation of one hundred and fifteen select church leaders, who unanimously affirmed that "the Presidency of the Church are set to govern and control the affairs of the Church and Kingdom of God . . . that upon their shoulders rests the responsibility of teaching, governing, controlling and counselling the Church and Kingdom of God in *all* things on the earth." [79]

Perhaps Woodruff was merely clutching at straws in a desperate attempt to evade the inevitable. But he was not the only one who attempted to keep alive the belief that the kingdom of God, and with it the church, would be delivered from the enemy in the near future. In 1900, Woodruff's successor, Lorenzo Snow affirmed at a special priesthood meeting in the Salt Lake Temple that "there are many here now under the sound of my voice, probably a majority, who will live to go back to Jackson County and assist in building that temple." [80]

By accepting polygamy as the major issue, the church leaders could always insist that the persecution of the Saints was of a *religious* nature, involving a violation of their constitutional rights. The enemies of Mormonism, of course, knew this. To repeat Dubois: "There was a universal detestation of polygamy, and inasmuch as the Mormons openly defended it we were given a very effective weapon with which to attack."[81]

"As the Mormons openly defended it"; this statement is the clue. For to the frustration of the Gentiles, the Saints always denied the allegations pertaining to the political kingdom. And they could do this most effectively without being technically untruthful, for, as mentioned previously, the political kingdom of God was not a church organization. Hence, Mormon leaders could keep the opposition somewhat in the dark. This, at least partially, explains the profound frustration of the Gentiles in their attacks on the kingdom. When, and if, the full story of the role of the kingdom of God in the anti-polygamy crusade is revealed, the verdict of future historians might well be that in 1890 the Saints merely lost a battle, being as yet undefeated in the war. The enemies of Mormonism, at any rate, apparently felt this way; the continued altercations with the Saints for at least another twenty years seem to indicate that the Gentiles were less than satisfied with their "victory" of 1890. The story of this subterranean war, much less spectacular than the history of the anti-polygamy crusade—copy was more difficult to obtain and harder to sell to the newspapers and journals that had thrived on the imaginary details of life in the gigantic seraglio that supposedly was Utah—promises to be in many ways far more important for an understanding of the transformation of Mormonism than the public cessation of polygamy. If a full record of this struggle were available to the historian, its account would undoubtedly fill a book. In the absence of crucial primary sources, the following and concluding chapter of this study can provide only a glimpse into certain episodes of that final struggle which ended in the metamorphosis of the political kingdom of God.

Epilogue: The Metamorphosis of the Kingdom of God

IX

Gentile persecution was one of the most important reasons why Mormon leaders relegated to an undetermined future their attempts to build the temporal kingdom of God on earth. There were, however, still other factors that contributed to the decline of the kingdom. The Mormon-Gentile conflict of the 1880's had generated the temporary revival of millennial fervor among the Saints, and stimulated the hope that the church would momentarily be delivered from its enemies. Lorenzo Hatch believed that the Edmunds Act was a harbinger of the millennium, and in 1890 many Saints recalled Joseph Smith's prediction of 1835 that fifty-six years should "wind up the scene." [1] John Mills Whitaker recorded in his journal in 1887: "Our only hope lies in the fact that the Lord has promised this as a Choice Land, that no King shall rule here, and it has an eternal future and will be the head of the world domination in His own due time, and for this we will pray and wait. For the promise is that it will not be given to another people." [2]

Epilogue: The Metamorphosis of the Kingdom of God

The optimism of Whitaker's remarks, however, appear to be dampened by a spirit of resignation. As the years wore on without deliverance, fatalism among the Saints became more pronounced. At a special priesthood meeting held in Salt Lake City in 1900, Mormon leaders apparently tried their best to counteract this spirit of defeatism. Church president Lorenzo Snow, as mentioned previously, affirmed that "there are many here now under the sound of my voice, probably a majority, who will live to go back to Jackson County and assist in building that temple." [3] The site, of course, was to be the original center stake of Zion. This event would herald the immediacy of the parousia. Although Snow's statements "created a profound feeling among all present," it was only too apparent that such enthusiasm was short-lived.[4] In 1903 Benjamin F. Johnson recalled that "we were over seventy years ago taught by our leaders to believe that the coming of Christ and the millennial reign was much nearer than we believe it to be now." [5] When Johnson, furthermore, felt that he could reveal important secrets of the Council of Fifty to a trusted friend, his action suggested that church leaders themselves no longer hoped for the immediate realization of the political kingdom of God, an event that definitely had to precede the ushering in of the millennium.[6] The decline of the idea of the political kingdom of God was thus an inevitable corollary of the decline of millennialism.

There were other and more practical reasons why the Council of Fifty ceased to function. The conception of a temporal kingdom that would dominate the world could provide a powerful motivation for a society of farmers and artisans to carve an inland empire out of a hostile environment, thus providing a physical basis of survival for Mormonism. In fact, the positive leadership of the Council of Fifty may well have been one of the primary reasons why Mormonism, unlike most sects originating early in the nineteenth century, not only survived but also continued to thrive. Yet, having successfully accomplished its important mission of establishing a home for the Saints, the Council may have found it difficult to employ the idealistic vision of a world empire as the justification for the more mundane direction of everyday Mormon endeavors, especially in view of the onslaught of a hostile world that attempted to crush this empire, partly in response to the ideas and activities of the very organization that had created it.

In giving up the idea of establishing a political kingdom of God in the near future, Mormon leaders also yielded to pressures from within the church. The paradoxical nature of the kingdom—its affiliation with concepts of national manifest destiny and its contrasting insistence on separatist Mormon nationalism—was a phenomenon largely unappreciated by the Saints. Nevertheless, it was patently apparent that the two concepts could not forever exist side by side. When, after the Civil War, it became more and more obvious that the chances for a separate Mormon kingdom of God were very remote, a younger generation of Latter-day Saints, recognizing the contradictory nature of the kingdom, were eager to identify Mormonism with the mainstream of American life without reservations. Such a desire placed increasing pressure on the kingdom.

The first important signs of internal discontent appeared in 1869, when, after the completion of the transcontinental railroad, a number of prominent Mormon businessmen and intellectuals believed that the time had come to end the isolation of the kingdom. Under the leadership of William Godbe, a prosperous merchant who had been close to Brigham Young, such liberal Mormons as E. L. T. Harrison, Edward W. Tullidge, W. H. Shearman, and Eli B. Kelsey called for cooperation with the Gentiles and for an end to church control over temporal affairs.

Tullidge later insisted that the idea of a separatist political kingdom of God was in fact a distortion of what he conceived to be the true meaning and destiny of Mormonism: "The idea never was that this Latter-day Israel was to be as a kingdom within a kingdom. It never was marked down in the divine programme that this Zion of America was in any sense a foreign power (even of divine cast) to be formed within the native galaxy of the American Republic—a Kingdom of God whose destiny it was to supersede and obliterate the present United States." [7] Rather, Tullidge affirmed, it was the divine mission of Mormonism "to give a more glorious destiny to the American nation itself." [8] This statement would seem to be directed against the Gentiles so as to counteract charges that the Saints were intent on establishing an independent kingdom of God. However, closer examination reveals that Tullidge was not speaking primarily to the Gentiles but to his fellow Mormons: "When Mormonism *is not* thus manifested," continued Tullidge, "*then it is not* fulfilling its own distinctive mission and divine calling." [9] To Tullidge the wish to identify Mormonism with the mainstream of American life had therefore become the father of the thought that the Saints never were fated to establish "a kingdom within a kingdom."

Brigham Young, understandably, could not allow the Godbeite heresy to threaten the kingdom from within. In an investigation before a High Council of the church, the insurgents were asked if they would acknowledge Brigham Young's right to dictate to them "in all things temporal and spiritual." [10] The followers of Godbe countered with the question of whether or not it was possible for them to honestly differ from the presiding priesthood. "The High Council affirmed that this was contrary to church doctrine," and that they "might as well ask whether [they] could honestly differ from the Almighty." [11] Refusing to accept this interpretation, the Godbeites were summarily excommunicated.

It is an ironic commentary on social change that the liberalism of the Godbeites has become the conservatism of twentieth-century Mormons. This change is vividly illustrated by the testimony of church leaders in the Smoot hearings. In 1903, a powerful group of senators instigated proceedings to remove Reed Smoot, a Mormon apostle, from his senate seat, on the grounds that the Mormon hierarchy still controlled political affairs in Utah, that separation of church and state were only practiced superficially, and that Smoot was therefore an emissary of the Mormon priesthood as well as a representative of the state.[12] Most of the leading Mormon authorities were subpoenaed to appear before the senate committee. Alleged church control of politics and attempts to establish a political kingdom of God were the major charges levelled against the Mormons. President Joseph F. Smith averred that the church, and not Smoot, was on trial. These hearings, more than anything else, forced Mormon leaders to come to a decision on church influence in politics, and on the future of the political kingdom of God. Smith's testimony would have startled Brigham Young considerably, for the son of Hyrum Smith testified that: "Our people are given the largest possible latitude for their convictions, and if a man rejects a message that I may give him but is still moral and believes in the main principles of the gospel and desires to continue his membership in the church, he is permitted to remain and he is not unchurched." [13] This assertion was an affirmation of future policy rather than past practice. The Godbeites had been by no means the only ones excommunicated for refusing to accept the temporal "counsel" of the hierarchy.

The political kingdom of God received considerable attention at these senate hearings, with the writings of Orson Pratt coming under particularly close scrutiny. No self-respecting critic of Mormonism could ignore Pratt's famous statement regarding the legitimacy of the kingdom of God:

> The Kingdom of God is an order of government established by divine authority. It is the only legal government that can exist in any part of the universe. All other governments are illegal and unauthorized. God, having made all beings and worlds, has the supreme right to govern them by His own laws,

and by officers of His own appointment. Any people attempting to govern themselves by laws of their own making, and by officers of their own appointment, are in direct rebellion against the kingdom of God.[14]

Perhaps no other statement by a Mormon leader gained as much notoriety in anti-Mormon literature.

The task of refuting Pratt before the committee fell to James E. Talmage, whom the church had appointed to digest the massive testimony of its witnesses and iron out any contradictions. Talmage drew support from a statement by Brigham Young, who had once dismissed Pratt's "vain philosophy" as being "no guide for Latter-day Saints."[15] To Talmage it was irrelevant that Young had levelled the charge in a totally different context, and that the Mormon leader shared Pratt's views about the kingdom of God.[16]

Talmage's approach, however, was the only realistic one, especially since church leaders in the past had defended the kingdom against the Gentiles only by pointing out that church and state were separate in Mormondom, and that the charge of church control of politics was a distortion because in a Mormon community political leaders inevitably belonged to the church. The Mormon leaders obviously could not publicly reverse their stand on a doctrine as fundamental as that of the political kingdom of God, especially since they had always denied its existence to the Gentiles. Hence church leaders could only continue to affirm that a political kingdom of God was in no way part of the Mormon dream. The hierarchy could exorcise the separatist tendencies of Mormonism best by insisting that they had never existed. The intellectual transformation of Mormonism could best be accomplished under the pretense that it was not going on.

Because Gentile accusations frequently distorted Mormon aims, and because the enemies of Mormonism were unaware of the technical distinction between church and kingdom, church leaders could quite effectively bury the political kingdom of God by taking refuge behind semantics without being technically guilty of untruthfulness. Even before Talmage took the stand, the First Presidency had published an article in the 1903 Christmas edition of the *Deseret News* which reaffirmed its traditional public stand on the kingdom of God. The Mormon church, the article asserted, "does not attempt to exercise the powers of a secular government, but its influence and effects are to strengthen and promote fidelity to the law and loyalty to the nation where its followers reside. The phrase 'church and kingdom' . . . [denotes] solely an ecclesiastical organization. It is separate and distinct from the state." [17]

The First Presidency could not have chosen its words more carefully. The word *kingdom,* as used in this context, had always been synonymous with *church* in Mormon usage. Any mention of the *political* kingdom of God was of course scrupulously avoided, although, ironically, the avowed purpose of the church "to strengthen and promote fidelity to the law and loyalty to the nation where its followers reside" was applicable to the political kingdom of God as well. The Mormon leaders must have known that this statement—introduced by Talmage as evidence for the defense in the Smoot hearings, and so reminiscent of the one issued shortly before the Manifesto, as well as foreshadowing the official declaration of the church regarding relations of church and state published in 1907— could be interpreted by the Gentiles as a Mormon concession; yet to those who understood the true purposes of the political kingdom, it was nothing of the kind.[18] In fact, the phrase could be viewed as a subtle statement of defense in behalf of the kingdom by those who were privy to its political philosophy. It was, of course, a supreme paradox that the Mormon leaders could apply a theoretical separation of church and state to the very purpose of preventing such a division.

The doctrine of polygamy provided another subtle means for defending the kingdom by serving as a foil to deflect the onslaught on political Mormonism. Dubois, for instance, charged that the Mormons were attempting to cloud the real issues [i.e., relationship of church and state in Mormon dominated areas] by "trying to force the protestants to issues which they themselves have never raised" [i.e., polygamy].[19]

Although Smoot's vindication might be interpreted as a victory for the Mormons, the church leaders would not have been able to survive many such victories. For with each new controversy the survival of the political kingdom depended increasingly on a private interpretation of words. As time went on, it became more and more apparent that the kingdom could not live by semantics alone, especially when it was being deserted by its own citizens.

Led by a vocal minority of intellectuals in the Godbeite tradition, a new generation of Mormons—ignorant of the political kingdom of God—began to identify with the mainstream of American culture. Frank Cannon, later to become a notorious enemy of his own people, illustrated through a description of his patriotic feelings sentiments that were most likely shared by many young members of the church. While in Washington, some time before the Manifesto, he remarked: "I wonder whether another American ever saw that city with such eyes of envy, of aspiration, of wistful pride, of daunted admiration. Here were all the consecrations of a nation's memories, and they thrilled me, even while they pierced me with the sense that I was not, and might well despair of ever being, a citizen of their glory." [20]

On a more intellectual level, Nels L. Nelson, Professor of English at Brigham Young University, attempted to show in his *Scientific Aspects of Mormonism* how much Joseph Smith had anticipated the thoughts of Charles Darwin, John Fiske, T. H. Huxley, and Herbert Spencer. Nelson was looking for evidence to demonstrate that Mormonism was in the mainstream of Western thought and culture, and in the forefront of those forces that were pushing America ever onward and upward in a cosmic process of scientific and moral evolution; he was satisfied that he had found this evidence in abundance.[21]

Even more important in this enterprise was the work of the historian. Liberal students of Mormon history such as Andrew Love Neff, for example, insisted that the separatist tendencies of Mormonism had existed only as a figment of the imagination of the enemies of the church. To Neff and others the Turner hypothesis provided a ready-made vehicle for the Americanization of Mormon history.[22] In fact, these scholars probably would have invented Turner had he not existed, so readily did they apply the frontier hypothesis to the Mormon past. By portraying the Saints as typical frontiersmen, they created the impression that Mormon social and political institutions, from their inception, reflected the values of American democracy. Whatever departures had occurred from the main currents of American thought and behavior were mere back eddies, explainable as temporary but necessary responses to a hostile environment. They believed that, once the Mormon pioneers had conquered this environment, the true American character of the pioneers, both socially and politically, would reveal itself. These historians had thus employed one of the most time-honored uses of history—that of reading the present into the past in order to reshape the future along ways parting from the old—to the reconstruction of the Mormon past.[23]

The history of Mormonism in the twentieth century reveals the extent of their success. As Ernst Troeltsch pointed out long ago, a visible, earthly kingdom of God has always been one of the chief criteria of the sects of Christianity. He also observed that the history of a sect is characterized by a subtle but continuous process of accommodation to the dominant environment, as a result of which the sect is finally transformed into a church.[24] The metamorphosis of the political kingdom of God in Mormon history provides, perhaps, one of the most striking examples for a further validation of this thesis. From a sociological point of view, Mormonism, in 1966, differs fundamentally from the Mormonism of 1890 even though no theoretical change in doctrine may have occurred. Yet it is a fact that doctrines such as plural marriage, economic communitarianism, and the political kingdom of God are either totally ignored or else "held in abeyance"—doctrines which throughout the nineteenth century were considered part of the very fiber and essence of Mormonism by the hierarchy, and, as far as they were aware of them, most of its followers.

One important criterion of a church is that it spawns sects whose initial intention it is to return the "church" to its former "sectarian" origins, and who refuse to accept the accommodation to the world. Since the cessation of polygamy and the disappearance of the political kingdom of God, Mormonism has given birth to numerous such sects, most of which, in spite of many other disagreements, are united in their belief that the church's alleged compromise with Babylon can be rectified only if the leaders reinstitute communitarianism, plural marriage, and the political kingdom of God under a revitalized Council of Fifty. Needless to say, church leaders in Salt Lake City vigorously attempt to disassociate themselves and the church from such movements.[25]

All history, in the final analysis, is irony, and the history of Mormonism makes no exception. When Brigham Young assumed the leadership of the Mormons in Nauvoo after the death of Joseph Smith, many Saints refused to follow him because they could not accept polygamy and the corporate notion of a political kingdom of God. Ultimately, in protest, they found themselves united in the Reorganized Church, whose leaders, officially, have since then categorically denied that Joseph Smith ever intended the creation of a political kingdom of God, or practiced plural marriage. From a doctrinal point of view, then, there are some striking parallels between the relationship of the Reorganized Church and Brigham Young, and present-day Mormon leaders in Salt Lake City and the various Fundamentalist sects. History always has the tendency to fold back upon itself. The challengers become defenders, and vice versa.

And yet, if it had been otherwise, Mormonism might not

have survived. It was best, perhaps, that the political kingdom of God and the Council of Fifty died in the heat of battle at a time when the American people could take such kingdoms seriously. The following incident, revealing how the Mormon kingdom might have fared in the twentieth century, implies that the violent opposition to the kingdom by the Gentiles was, in a sense, a compliment in disguise.

In the election year of 1960, a Bishop Homer Tomlinson, founder and leader of the Theocratic Party, campaigned for the establishment of a political kingdom of God in the United States, with himself as king and president. Appearing before a cheering crowd of fifteen hundred Princeton undergraduates, Tomlinson proclaimed that the kingdom of God was at hand. In a triumphant tour, the students paraded the candidate around the campus. The editors of *The Daily Princetonian* thought it a great joke to have Tomlinson's picture appear on the front page the following day.[26] His reception on other campuses seems to have followed the Princeton pattern.

Mormonism was spared such a fate—a fate far worse than persecution—because at one of the most crucial periods of its history it responded to the values of twentieth-century American culture, at the same time preserving much of its identity. There is a final paradox, however; for without the existence and activities of the Council of Fifty, which contributed significantly to the building of the Rocky Mountain kingdom, Mormonism might well have failed to enjoy its present stature and prestige within the framework of accepted American religious values and persuasions.

Notes

I. The Kingdom of God and the Millennial Tradition

1. Parley P. Pratt, *To Her Gracious Majesty, Queen Victoria* (Manchester, England, 1841), p. 5.

2. *The Latter-day Saints' Millennial Star*, XXIII (1862), 422.

3. The term *Gentile*, in Mormon usage, usually refers to anyone who is not a member of The Church of Jesus Christ of Latter-day Saints. More specifically, it refers to anyone not a member of the House of Israel. But, in Mormon theology, all Latter-day Saints in good standing belong to the House of Israel, either through direct lineage, or by adoption.

4. Joseph Smith, *The Doctrine and Covenants of the Church of Jesus Christ of Latter-day Saints* (Salt Lake City, 1951 ed.), 6:1–4.

5. Joseph Smith, *History of the Church of Jesus Christ of Latter-day Saints* (6 vols., 2d ed.; Salt Lake City, 1950), I, 77. In 1838, the name was officially changed to "The Church of Jesus Christ of Latter-day Saints."

6. *Journal of Discourses*, XII (1870), 56–57.

7. For a discussion of the dualistic metaphysics of Descartes, see James Collins, *A History of European Philosophy* (Milwaukee, 1954), pp. 175–195. *Doctrine and Covenants*, 131:7–8. The metaphysical implications of Smith's monistic philosophy were analyzed by Orson Pratt in *Absurdities of Immaterialism* (Liverpool, 1849). But his proposal of an atomistic materialism as the basis for a Mormon metaphysics, more comprehensively expressed in *The Great First Cause* (Liverpool, 1851), was rejected by Brigham Young as unorthodox. More recently, Mormon apostle John A. Widstoe, in an analysis of this aspect of Mormon philosophy, paraphrased Smith succinctly: "Spiritual matter is but a refined form of gross matter." See *A Rational Theology* (Salt Lake City, 1915), p. 11. A recent and very concise discussion of the monistic aspect of Mormon qualitative metaphysics is Sterling McMurrin's *The Philosophical Foundations of Mormon Theology* (Salt Lake City, 1959).

8. *Millennial Star*, VI (1845), 19.

9. Parley P. Pratt implied this in *Key to the Science of Theology* (Liverpool, 1855), pp. 27–28, 122.

10. S. A. Davis, in *Messenger and Advocate*, III (1837), 489–491, as quoted in Leonard J. Arrington, *Great Basin Kingdom* (Cambridge, Mass., 1958), p. 6.

11. *Doctrine and Covenants*, 27:12; Section 107.

12. Smith, *History of the Church*, V, 256–259.

13. *Journal of Discourses*, XVII (1875), 156. See also *Times and Seasons*, IV (1842), 24–25; John Taylor, *Journal of Discourses*, X (1865), 54–58; Wilford, Woodruff, *ibid.*, XXI (1881), 281–286.

14. Bruce R. McConkie, "Keys of the Kingdom," address at Brigham Young University, April 23, 1957 (mimeographed). The author sees the kingdom of God as synonymous with the church in spiritual as well as temporal matters.

15. Smith, *History of the Church*, V, 256–259.

16. William Bradford, *History of Plimouth Plantation* (Boston, 1898), pp. 94–95.

17. Smith, *History of the Church*, VI, 318–322.

18. *Ibid.*, I, 402; *Doctrine and Covenants*, 97:21.

19. *Millennial Star*, I (1840), 5.

20. *Ibid.*, XXIV (1862), 103.

21. Norman Cohn, *The Pursuit of the Millennium* (2d ed.; New York, 1961), pp. 1–21; Walter Nigg, *Das Ewige Reich* (Erlenbach-Zuerich, 1944), pp. 9–31.

22. Cohn, p. 14.

23. *Ibid.*, 286–306; an excellent discussion of the political and religious thought of the English Fifth Monarchists is Alfred Cohen, "The Kingdom of God in Puritan Thought: A Study of the Quest for the Fifth Monarchy" (doctoral dissertation, Indiana University, 1961).

24. John Davenport, "An Epistle to the Reader," in Increase Mather, *The Mystery of Israel: Salvation Explained and Applyed* (London, 1669).

25. Ira V. Brown, "Watchers for the Second Coming: The Millennial Tradition in America," *The Mississippi Valley Historical Review*, 39 (1952), 451.

26. *Ibid.*, pp. 452–453; Arthur E. Bestor, Jr., *Backwoods Utopia: The Sectarian and Owenite Phases of Communitarian Socialism in America, 1663–1829* (Philadelphia, 1950), p. 91.

27. Whitney R. Cross, *The Burned-Over District: The Social and Intellectual History of Enthusiastic Religion in Western New York, 1800–1850* (Ithaca, N.Y., 1950).

28. *Doctrine and Covenants*, Sections 65 and 78.

29. *Painesville Telegraph*, March 15, 1831.

30. In 1832, Smith predicted the "desolation and utter abolishment" of New York, Albany, and Boston unless they accepted Mormonism. See *Doctrine and Covenants*, 84:114–115.

31. *Millennial Star*, VI (1845), 140–142. Actually, this account most likely was not an authentic dream. The editors probably provided the Saints

with this vicarious excursion to the New Jerusalem in order to help them endure the hardships of the impending exodus to the Great Basin by directing their hopes toward a better future.

32. See especially *Doctrine and Covenants*, 34:7; 35:27; 38:8; 39:21; 43:17–35; 45:63; 49:7; 52:43; 58:4; 63:37, 53, 58; 112:24, 34.

33. *Ibid.*, 63:53.

34. Smith, *History of the Church*, V, 336–337.

35. *Millennial Star*, LII (1890), 675; Smith, *History of the Church*, II, 182.

36. *Doctrine and Covenants*, 39:21; 49:7; 133:11.

37. Smith, *History of the Church*, VI, 254.

38. *Ibid.*, V, 336; *Doctrine and Covenants*, 130:14–17.

39. Smith, *History of the Church*, V, 291, in Richard Lloyd Anderson, "Joseph Smith and the Millenarian Timetable," *Brigham Young University Studies*, III (1961), 61.

40. T. B. H. Stenhouse, *The Rocky Mountain Saints* (New York, 1874), p. 489.

41. See especially *Doctrine and Covenants*, Section 87; see also 38:29; 45:63; 63:33.

42. *Journal of Discourses*, XIX (1878), 38.

43. *Doctrine and Covenants*, 133:9–13, 21.

44. *Journal of Discourses*, III (1854), 67.

45. The belief that the parousia was to come by miraculous means was by far the most common belief throughout the history of millennial expectations. See Nigg, p. 38. See also Sigmund Mowinckel, *He That Cometh*, trans. G. W. Anderson (New York, 1954), p. 126; "Eschatology also includes the thought that this drama has a universal cosmic character. The universe itself, heaven and earth, is thrown into the melting pot. It follows that this is not brought by human or historical forces, or by any immanent evolutionary process."

46. William Mulder, *Homeward to Zion; the Mormon Migration from Scandinavia* (Minneapolis, 1957), p. 21.

47. Richard Niebuhr, *The Social Sources of Denominationalism* (Hamden, Conn., 1954), p. 160.

48. The idea of disillusion is one of the major themes of Nigg's work, as exemplified by its subtitle, "Geschichte einer Sehnsucht and einer Enttaeuschung."

49. Benjamin F. Johnson to George S. Gibbs, April to October, 1903 (typed MS, Brigham Young University Library).

50. *Millennial Star*, XII (1850), 358.

51. This famous sentence, which all Mormons are able to quote, was coined by Lorenzo Snow.

52. See especially Nels L. Nelson, *Scientific Aspects of Mormonism* (New York, 1904). Nelson, an English professor at Brigham Young University, was strongly influenced by Herbert Spencer, John Fiske, and other Social Darwinists.

53. See *Doctrine and Covenants*, 93:36: "The Glory of God is intelligence." 130:18–19: "Whatever principle of intelligence we attain unto in this life, it will rise with us in the resurrection. And if a person gains

more knowledge and intelligence in this life through his diligence and obedience than another, he will have so much the advantage in the world to come." These scriptures, however, have been widely misinterpreted by both Mormons and non-Mormons. The first requirement of any Saint was to learn the principles and doctrines of salvation. And, since even this might take a lifetime, an overemphasis on the acquisition of secular knowledge might well endanger an individual's salvation.

54. Ernest Tuveson, *Millennium and Utopia* (Berkeley, 1949).

55. Timothy Dwight, *Sermon, Delivered in Boston* (Boston, 1813), pp. 25–26.

56. During the nineteenth century, the Saints, for the most part, understandably believed that the growth of the kingdom of God would be rapid. Although this optimism was occasionally dampened, a more cautious attitude arose around the turn of the century, even though church leaders would occasionally caution the Saints as early as the 1880's that the development of the kingdom would be gradual and difficult. See H. W. Naisbitt, *Journal of Discourses,* XII (1881), 74–82.

57. Shirley Jackson Case, *The Millennial Hope* (Chicago, 1918), p. 99.

58. Therald N. Jensen, "Mormon Theory of Church and State" (doctoral dissertation, University of Chicago, 1938), pp. 67–68.

59. *Lorenzo Hill Hatch Journal,* ed. Ruth Savage Hilton (Provo, Utah, 1958), p. 125.

60. *Millennial Star,* LII (1890), 657, 692–693.

II. Mormonism and the American Dream

1. Stow Persons, *American Minds; A History of Ideas* (New York, 1958), p. 183.

2. Thomas J. Yates, "Count Tolstoi and the 'American Religion,'" *The Improvement Era,* XLII (1939), 94; *The Autobiography of Andrew Dickson White* (2 vols.; New York, 1907), II, 87.

3. *Burned-Over District.*

4. Fawn M. Brodie, *No Man Knows My History: The Life of Joseph Smith the Mormon Prohpet* (New York, 1945), p. viii.

5. *The Works of John Adams,* ed. Charles Francis Adams (Boston, 1856), I, 66.

6. *The Writings of James Madison,* ed. Gaillard Hunt (New York, 1902), III, 359.

7. *The Writings of Thomas Jefferson,* ed. H. A. Washington (New York, 1859), IV, 440–441.

8. See especially Edward McNall Burns, *The American Idea of Mission* (New Brunswick, N. J., 1957).

9. Sherwood Eddy, *The Kingdom of God and the American Dream. The Religious and Secular Ideals of American History* (New York and London, 1941), p. 116.

10. A. Leland Jamison, "Religions on the Christian Perimeter," in *The Shaping of American Religion,* ed. James Ward Smith and A. Leland Jamison (Princeton, N. J., 1961), p. 214.

Notes

11. "If any of you lack wisdom, let him ask of God, that giveth to all men liberally, and upbraideth not; and it shall be given him."

12. *The Pearl of Great Price* (Salt Lake City, 1951 ed.), Joseph Smith 2:19.

13. *Ibid.*, The Articles of Faith, article 8.

14. *Book of Mormon*, I Nephi, 14:9.

15. *Pearl of Great Price*, Joseph Smith, 2:66–75.

16. *Ibid.*, The Articles of Faith, article 8.

17. The most notable book advancing this theory was Ethan Smith, *View of the Hebrews: Or the Ten Tribes of Israel in America* (Poultney, Vt., 1823).

18. Peter Meinhold, "Die Anfaenge des Amerikanischen Geschichtsbewusstseins," *Saeculum*, V (1954), 65–86.

19. *Doctrine and Covenants*, Section 116.

20. Charles L. Sanford claims in *The Quest for Paradise. Europe and the American Moral Imagination* (Urbana, Ill., 1961), that the myth of the Garden of Eden is the driving force in American culture. Strangely enough, Sanford fails to mention the Mormons with so much as a word.

21. *Book of Mormon*, Ether 2:21.

22. *Ibid.*

23. *Ibid.*, II Nephi, 10:11; III Nephi, 21:4.

24. *Doctrine and Covenants*, 101:80.

25. Parley P. Pratt, *Key to Theology*, pp. 76–77.

26. *Ibid.*, pp. 79–81.

27. Quoted in *Truth*, II (1936), 37.

28. *Doctrine and Covenants*, 134:9: "We do not believe it just to mingle religious influence with civil government, whereby one religious society is fostered and another proscribed in its spiritual privileges, and the individual rights of its members, as citizens, denied."

29. U.S. Congress. *Congressional Record*, 47th Congress, 1st Sess., April 19, 1882, p. 3068.

30. See Klaus Hansen, "The Political Kingdom of God as a Cause for Mormon-Gentile Conflict," *Brigham Young University Studies*, II (1960), 241–260.

31. Quoted in *Truth*, II (1936), 37; see also *Juvenile Instructor*, XXXI (1896), 140.

32. *Deseret News*, August 1, 1856.

33. Mark Cannon, "The Mormon Issue in Congress, 1872–1882" (doctoral dissertation, Harvard University, 1960), pp. 238–239.

34. *Journal of Discourses*, II (1855), 317; see also Heber C. Kimball, *ibid.*, X (1865), 240–241; Wilford Woodruff, *ibid.*, II (1855), 192–193; Orson Pratt, *ibid.*, XIII (1871), p. 126.

35. *Ibid.*, XVII (1875), 137.

36. *Key to Theology*, p. 70.

37. Orson Pratt, *The Kingdom of God* (Liverpool, 1851), p. 1. See also John Taylor's statement in *Journal of Discourses*, I (1854), 230: "Let us now notice our political position in the world. What are we going to do? We are going to possess the earth. Why? Because it belongs to Jesus

Christ, and he belongs to us, and we to him. We are all one, and will take the kingdom and possess it under the whole heavens, and reign over it for ever and ever. Now, ye kings and emperors, help yourselves, if you can. This is the truth, and it may as well be told at this time as at any other."

38. *Journal of Discourses*, I (1851), 173–174.

39. *Ibid.*

40. Alexis de Tocqueville, *Democracy in America*, trans. Henry Reeves I (New York, n.d.), 280–294.

41. Gaylon L. Caldwell, "Mormon Conceptions of Individual Rights and Political Obligation" (doctoral dissertation, Stanford, 1952), p. 242; Hyrum L. Andrus, *Joseph Smith and World Government* (Salt Lake City, 1958), pp. 33–35.

42. *Journal of Discourses*, XVII (1875), 156–157; see also *ibid.*, II (1855), 309–310; II (1856), 256; XI (1867), 275; XII (1869), 113–114.

43. *Journal of Discourses*, I (1854), 83.

44. *Ibid.*, VI (1859), 129.

45. Smith, *History of the Church*, V, 61.

46. *Journal of Discourses*, VII (1860), 326.

47. *Book of Mormon*, Mosiah, 29:13.

48. *Millennial Star*, V (1844), 150.

49. Journal History, July 12, 1865. George A. Smith's statement, and numerous others like it by other church leaders, were all based on Joseph Smith's pronouncement, made in 1844: "I go for a theo-democracy." Journal History, April 15, 1844. See also *Times and Seasons*, IV (December 1, 1842), 24–25.

50. See Chapter VII, pp. 138–139.

51. *Journal of Discourses*, XIV (1872), 93.

52. *Ibid.*

53. *Ibid.*, p. 93.

54. *Deseret News*, July 19, 1865.

55. *Millennial Star*, XXVI (1876), 744, 746.

56. Smith, *History of the Church*, VI, 203–204.

57. Perhaps no other statement of Smith has become as permanent a part of Mormon folklore. It can be found in scores of pioneer diaries. As an example see "The Life Story of Mosiah Lyman Hancock" (MS, Brigham Young University Library), p. 29: "The Mormons will save the country when its liberty hangs by a hair, as it were." See also Preston Nibley, "What of Joseph Smith's Prophesy?" *Deseret News*, Church Section, December 5, 1948.

58. *Journal of Discourses*, VI (1859), 342. Young, in elaborating on this theory, declared that the kingdom would be a "true democratic theocracy" (*ibid.*, p. 346), and that the people would "find it a Republican Democratic Government" (*ibid.*, VII (1860), 8). He defined "a true Republican Government" as being "a government or institution that is perfect —perfect in its laws and ordinances, having for its object the perfection of mankind in righteousness. This is a true Democracy. But Democracy as it is now is another thing. True Democracy or Republicanism, if it

Notes

were rightly understood, ought to be Government of the United States"
(*ibid.*, p. 10).

59. *Journal of Discourses*, VI (1859), 342.

60. *Ibid.*, VII (1860), 14.

61. Albert Carrington, *ibid.*, XVII (1875), 165–166; Orson Pratt, III
(1856), 71; John Taylor, XXI (1881), 31.

62. Parley P. Pratt, *ibid.*, III (1856), 71–73.

63. Minutes of Council of Fifty, 1880 (Brigham Young University
Library). Joseph Smith stated: "The only fault I find with the Constitution is it is not broad enough to cover the whole ground. Although it
provides that all men shall enjoy religious freedom, yet it does not
provide the manner by which that freedom can be preserved, nor for
the punishment of government officers who refuse to protect the people
in their religious rights, or punish those mobs, states, or communities
who interfere with the rights of the people on account of their religion."

64. Johnson to Gibbs, p. 7.

65. *Journal of Discourses*, III (1856), 71–73.

III. The Establishment of the Government of God

1. Smith, *History of the Church*, VI, 364.

2. *Ibid.*, p. 290.

3. *Ibid.*, pp. 288–289.

4. *Doctrine and Covenants*, 37:3.

5. *Millennial Star*, X (1848), 247.

6. Ray B. West, *Kingdom of the Saints; The Story of Brigham Young
and the Mormons* (New York, 1957), p. 39. An excellent study of the
Ohio period is R. Kent Fielding, "The Growth of the Mormon Church
in Kirtland, Ohio" (doctoral dissertation, Indiana University, 1957).

7. For studies of Mormon communitarianism in this period see espe-
cially Leonard J. Arrington, "Early Mormon Communitarianism: The
Law of Consecration and Stewardship," *Western Humanities Review*, VII
(1953), 341–369; Mario S. DePillis, "The Development of Mormon Com-
munitarianism, 1826–1846" (doctoral dissertation, Yale University, 1960);
Hamilton Gardner, "Communism Among the Mormons," *Quarterly
Journal of Economics*, XXXVII (1922), 134–174; and Joseph A. Geddes, *The
United Order Among the Mormons; Missouri Phase* (Salt Lake City, 1924).

8. Smith, *History of the Church*, I, 357–359; for the influence of Smith's
ideas on later Mormon settlements see Lowry Nelson, *The Mormon
Village: A Pattern and Technique of Land Settlement* (Salt Lake City,
1952). The most detailed account of these events is in Warren A. Jennings,
"Zion is Fled; The Expulsion of the Mormons from Jackson County,
Missouri" (doctoral dissertation, University of Florida, 1962).

9. In 1838, when Smith and some of his associates were ordered to be
shot by a court martial of the Missouri militia, Doniphan, a colonel in
the militia, refused to carry out the order and thus saved the prophet's
life.

10. *Doctrine and Covenants*, 103:15–17.

11. *Ibid.*, 103:34–35.

12. Roberts, in Smith, *History of the Church*, II, p. xxiii.

13. *Ibid.*, p. xxiv.

14. An important account by a contemporary witness is Thomas Ford, *A History of Illinois* (Chicago, 1854); George R. Gayler's "A Social, Economic, and Political Study of the Mormons in Western Illinois, 1839–1846; A Re-evaluation" (doctoral dissertation, Indiana University, 1955), contributes little to previous scholarship, and is superseded by Robert B. Flanders, *Nauvoo: Kingdom on the Mississippi* (Urbana, Ill., 1965). Still valuable is Brigham H. Roberts, *The Rise and Fall of Nauvoo* (Salt Lake City, 1900).

15. Smith, *History of the Church*, VI, 239–245.

16. *Millennial Star*, III (1842), 69.

17. *Ibid.*

18. John C. Bennett, *The History of the Saints* (Boston, 1842), p. 293.

19. Smith, *History of the Church*, VI, 365.

20. Quoted in Brodie, *No Man Knows My History*, pp. 357–358.

21. *Ibid.*, p. 358.

22. *Journal of Discourses*, IX (1863), 294.

23. Minutes of the Council of Fifty, 1880.

24. Smith, *History of the Church*, II, 247: "Inasmuch as this Church of Christ has been reproached with the crime of fornication and polygamy, we declare that we believe that one man should have one wife, and one woman but one husband except in case of death, when either is at liberty to marry again."

25. See statement by Joseph Smith III, son of the Mormon prophet, who became head of the Reorganized Church of Jesus Christ of Latter Day Saints, in his autobiography, as quoted in Edward W. Tullidge, *Life of Joseph the Prophet* (rev. ed.; Plano, Ill., 1880), pp. 798–800; see also Inez Smith Davis, *The Story of the Church* (4th ed. rev.; Independence, Mo., 1948), pp. 486–490.

26. Brodie, p. 301. Brodie gathered evidence showing that Smith may have had as many as forty-eight plural wives. See *ibid.*, 434–465.

27. *Ibid.*, 181–184.

28. Quoted in William Alexander Linn, *The Story of the Mormons* (New York, 1902), p. 280.

29. Eliza R. Snow, *Biography of Lorenzo Snow* (Salt Lake City, 1884), p. 70.

30. Quoted in *The True Latter Day Saints Herald*, I (1860), 22–23.

31. For Smith's public condemnations of polygamy, see *Time and Seasons*, III (1842), 709–710; V (1844), 423.

32. The official revelation concerning plural marriage was recorded on July 12, 1843. See *Doctrine and Covenants*, Section 132. The revelation concerning the political kingdom of God was given on April 7, 1842. See Minutes of the Council of Fifty, 1880.

33. Polygamy was officially announced by the church on August 29, 1852 in a missionary conference, and published in a special edition of the *Deseret News* on September 14, 1852.

Notes

34. See below, pp. 170–172, 178–179, 186–187.

35. Milo M. Quaife, *The Kingdom of Saint James* (New Haven, 1935), pp. 49–50.

36. *Ibid.*

37. Ether, 8:18–26; Helaman, 6:18–30.

38. James C. Bilderback, "Masonry and Mormonism, Nauvoo, Illinois, 1841–47" (master's thesis, University of Iowa, 1937); Anthony Woodward Ivins, *The Relationship of "Mormonism" and Freemasonry* (Salt Lake City, 1934); E. Cecil McGavin, *Mormonism and Masonry* (4th ed.; Salt Lake City, 1956).

39. Smith, *History of the Church*, VI, 261, 263.

40. Some other prominent Freemasons initiated into the Council of Fifty were Heber C. Kimball, George Miller, Hyrum Smith, John Smith, Newel K. Whitney, and Brigham Young. Unfortunately, I have been unable to gain access to a complete list of members of the Nauvoo Lodge. It would be interesting to learn the names of the fifty prominent Mormon Freemasons who attended the laying of the cornerstone of the masonic temple at Nauvoo on June 24, 1843, and who signed a document deposited in the cornerstone.

41. *William Clayton's Journal* (Salt Lake City, 1921), pp. 40, 202; Journal of Amasa Lyman (typed MS, Bringham Young University Library), p. 37.

42. *Sangamon Journal*, July 29, 1842.

43. As quoted in M. W. Montgomery, *The Mormon Delusion* (Minneapolis, 1890), p. 44.

44. Smith, *History of the Church*, III, 180.

45. These included Reynolds Cahoon, Benjamin F. Johnson, John D. Lee, Cornelius P. Lott, Amasa Lyman, John Pack, Orrin Porter Rockwell, Albert P. Rockwood, Shadrach Roundy, John Scott, and Lyman Wight.

46. Ford, *History of Illinois*, p. 322.

47. Smith, *History of the Church*, IV, 500, VI, 39, 45.

48. *Ibid.*, VI, 39.

49. *Ibid.*

50. Quoted in *ibid.*, pp. 39–41.

51. *Ibid.*, p. 41.

52. Roberts made it a special point to note the failure of Law and Rigdon to sign the letter. *Ibid.*

53. *Ibid.*, pp. 260–261, 263–264, 267.

54. Minutes of the Council of Fifty, 1880.

55. *A Mormon Chronicle: The Diaries of John D. Lee, 1848–1876*, ed. Robert Glass Cleland and Juanita Brooks (2 vols.; San Marino, Calif., 1955), I, 98.

56. *Ibid.*

57. B. H. Roberts, ed., *History of the Church of Jesus Christ of Latter-Day Saints, Period II, from the Manuscript History of Brigham Young and other Original Documents* (Salt Lake City, 1932), pp. 213, 379, 381–382; Lee, *Mormon Chronicle*, I, 97, 98, 104; John D. Lee, *Mormonism Unveiled* (St. Louis, 1877), p. 173; *Millennial Star*, XXV (1863), 136;

XXVI (1864), 328; George Miller, *Correspondence of Bishop George Miller with the Northern Islander* (Burlington, Wisconsin, 1916 [?]), pp. 20, 35.

58. Johnson to Gibbs, p. 9.

59. Lee, in *Mormonism Unveiled*, p. 173, mentioned a man named Jackson, whose identity cannot be determined. See also *Millennial Star*, XXVI (1864), 328.

60. "Diaries and Official Records of John D. Lee" (typed MS at Brigham Young University Library), pp. 166–168.

61. *Millennial Star*, XXIII (1861), 423; Roberts, ed., *History of the Church, Period II*, p. 614.

62. Johnson to Gibbs, p. 10.

63. *Journal of Discourses*, XII (1869), 164.

64. Johnson to Gibbs, p. 9.

65. Lee, *Mormon Chronicle*, I, 104.

66. *Ibid.*

67. Lee, *Mormonism Unveiled*, p. 173.

68. Clayton, pp. 74, 202.

69. *Journal of Discourses*, IV (1857), 371–372.

70. *Doctrine and Covenants*, 45:72.

71. Lee, *Mormon Chronicle*, I, 80.

72. Minutes of the Council of Fifty, 1880.

73. George Miller to unidentified correspondent, June, 1855, in the John Zahnd MS (Mormon Papers, Manuscript Division, New York Public Library), pp. 17–18; *Zion's Harbinger and Baneemy's Organ*, III (July, 1853), 53, in Flanders, *Nauvoo*, p. 292.

74. Former Bishop Andrew Cahoon, whose father Reynolds Cahoon had been a member of the Council of Fifty, testified in 1889: "The King of that Kingdom that was set up on the earth was the head of the Church. Brigham Young proclaimed himself King here in Salt Lake Valley before there was a house built, in 1847." Quoted in Reginald W. Kauffman and Ruth H. Kauffman, *The Latter Day Saints: A Study of the Mormons in the Light of Economic Conditions* (London, 1912), p. 83.

75. II Nephi, 10:11.

76. Charles Duffy, "The Vocabulary of Royalty: Fossilized Figures of Speech," *The Western Humanities Review*, V (1950), 118–119.

77. *Doctrine and Covenants*, 38:32.

78. *Ibid.*, 105:32.

79. Smith, *History of the Church*, VI, 57.

80. See Chapter VII, p. 129–130.

81. James Holt, "The Reminiscences of James Holt. A Narrative of the Emmett Company," ed. Dale Morgan, *Utah Historical Quarterly*, XXV (1957), 107.

82. Minutes of the Council of Fifty, 1880.

83. Lee, *Mormonism Unveiled*, p. 173.

84. *Ibid.*

85. Mormons regarded lawyers with great suspicion. None of the judicial officers of the State of Deseret, for instance, had any legal training. This was considered to be an advantage rather than an encum-

Notes

brance. See Dale Morgan, "The State of Deseret." *Utah Historical Quarterly,* VIII (1940), 87.

86. See extra edition of *Deseret News,* September 14, 1852.

87. See Charles W. Penrose, *Blood Atonement as Taught by Leading Elders of the Church of Jesus Christ of Latter-day Saints* (Salt Lake City, 1884); Joseph Fielding Smith, Jr., *Blood Atonement and the Origin of Plural Marriage* (Salt Lake City, 1905).

88. Lee, *Mormon Chronicle,* I, 103.

89. Penrose, *Blood Atonement,* p. 43.

90. *Journal of Discourses,* IV (1857), 219–220. Gustive O. Larson, "The Mormon Reformation," *Utah Historical Quarterly,* XXVI (1958), 60–63.

91. Lee, *Mormon Chronicle,* I, 98.

92. *Ibid.,* pp. 98–99.

IV. Quest for Empire

1. Quoted in William A. Mulder and A. Russell Mortensen, *Among the Mormons* (New York, 1958), p. 131.

2. It is significant that the majority of those Mormons who rejected the idea of a literal, temporal kingdom of God did not participate in the exodus. The Reorganized Church, for example, officially denies that Smith attempted to establish a political kingdom of God.

3. Smith, *History of the Church,* V, 85–86.

4. *Ibid.,* p. 389.

5. Mulder and Mortensen, p. 142.

6. See above, p. 59.

7. Smith, *History of the Church,* VI, 40.

8. *Ibid.,* pp. 64–65.

9. *Ibid.,* p. 156.

10. Linn, *The Story of the Mormons,* p. 251.

11. Smith, *History of the Church,* VI, 188.

12. Roberts, *ibid.,* pp. xxxii-xxxiii.

13. Ford, *History of Illinois,* p. 364.

14. Roberts, in *History of the Church,* VI, xxxiv.

15. G. Homer Durham, *Joseph Smith, Prophet-Statesman* (Salt Lake City, 1944), p. 145; Roberts, *The Rise and Fall of Nauvoo,* p. 252.

16. Roberts, in *History of the Church,* VI, xxxiv.

17. *Ibid.,* VI, 188.

18. *Ibid.,* VI, xxxiv.

19. Miller, *Correspondence,* p. 23.

20. Smith, *History of the Church,* VI, 232.

21. *Ibid.,* p. xxxiv.

22. *VII Peters,* p. 243.

23. Smith, *History of the Church,* VI, 95.

24. *Ibid.,* pp. 130–132.

25. *Doctrine and Covenants,* 101:86–89.

26. *Millennial Star,* XXVI (1846), 328.

27. *Ibid.*, p. 727.

28. Orson Hyde to John E. Page, May 6, 1844 (Mormon Papers, Woodward folder, Manuscript Division, New York Public Library).

29. *Ibid.*

30. *Millennial Star*, XXVI (1846), 328.

31. Smith, *History of the Church*, VI, 255–260.

32. *Ibid.*, 260–261.

33. *Ibid.*, p. 264; Miller, *Correspondence*, p. 20.

34. Smith, *History of the Church*, VI, 222.

35. William C. Binkley, *The Expansionist Movement in Texas, 1836–1850* (Berkeley, 1925), pp. 43–67; Joseph William Schmitz, *Texan Statecraft, 1836–1845* (San Antonio, 1941), pp. 202–204.

36. Smith, *History of the Church*, VI, 326.

37. *Ibid.*, p. 371.

38. *Ibid.*, p. 374.

39. *Ibid.*, p. 354.

40. Ephraim D. Adams, *British Interests and Activities in Texas* (Baltimore, 1910), pp. 176–196.

41. Miller, *Correspondence*, p. 20.

42. *Ibid.*

43. *Millennial Star*, XXIV (1862), 103.

44. Miller, *Correspondence*, pp. 20–21.

45. *Ibid.*; Smith, *History of the Church*, VI, 351, 356.

46. Smith, *History of the Church*, VI, 356.

47. *Ibid.*

48. The idea that Babbitt may have been sent as a diplomatic agent to France was first suggested by Andrus, *Joseph Smith and World Government*, p. 62.

49. Smith, *History of the Church*, VI, 353.

50. See *ibid.*, p. 391, for Smith's identification with Jeffersonianism; p. 276 for his dislike of the British; p. 275 for his reverence for Lafayette.

51. *Ibid.*, pp. 275–277.

52. *Ibid.*, p. 372.

53. Miller, *Correspondence*, p. 23.

54. Orson Hyde to Joseph Smith, April 30, 1844 (typed MS, Brigham Young University Library).

55. Miller, *Correspondence*, p. 23.

V. The Mantle of the Prophet

1. *Sacred Hymns and Spiritual Songs for the Church of Jesus Christ of Latter-day Saints* (Salt Lake City, 1890 ed.), Hymn 297.

2. Davis, *Story of the Church*, pp. 288, 385, 386, 444, 445.

3. Roberts, ed., *History of the Church*, Period II, pp. 231–243; Roberts, *Comprehensive History*, II, 416–418.

4. Roberts, *Comprehensive History*, II, 418.

5. See Chapter VIII, pp. 156–158.

6. Smith, *History of the Church*, VI, 213.

Notes

7. "The Reminiscences of James Holt," *Utah Historical Quarterly,* XXIII (1955), 7.

8. Roberts, ed., *History of the Church, Period II,* pp. 377, 383–384, 434, 618.

9. Joseph Smith III and Heman C. Smith, *The History of the Reorganized Church of Jesus Christ of Latter Day Saints* (4 vols.; Lamoni, Iowa, 1896–1903), II, 90–91.

10. *Ibid.*

11. Roberts, ed., *History of the Church, Period II,* pp. 248–249, 254–255; Heman Hale Smith, "The Lyman Wight Colony in Texas, 1846–1858" (typescript, Brigham Young University Library).

12. Journal of William Leyland, quoted in Heman Hale Smith, p. 22; Stout, II, 336.

13. Stout, I, 245.

14. Miller, *Correspondence,* pp. 35–36.

15. George Miller to James J. Strang, June 12, 1849, in Smith and Smith, *History of the Reorganized Church,* I, 793.

16. Sarah Scott to Abigail Hall, March 31, 1848, in "The Death of a Mormon Dictator, Letters of Massachusetts Mormons, 1843–1848," ed., George F. Partridge, *The New England Quarterly,* IX (1936), 614. See also Roberts, *Comprehensive History,* II, 429–445.

17. *The Diary of James J. Strang,* ed., Mark A. Strang (East Lansing, Mich., 1961), pp. 15, 17, 18, 19, 22, 32.

18. Smith, *History of the Church,* VI, 318–321; S. George Ellsworth, "A History of Mormon Missions in the United States and Canada, 1830–1860" (doctoral dissertation, University of California, Berkeley, 1950), pp. 260–270.

19. See Dale Morgan's anonymous introduction to the Strang Papers (Coe Collection, Yale University Library). The letter is part of the Strang Papers.

20. Milo M. Quaife, *The Kingdom of Saint James; A Narrative of the Mormons* (New Haven, Conn., 1930), pp. 31–78.

21. *Ibid.*

22. Quaife claims that Sidney Rigdon based his claims to church leadership on this purported revelation. See pp. 49–50.

23. James J. Strang, "Secret Covenant of the Illuminati" (Coe Collection, Yale University Library).

24. Thus Russel B. Nye, in *Diary of James J. Strang,* p. xiii.

25. In addition to the five individuals already mentioned, there was George J. Adams, who, though not a member of the Council of Fifty, seems to have been privy to some important business in connection with the kingdom of God. See *Millennial Star,* VII (1844), 5.

26. No copies of the original are known to be extant. A more complete edition was issued in 1856, a reprint of which appeared at Burlington, Wisconsin, 1948. It may be more than coincidental that Joseph Smith's clerks kept some sort of record or journal called "Book of the Law of the Lord."

27. Quaife, p. 93.

28. James J. Strang, *The Book of the Law of the Lord* (Saint James, 1856), p. 171.

29. *Ibid.*, p. 21.

30. *The Kingdom of God*, p. 1.

31. Flanders, *Nauvoo*, pp. v-vi.

32. February 1, 1847, in Strang Papers (Coe Collection, Yale University Library).

33. *Zion's Harbinger and Baneemy's Organ*, III (July, 1853), 53, quoted in Flanders, p. 292.

34. Stephen Post to Warren Post, March 7, 1856, Warren Post Papers (Graceland College Library, Lamoni, Iowa).

VI. Exodus

1. Quoted in Brodie, p. 397.

2. *Ibid.*

3. Roberts, ed., *History of the Church, Period II*, pp. 449–450.

4. Lee, *Mormonism Unveiled*, p. 173; Stout, I, 21–22.

5. Roberts, ed., *History of the Church, Period II*, pp. 399–400.

6. *Ibid.*, p. 380.

7. *Ibid.*, pp. 406–407.

8. *Ibid.*, pp. 449–453.

9. *Ibid.*, p. 435.

10. Bernard DeVoto, *The Year of Decision, 1846* (Boston, 1943), pp. 73–89; Roberts, *Comprehensive History*, II, 473 ff; Ray B. West, *Kingdom of the Saints; The Story of Brigham Young and the Mormons* (New York, 1957), pp. 156–164. Neither, however, discusses the role of the Council of Fifty.

11. For the role of the Council of Fifty in the exodus see especially Andrus, *Joseph Smith and World Government*, pp. 67–86; Bush and Hansen, "Notes Towards a Definition of the Council of Fifty."

12. Roberts, ed., *History of the Church, Period II*, p. 379.

13. *Ibid.*, p. 480.

14. *Ibid.*, p. 379.

15. *Ibid.*, pp. 454–455.

16. *Ibid.*, p. 567. Stout recorded in his diary under entry of January 13 (I, 105): ". . . met with the Council of Fifty. This is the first time I ever met with that Council. The subject of our removal West was discussed & I was well entertained."

17. Stout, I, 107; Roberts, *Comprehensive History*, III, 40.

18. Johnson to Gibbs, p. 23.

19. Clayton, pp. 40, 202; Lee, "Diaries and Official Records," pp. 103, 104, 110, 163.

20. *Doctrine and Covenants*, Section 136.

21. *Journals of John D. Lee, 1846–47 and 1859*, ed. Charles Kelly (Salt Lake City, 1938), p. 53.

22. Those belonging to the Council of Fifty in the first pioneer group were Ezra T. Benson, Thomas Bullock, Albert Carrington, William Clay-

ton, Heber C. Kimball, Amasa Lyman, Orson Pratt, John Pack, Willard Richards, Orrin Porter Rockwell, Albert P. Rockwood, Shadrach Roundy, Charles Shumway, George A. Smith, Erastus Snow, Wilford Woodruff, Phineas H. Young, and Brigham Young. See Clayton, p. 202; Journal of Amasa Lyman (typescript, Brigham Young University Library), p. 37.

23. Benjamin F. Ferris, *Utah and the Mormons* (New York, 1856), p. 165.

24. Frederick Logan Paxson, *History of the American Frontier, 1763–1893* (New York, 1924), p. 349.

25. Quoted in Arrington, *Great Basin Kingdom*, p. 435.

26. *Ibid.*

27. Leland H. Creer, *The Founding of an Empire: The Exploration and Colonization of Utah, 1776–1856* (Salt Lake City, 1947), pp. 335–336.

28. Jensen, "Mormon Theory of Church and State," pp. 49–53.

29. *Ibid.*, p. 55.

30. Thus Leland H. Creer, *Utah and the Nation*, (Seattle, Wash., 1929); Andrew L. Neff, "The Mormon Migration to Utah" (doctoral dissertation, University of California, Berkeley, 1918). These two works were doctoral dissertations written under Herbert E. Bolton at the University of California. See also DeVoto, p. 87.

31. Smith, *History of the Church*, VI, 206.

32. Jensen, p. 55.

33. *Ibid.*, p. 20. See also Durham, *Joseph Smith, Prophet-Statesman*, p. 101; J. Keith Melville, "Mormon Theory of Church and State" (doctoral dissertation, University of Utah, 1956), p. 11.

34. "Separatism in Utah, 1847–1870," *Annual Report of the American Historical Association for the Year 1917* (Washington, 1920), pp. 333–343. *The Mormons* (Chicago, 1957), p. 171.

35. Roberts, ed., *History of the Church, Period II*, pp. 478–479.

36. The interpretation by Richard Vetterli, *Mormonism, Americanism, and Politics* (Salt Lake City, 1961), pp. 329–332, is typical of this point of view.

37. Roberts, ed., *History of the Church, Period II*, pp. 612–613.

38. James K. Polk, *Diary*, ed. Milo M. Quaife (4 vols.; Chicago, 1910), I, 449–450.

39. Stout, I, 172; Arrington, *Great Basin Kingdom*, pp. 21–22.

40. Irene Haskall Pomeroy to Ashbel G. Hascall, July 6, 1845, in "Letters of a Proselyte. The Hascall-Pomeroy Correspondence," *Utah Historical Quarterly*, XXV (1957), 63.

41. *Ibid.*, p. 254.

42. Quoted in Dale Morgan, *The Great Salt Lake* (New York, 1947), p. 223. Lobelia was an herb occasionally used by the pioneers. The cure, however, was frequently worse than the disease.

43. *Times and Seasons*, VI (1846), 1096–97.

44. Journal History, September 8, 1851, p. 4.

45. Irene H. Pomeroy to Ophelia M. Andrews, March 5, 1848, in "Hascall-Pomeroy Correspondence," p. 243.

46. *Deseret News*, July 28, 1858.

47. *Doctrine and Covenants*, 58:21.

48. *Journal of Discourses*, XX (1879), 166.

49. Quoted in Montgomery, *The Mormon Delusion*, p. 310.

50. *Journal of Discourses*, II (1852), 172.

51. "Journal of the Iron County Mission," ed. Gustive O. Larson, *Utah Historical Quarterly*, XX (1952), 260.

VII. "Exalted Above the Hills"

1. Kelly, ed., *Journals of John D. Lee*, p. 25.

2. Roberts, *Comprehensive History*, III, 270–278; IV, xxiii; Norman C. Pierce, *The 3½ Years* (Salt Lake City, 1963), p. 211. In keeping with the universal character of the kingdom, the standard was to represent all the nations of the earth.

3. (New York, 1951), pp. 18–20.

4. Smith, *History of the Church*, VI, 318–319.

5. Isa. 2:2–3; Dan. 2:44–45.

6. XIX (1857), 630.

7. *Latter-Day Kingdom* (Liverpool, 1856), p. 117.

8. *Journal of Discourses*, II (1855), 310.

9. Andrus, *Joseph Smith and World Government*, pp. 87–122; Arrington, *Great Basin Kingdom*, pp. 31–32, 50–51, 55, 57–63; Bush and Hansen, "Notes Towards a Definition of the Council of Fifty"; Clark, "The Kingdom of God, the Council of Fifty, and the State of Deseret"; Klaus J. Hansen, "The Theory and Practice of the Political Kingdom of God in Mormon History, 1829–1890" (master's thesis, Brigham Young University, 1959), pp. 138–175.

10. "Separatism in Utah," p. 336; *Founding of an Empire*, p. 310.

11. Journal of Charles C. Rich, October 10, 1847, quoted in Hyrum L. Andrus, "Joseph Smith and the West," *Brigham Young University Studies*, II (1960), 146.

12. Journal History, January 20, 1849.

13. Lee, *Mormon Chronicle*, I, 80.

14. "The State of Deseret," *Utah Historical Quarterly*, VIII (1940), p. 79.

15. *My Life's Review* (Independence, Mo., 1947), p. 124.

16. Lee, *Mormon Chronicle*, I, 88.

17. Journal History, June 26, 1848. It should be noted that the term "kingdom of God and his Laws" is the identical phrase used in the Minutes of the Council of Fifty.

18. *Ibid.*

19. Journal History, October 10, 1848.

20. Lee, *Mormon Chronicle*, I, 80; Stout, II, 337.

21. Morgan, "State of Deseret," p. 82.

22. *Founding of an Empire*, p. 313.

23. Creer, *Utah and the Nation*, p. vii.

24. Creer, *Founding of an Empire*, p. 312; Andrew L. Neff, *History of Utah, 1847–1869*, ed. Leland H. Creer (Salt Lake City, 1940), p. 108.

25. Quoted in Morgan, *The Great Salt Lake*, p. 202.

26. Morgan, "The State of Deseret," p. 84; Neff, p. 115.

27. Quoted in Morgan, "The State of Deseret," p. 156.

28. *Ibid.,* p. 162.

29. *Ibid.,* p. 160.

30. Lee, *Mormon Chronicle,* I, 99; Journal History, March 4, 1849.

31. *History of Utah,* p. 121.

32. Quoted in Morgan, "State of Deseret," p. 157.

33. Stout, II, 358.

34. Lee, *Mormon Chronicle,* I, 92.

35. "State of Deseret," pp. 96–113.

36. James B. Allen, "The Development of County Government in the Territory of Utah, 1850–1896" (master's thesis, Brigham Young University, 1956); Thomas G. Alexander, "The Utah Federal Courts and the Areas of Conflict, 1850-1896" (master's thesis, Utah State University, 1961).

37. Gustive O. Larson, *Prelude to the Kingdom; Mormon Desert Conquest, A Chapter in American Cooperative Experience* (Francestown, N. H., 1947), p. 106.

38. *Ibid.,* p. 127.

39. *An Expedition to the Valley of the Great Salt Lake* (London, 1852), pp. 331–332.

40. Morgan, "State of Deseret," p. 156.

41. Leonard J. Arrington, "Coin and Currency in Early Utah," *Utah Historical Quarterly,* XX (1952), 56–57; Ralph Hansen, "Administrative History of the Nauvoo Legion in Utah" (master's thesis, Brigham Young University, 1954).

42. Journal History, July 19, 1849.

43. *Ibid.*

44. In the light of these events, Leland Creer's recent interpretation that the Saints petitioned for a territorial government because they seemed to be "mistrustful of their application for a sovereign state government being favorably received" will have to be reversed. "The Evolution of Government in Early Utah," *Utah Historical Quarterly,* XXVI (1958), 37.

45. Frank J. Cannon and George L. Knapp, *Brigham Young and His Mormon Empire* (New York, 1913), p. 117.

46. Richard D. Poll, "The Mormon Question Enters National Politics, 1850–1856," *Utah Historical Quarterly,* XXV (1957), 117.

47. *Deseret News,* March 8, 1851.

48. Roberts, *Comprehensive History,* III, 509–510.

49. Morgan, "State of Deseret," pp. 130–131.

50. Roberts, *Comprehensive History,* III, 501.

51. Determined by comparison with membership list of Council of Fifty. See Appendix.

52. Neff, pp. 168–177; U.S., President, 1850–53 (Fillmore), *Message from the President of the United States Transmitting Information in Reference to the Condition of Affairs in the Territory of Utah,* 34th Cong., 1st Sess., Executive Doc. No. 25.

53. *Utah and the Mormons* (New York, 1856), p. 167.

54. Determined by a comparison of Council of Fifty membership lists (see Appendix) with "Journals of the Legislative Council and House of Representatives, 1851–1894" (microfilm, Utah State Historical Society).

55. "The Moses Thatcher Case" (MS, Utah State Historical Society), p. 3.

56. George William and Helen Pruitt Beattie, *Heritage of a Valley, San Bernardino's First Century* (Pasadena, Calif., 1939), p. 230.

57. *Mormonism: Its Leaders and Designs* (New York, 1857), p. 189; Stout, II, 524.

58. Stout, II, 559.

59. *Deseret News*, November 7, 1860.

60. There are those, however, who argue that even a democracy is in reality run by an oligarchy. See John H. Schaar, *Loyalty in America* (Berkeley, Calif., 1957), p. 50.

61. Abraham, 3:22–23.

62. Smith, *History of the Church*, VI, 364.

63. Leonard J. Arrington, "Taxable Income in Utah, 1862–1872," *Utah Historical Quarterly*, XXIV (1956), 37.

64. *Ibid.*, pp. 42–43.

65. The most precise estimates are in Stanley S. Ivins, "Notes on Mormon Polygamy," *Western Humanities Review*, X (1956), 229–239.

66. Lee, "Journal of the Iron County Mission," p. 358.

67. Cited in *Truth*, II (1936), 22.

68. *Acts, Resolutions and Memorials Passed at the Fifth Annual Session of the Legislative Assembly of the Territory of Utah* (Great Salt Lake City, 1855), pp. 35–37, 235.

69. Clark, "Church and State Relationships in Education in Utah," p. 78.

70. Arrington, *Great Basin Kingdom*, pp. 245–251.

71. These were Robert T. Burton, Dr. Jeter Clinton, Edward Hunter, Charles Kimball, David P. Kimball, Parley P. Pratt, Jr., Joseph Rich, John T. Sharp, Abraham O. Smoot, Hosea Stout, and George J. Taylor. History of Brigham Young, January 25, 1867 (L.D.S. Church Historian's Office).

72. Arrington, *Great Basin Kingdom*, p. 245.

73. *Ibid.*

74. *Millennial Star*, XXX (1868), 443.

75. Journal History, October 3, 1868.

76. Stout, II, 721.

77. Arrington, *Great Basin Kingdom*, p. 250; for the "Word of Wisdom," see *Doctrine and Covenants*, Section 89.

78. Minutes of the Provo School of the Prophets, October 13, 1868 (microfilm, Brigham Young University Library).

79. Records of the Bishops' Meetings, Provo, 1868–1875, October 15, 1868 (microfilm, Brigham Young University Library).

80. Cited in *Truth*, II (1936), 22.

81. *Journal of Discourses*, XVII (1875), 157.

VIII. The Kingdom of God vs. the Kingdoms of the World

1. Smith, *History of the Church*, III, 183–186.

2. *Ibid.*, VI, 366.

3. *Doctrine and Covenants*, 103:4.

Notes

4. *Ibid.*, 103:2–3.

5. Richard L. Bushman, "Mormon Persecutions in Missouri, 1833," *Brigham Young University Studies*, III (1960), 20; Mark W. Cannon, "The Mormon Issue in Congress," p. 37; Creer, *Utah and the Nation*, pp. vii, 13–14; B. H. Roberts, *The Missouri Persecutions* (Salt Lake City, 1900).

6. Mark W. Cannon, "The Crusades Against the Masons, Catholics, and Mormons: Separate Waves of a Common Current," *Brigham Young University Studies*, III (1961), 23–40; for a treatment of the same topic by a non-Mormon see David Brion Davis, "Some Themes of Counter-subversion: An Analysis of Anti-Masonic, Anti-Catholic, and Anti-Mormon Literature," *Mississippi Valley Historical Review*, XLVII (1960), 205–224.

7. John A. Beadle, *Brigham's Destroying Angel* (n.p., 1872), p. 15.

8. John Hyde, *Mormonism: Its Leaders and Designs* (New York, 1857), pp. 307–308.

9. *Millennial Star*, XXIII (1861), 125.

10. T. B. H. Stenhouse, *The Rocky Mountain Saints* (New York, 1873), p. 3.

11. Roberts, *Comprehensive History*, I, 431–432.

12. *Ibid.*, p. 433.

13. Quoted in Warren Abner Jennings, "Zion is Fled; The Expulsion of the Mormons from Jackson County, Missouri," p. 306.

14. Samuel M. Smucker, *The Religious, Social, and Political History of the Mormons, or Latter-day Saints, from their Origin to the Present Time* (New York, 1860), pp. 108–109.

15. U.S., Congress, Senate, *Testimony in Trial of Joseph Smith, Jr., for High Treason*, 26th Cong., 2d Sess., 1841, Senate Doc. 189, p. 23.

16. Smith, *History of the Church*, III, 211.

17. October 29, 1838, Albert P. Rockwood Papers (Coe Collection, Yale University Library).

18. (Chicago, 1880), p. 276.

19. (Chicago, 1854), pp. 321–322.

20. George T. M. Davis, *An Authentic Account of the Massacre of Joseph Smith, the Mormon Prophet, and Hyrum Smith, His Brother . . .* (St. Louis, 1844), p. 7.

21. February 15, 1844, The Thomas C. Sharp and Allied Anti-Mormon Papers, 1844–1846 (Coe Collection, Yale University Library).

22. *Millennial Star*, XXIV (1862), 359.

23. Smith, *History of the Church*, VI, 341.

24. George R. Gayler, "The *'Expositor'* Affair. Prelude to the Downfall of Joseph Smith," *The Northwest Missouri State College Studies*, XXV (1961), 6–7.

25. *Ibid.*

26. Smith, *History of the Church*, VI, 443.

27. Gayler, p. 12.

28. *Ibid.*, p. 11; Davis, *The Story of the Church*, p. 335: "The Saints never did a more unwise thing than order the destruction of the *Expositor.*"

29. Smith, *History of the Church*, VI, xxxvii–xxxix.

30. Roberts, ed., *History of the Church, Period II*, p. 444.

31. *Ibid.*, p. 498.

32. U.S., Congress, Senate, Territorial Papers, 1789–1873; Utah, December 13, 1849–June 11, 1870: "Petition of Wm. Smith and others, members of the Church of Latter-day Saints, against the admission of the Salt Lake Mormons into the Union as a State" (National Archives).

33. Enos Goodrich to Charles E. Stuart, March 7, 1853, Strang Papers, (Coe Collection, Yale University Library).

34. Norman F. Furniss, *The Mormon Conflict, 1850–1859* (New Haven, 1960), pp. 21–29.

35. Richard D. Poll, "The Mormon Question Enters National Politics, 1850–1856," *Utah Historical Quarterly*, XXV (1957), 131.

36. *Ibid.*, p. 118.

37. Richard D. Poll, "The Political Reconstruction of Utah Territory, 1866–1890," *Pacific Historical Review*, XXVII (1958), 111–112.

38. Journal History, August 2, 1857.

39. Furniss, p. 136.

40. September 1, 1858, in Edward Eberstadt and Sons, *Western America in Documents; From the Mississippi to the Pacific, 1669–1890* (New York, 1963), p. 111.

41. Ellerbeck Papers, *ibid.*, p. 106.

42. Orson F. Whitney, *History of Utah* (4 vols.; Salt Lake City, 1892–1904), II, 24–25.

43. *New York Daily Tribune*, October 19, 1861, p. 4.

44. *Doctrine and Covenants*, Section 87.

45. Smith, *History of the Church*, V. 394.

46. January 3, 1861, Brigham Young Papers (Coe Collection, Yale University Library).

47. February 7, and February 14, 1861, *ibid.*

48. Diary of Charles Walker, April 28, 1861 (typescript, Utah State Historical Society).

49. *Deseret News*, May 1, 1861. My italics. Kimball's choice of words is significant in view of the distinctions Mormons made between the government and the Constitution of the United States. The South, of course, could use the same argument. Many southerners, it will be remembered, justified secession on the grounds that they were defending the Constitution.

50. Journal History, January 19, 1863.

51. January 28, 1865, in U.S., Dept. of State, Territorial Papers, Utah Series (National Archives).

52. Frances P. Dyer to Addison Pratt, August 19, 1866, Addison Pratt Family Papers (in possession of S. George Ellsworth, Logan, Utah).

53. Quoted in Gustive O. Larson, *Outline History of Utah and the Mormons* (Salt Lake City, 1958), p. 201.

54. April 27, 1870, in U.S., Dept. of State, Territorial Papers, Utah Series (National Archives).

Notes

55. Sixty signed letters, 1859–1866, Brigham Young Papers (Coe Collection, Yale University Library).

56. Clark, "Church and State Relationships in Education in Utah"; T. Edgar Lyon, "Evangelical Protestant Missionary Activities in Mormon Dominated Areas: 1865–1900" (doctoral dissertation, University of Utah, 1962).

57. Autobiography of Frederick T. Dubois (typescript in Idaho Historical Society), p. 29.

58. (Philadelphia, 1870), pp. 400–401.

59. Joseph Nimmo, Jr., *The Mormon Usurpation* (Huntington, N.Y., 1899), pp. 6–7.

60. (Salt Lake City, n.d.), pp. 15–16.

61. Cannon, "The Mormon Issue in Congress," p. 162; Robert J. Dwyer, *The Gentile Comes to Utah; A Study in Religious and Social Conflict, 1862–1890* (Washington, 1941); Poll, "The Mormon Question Enters National Politics," p. 119.

62. Richard D. Poll's much neglected "The Twin Relic; A Study of Mormon Polygamy and the Campaign by the Government of the United States for its Abolition, 1852–1890" (master's thesis, Texas Christian University, 1939) is still the best account of the controversy.

63. Cannon, "The Mormon Issue in Congress," pp. 4–5.

64. L. John Nuttall Letterpress Book, 1879–1881 (Brigham Young University Library).

65. *Ibid.*

66. (Brigham Young University Library)

67. *Ibid.*

68. *Ibid.*

69. Francis M. Lyman and Moses Thatcher. The others were Angus M. Cannon, William W. Cluff, William Jennings, Feramorz Little, L. John Nuttall, William B. Preston, Franklin S. Richards, William R. Smith, Silas S. Smith, John Henry Smith, William W. Whittaker, and Junius F. Wells.

70. *Diary and Letters of Rutherford Birchard Hayes*, ed. Charles Williams (5 vols.; Columbus, Ohio, 1922–26), III, 583-584.

71. Larson, *Outline History*, p. 207.

72. Nuttall, Letterpress Book, 1879–1881.

73. *Doctrine and Covenants*, Official Declaration, pp. 256–257.

74. February 12, 1886, John W. Young Papers (Coe Collection, Yale University Library).

75. To F. D. Richards, April 20, 1886, *ibid.*

76. To H. J. Grant and J. F. Wells, February 10, 1886, *ibid.*

77. January 17, 1888, John W. Young Railroad Correspondence (L.D.S. Church Historian's Office).

78. "Official Declaration," Salt Lake City, December 12, 1889.

79. L. John Nuttall Diary, April 19, 1893.

80. John Mills Whitaker, Journal No. 5, October 16, 1887 (University of Utah Library).

81. See above, p. 170.

IX. Epilogue

1. *Lorenzo Hill Hatch Journal,* p. 125.
2. Journal No. 5, October 16, 1887.
3. Journal No. 10, November 10, 1900.
4. *Ibid.*
5. Johnson to Gibbs, p. 18.
6. *Ibid.*
7. *Tullidge's Histories* (Salt Lake City, 1889), II, 154.
8. *Ibid.*
9. *Ibid.,* p. 155.
10. Edward W. Tullidge, "The Godbeite Movement," *Tullidge's Quarterly Magazine,* I (1880), 32.
11. *Ibid.*
12. U.S., Congress, Senate, *Proceedings Before the Committee on Privileges and Elections of the United States Senate in the Matter of the Protest Against the Right Hon. Reed Smoot, A Senator from the State of Utah, to Hold His Seat* (4 vols.; Washington, 1904–1907), I *passim.*
13. *Ibid.,* 97–98.
14. *The Kingdom of God,* p. 1.
15. *Deseret News,* August 23, 1865.
16. Brigham H. Roberts to "Brother Joseph," n.d., James E. Talmage Papers (Brigham Young University Archives). The letter is a request for information that would minimize the temporal and political aspects of the kingdom of God: "The above references are wanted to aid Brother Talmage in forming testimony to be given before the Senate Investigating Committee." Cf. *Smoot Proceedings,* III, 25–34, for Talmage's testimony.
17. December 19, 1903; cf. *Smoot Proceedings,* III, 35–38.
18. *Smoot Proceedings,* III, 35–38.
19. *Ibid.,* I, 126.
20. Cannon and O'Higgins, *Under the Prophet in Utah,* p. 66.
21. (New York, 1904)
22. See for example, Neff to George H. Brimhall, April 1, 1906, Brimhall Papers (Brigham Young University Archives).
23. Representative Mormon works in this tradition are Creer, *Utah and the Nation,* and *The Founding of an Empire;* Milton R. Hunter, *Utah in Her Western Setting* (Salt Lake City, 1943); Neff, *History of Utah;* Levi Edgar Young, *The Founding of Utah* (New York, 1923). Others following this same interpretation are Ray Allen Billington, *Westward Expansion, A History of the American Frontier* (New York, 1949), p. 532 ff.; Dean D. McBrien, "The Influence of the Frontier on Joseph Smith" (doctoral dissertation, George Washington University, 1929); Thomas Weldon, "The Turner Thesis and the Mormon Frontier" (master's thesis, Stetson University, 1964). Two carefully reasoned studies refuting the concept of Mormonism as a frontier religion are Whitney R. Cross, *The Burned-over District,* pp. 138–150; and Ellsworth, "A History of Mormon Missions in the United States and Canada, 1830–1860," pp. 327–342.

Notes

24. Ernst Troeltsch, *The Social Teachings of the Christian Churches*, trans. Olive Wyon (2 vol.; London, 1931), II, 461–465. See also Thomas F. O'Dea, "Mormonism and the Avoidance of Sectarian Stagnation: A Study of Church, Sect, and Incipient Nationality," *American Journal of Sociology*, LX (1954), 285–293.

25. Perhaps the most important mouthpiece of Mormon fundamentalism was for many years the periodical *Truth*, founded and edited by Joseph W. Musser (21 vols.; 1935–56). A recent, compact source on most fundamentalist doctrines, and a veritable gold mine on the Council of Fifty and the kingdom of God is Norman C. Pierce, *The 3½ Years*.

26. December 2, 1960.

Essay On Sources

A COMPREHENSIVE bibliography of the primary and secondary sources relating to the Council of Fifty and the political kingdom of God would require too much space for inclusion here. This essay will therefore be limited to a description and evaluation of the major source materials used in this study, with emphasis on published and unpublished primary sources directly related to the kingdom of God and the Council of Fifty. All significant sources, both primary and secondary, have been cited in the footnotes.

Manuscripts

The most important collection of Mormon materials is located at the Church Historian's Office of the Church of Jesus Christ of Latter-day Saints in Salt Lake City. This is an archives, not a research library. Nevertheless, I was grateful for permission to use the Journal History of the Church, a gigantic scrapbook of about 750 volumes containing excerpts from diaries, journals, letters, and newspapers, forming a day-by-day account from the founding of the church in 1830 to the present.

The official records of the Council of Fifty, with one small significant exception, are not available for research at the present time, although their existence cannot be doubted. The fact that the Council kept records of its proceedings has been substantiated from numerous sources in this study. The Council had an official clerk and historian. Although John D. Lee indicated that records were at times burned, it seems unlikely that this was a common procedure. Moreover, the possibility that such records were lost or destroyed by accident seems very remote, indeed, in view of the deserved reputation which stamps the Mormons as most meticulous keepers and preservers of records.

Fortunately, important manuscripts located in various other archives and libraries give significant information on both the Council of Fifty and the kingdom of God. Perhaps the most important of these is a typewritten copy of minutes of Council of Fifty meetings held in Salt Lake City in 1880. Although the provenance of these manuscripts cannot be determined, the correctness of the information contained therein is corroborated by numerous unimpeachable sources. They are found at Brigham Young University Library. Other manuscripts at the same library paticularly useful for this study were a lengthy autobiographical letter by Benjamin F. Johnson—a member of the Council of Fifty—to George S. Gibbs, written between April and October 1903; a typescript of unpublished Diaries and Official Records of John D. Lee; a typescript of the journal of Amasa Lyman; microfilms of the "Minutes of the Provo School of the Prophets," and of "Records of the Bishops' Meetings, Provo, 1868–1875"; typescript of the diary of L. John Nuttall; and L. John Nuttall's letterpress books, 1879–1881. In the Brigham Young University Archives, I gained helpful insights from the papers of George H. Brimhall, Benjamin Cluff, and James E. Talmage.

At the University of Utah Library, I was particularly pleased to gain access to the journals of John Mills Whitaker, one of the most comprehensive records of its period, giving much inside information on the anti-polygamy raids, the events leading up to the Manifesto, and early twentieth-century Mormonism.

The Utah State Historical Society has among its numerous sources the particularly valuable records of the Nauvoo Legion in Utah. A typescript of the diary of Charles Walker proved a most helpful source. A microfilm of the "Journals of the Legislative Council and House of Representatives, 1851–1894," of Utah Territory, was indispensable for comparing members of the legislature with membership lists of the Council of Fifty.

I had access to the manuscript collection of the Bancroft Library at the University of California through the microfilms available at Utah State University.

The manuscripts of the Coe Collection of Western Americana at Yale University Library contained the largest number of significant items in any single library helpful to this study. Of particular importance were the Strang Papers; a series of sixty letters addressed by Brigham Young to Council of Fifty member and Congressional Delegate William H. Hooper, 1859–66; the Albert P. Rockwood Papers; the Thomas C. Sharp and Allied Anti-Mormon Papers, 1844–46; and the letterbooks of John W. Young, a member of the Council of Fifty in its later period.

The Manuscript Division of the New York Public Library made available the John Zahnd MS, containing one of the few references to Joseph Smith's kingship. Also helpful was the Orson Hyde–John E. Page Correspondence, Mormon Papers, Woodward folder.

The National Archives contains a number of significant letters from the Territorial Papers, 1789–1873, Utah Series.

Public Documents

In addition to those already cited, the following published documents were of special significance for this study: U.S., Congress, Senate, *Testimony in Trial of Joseph Smith, Jr., for High Treason*, 26th Cong., 2d Sess.,

1841, Senate Doc. 189, which is an account of the trial of Joseph Smith and his associates before Judge Austin A. King in Missouri in 1838; U.S., Congress, Senate, *Proceedings Before the Committee on Privileges and Elections of the United States Senate in the Matter of the Protests Against the Right Hon. Reed Smoot, a Senator from the State of Utah, to Hold His Seat* (4 vols.; Washington, 1904–1907).

Mormon Scriptures

These are fundamental to an understanding of the idea of the political kingdom of God. Mormons accept the King James version as the most authoritative translation of the Bible. *The Book of Mormon* was first published in 1830, at Palmyra, New York. An early version of *The Doctrine and Covenants of the Church of Jesus Christ of Latter-day Saints* was first published in 1833, at Zion, Jackson County, Missouri, under the title *Book of Commandments for the Government of the Church of Christ;* several enlarged editions, adding further revelations of Joseph Smith, were subsequently issued. In its present form, it has been published in Salt Lake City since 1921. *The Pearl of Great Price,* "a selection from the Revelations, Translations, and Narrations of Joseph Smith," has been published in its present form in Salt Lake City since 1921.

Published Diaries, Journals, Letters, Memoirs, and Source Collections

The most important published collection of Mormon sources is Joseph Smith's journal, published as *History of the Church of Jesus Christ of Latter-day Saints,* ed. B. H. Roberts (6 vols., 2d ed.; Salt Lake City, 1950); this is supplemented by a seventh volume, covering the period from Smith's death to the exodus, taken from the Manuscript History of Brigham Young and other documents (Salt Lake City, 1956). *Among the Mormons; Historical Accounts by Contemporary Observers,* ed. William Mulder and A. Russell Mortensen (New York, 1958), makes available much material otherwise difficult to obtain.

William Clayton's Journal. A Daily Record of the Original Company of "Mormon" Pioneers from Nauvoo, Illinois to the Valley of the Great Salt Lake (Salt Lake City, 1921) contains extremely valuable information on the Council of Fifty by a man who served as its clerk. Benjamin F. Johnson, *My Life's Review* (Independence, Mo., 1947), is an autobiography by an original member of the Council. The diaries of John D. Lee constitute perhaps the most important single source on the Council of Fifty and the kingdom of God. The most important of his published diaries is *A Mormon Chronicle; The Diaries of John D. Lee, 1848–1876,* ed. Robert Glass Cleland and Juanita Brooks (2 vols.; San Marino, Calif., 1955); also significant are *Journals of John D. Lee, 1846–47 and 1859,* ed. Charles Kelly (Salt Lake City, 1938); "Journal of the Iron County Mission, John D. Lee, Clerk," ed. Gustive O. Larson, *Utah Historical Quarterly,* XX (1952), 109–134, 253–282, 353–383. Less reliable, because it was written in bitterness against church leaders for having made him the scapegoat in the Mountain Meadows Massacre, is his *Mormonism Unveiled* (St. Louis, 1877). Extremely valuable on the Nauvoo period of the Council of Fifty are the letters of George Miller, probably published by Wingfield Watson in 1916 under *Correspondence of Bishop George Miller with the Northern Islander from his First Acquaintance with Mormonism up to Near the Close of his Life. Written by Himself in the Year 1855;* these letters were also published by H. W. Mills, "De Tal Palo Tal Astilla," *Annual Publications of the Historical Society of Southern California* (1917), pp. 86–172, and separately under the title, *A Mormon Bishop and His Son, Fragments of a Diary Kept by George Miller, Sr., Bishop in the Mormon Church, and Some Records of Incidents in the Life of G. Miller, Jr., Hunter and Pathfinder* (London, n.d.); the most important Mormon diary to appear in print thus far is *On the Mormon Frontier; The Diary of Hosea Stout, 1844–1861,* ed. Juanita Brooks (2 vols.; Salt Lake City, 1964).

Magazines, Newspapers, and Serial Publications

Among numerous Mormon newspapers and periodicals the most helpful were the *The Deseret News,* published in Salt Lake City as a weekly since 1850, and as a daily since 1867; *The Latter-day Saints' Millennial Star,* which began publication at Liverpool in 1840 and became the major church organ in the British Mission, containing many articles and editorials on the Kingdom of God and the Second Coming; *The Journal of Discourses,* ed. George D. Watt *et al.* (26 vols.; Liverpool, 1854–1886), an indispensable source for the study of the thought of Mormon leaders, containing many sermons on the kingdom of God and numerous veiled allusions to the Council of Fifty; and *Truth* (21 vols.; Salt Lake City, 1935–1956), a fundamentalist publication placing great emphasis on the Council of Fifty and the kingdom of God. Significant for an understanding of the intellectual transformation of Mormonism are particularly *The Utah Magazine* (3 vols.; Salt Lake City, 1868–1869); *Tullidge's Quarterly Magazine* (5 vols.; 1880–1885); and the leading Gentile newspaper, the *Salt Lake Tribune,* founded in 1871, which took a vigorous anti-Mormon stand in the nineteenth century.

Treatises on Mormon Theology

Important aspects of the kingdom of God are discussed in Charles W. Penrose, *Mormon Doctrine* (Salt Lake City, 1888); Orson Pratt, *The Kingdom of God* (Liverpool, 1851); Orson Pratt, *Latter-day Kingdom* (Liverpool, 1856); Parley P. Pratt, *To Her Gracious Majesty, Queen Victoria* (Manchester, 1841). The metaphysical implications of the kingdom of God are discussed in Orson Pratt, *Absurdities of Immaterialism* (Liverpool, 1849); Orson Pratt, *The Great First Cause* (Liverpool, 1851); and Parley P. Pratt, *Key to the Science of Theology* (Liverpool, 1855).

Contemporary Accounts by Non-Mormons

Most non-Mormon accounts are strongly biased against the Saints, and highly unreliable. Some notable exceptions are Samuel Bowles, *Across the Continent* (Springfield, Mass., 1856), who observed the Saints as a member of the entourage of Schuyler Colfax and made some penetrating observation about polygamy and the Mormon theocracy; and Sir Richard F. Burton's classic account, *The City of the Saints, and Across the Moun-*

tains to California (London, 1861). George T. M. Davis, *An Authentic Account of the Massacre of Joseph Smith, the Mormon Prophet, and Hyrum Smith, His Brother* (St. Louis, 1844), is an extremely rare imprint found in the Princeton University Library; it reveals how much the Gentiles knew or suspected about the Council of Fifty and the kingdom of God; Thomas A. Ford's *A History of Illinois from Its Commencement as a State in 1818 to 1847* (Chicago and New York, 1854) is important for that same reason; Howard Stansbury, *An Expedition to the Valley of the Great Salt Lake* (London, 1852), is a sympathetic view of the Mormon theocracy by the commanding officer of the U.S. Topographical Engineers surveying Utah in the early period of settlement; T. B. H. Stenhouse's *The Rocky Mountain Saints* (New York, 1873), though written in the heat of apostate repudiation, contains valuable information about the kingdom of God.

The following works, of a more vitriolic character, give a highly distorted view of Mormonism and cannot be taken seriously on many counts; nevertheless, they are extremely important because they reveal Gentile reaction to the kingdom of God, and how much they suspected about the secrets of the kingdom: J. H. Beadle, *Life in Utah* (Philadelphia, 1870); John C. Bennett, *The History of the Saints* (Boston, 1842); Frank J. Cannon and Harvey J. O'Higgins, *Under the Prophet in Utah* (Boston, 1911); Frank J. Cannon and George L. Knapp, *Brigham Young and His Mormon Empire* (New York, 1913); John Corrill, *A Brief History of the Church of Latter-day Saints* (St. Louis, 1839); Benjamin G. Ferris, *Utah and the Mormons; The History of Government, Doctrines, Customs, and Prospects of the Latter-day Saints* (New York, 1856); John W. Hill, *Mormonism vs. Americanism* (Salt Lake City, 1889); John Hyde, Jr., *Mormonism: Its Leaders and Designs* (New York, 1857); M. W. Montgomery, *The Mormon Delusion* (Minneapolis, 1890). Needless to say, these are but representative examples of a veritable flood of such works emanating from the presses in the nineteenth century.

Biographical Aids

The most helpful source for biographical information on the Council of Fifty was Andrew Jenson, *Latter-day Saint Biographical Encyclopedia* (4 vols.; Salt Lake City, 1901–1936); Frank E. Esshom, *Pioneers and Prominent Men of Utah* (Salt Lake City, 1913), is of some limited value; Warrum Noble, *Utah Since Statehood, Historical and Biographical* (4 vols.; Chicago, 1919), is a typical "mugbook." Numerous family biographies, usually by pious descendants, were helpful for factual information, though of limited value from an interpretive point of view. In fact, the dearth of good biographies of members of the Council of Fifty is astonishing. Fawn Brodie's *No Man Knows My History, the Life of Joseph Smith the Mormon Prophet* (New York, 1945), in spite of its limitations, is still the best study of the founder of Mormonism. There is no adequate biography of Brigham Young. A superior biography of a member of the Council of Fifty is Juanita Brooks, *John Doyle Lee. Zealot—Pioneer Builder—Scapegoat* (Glendale, Calif., 1962).

Essay On Sources

Studies of the Kingdom of God and the Council of Fifty

Brigham H. Roberts made occasional reference to the Council of Fifty and the political kingdom of God in the footnotes of his *A Comprehensive History of the Church of Jesus Christ of Latter-day Saints* (6 vols.; Salt Lake City, 1930). Dale Morgan produced an unpublished study in 1940, which has not been available to scholars. In 1944, G. Homer Durham suggested that the idea of a political kingdom of God was of far greater significance than had been suspected by most historians up to that time in his article "A Political Interpretation of Mormon History," *The Pacific Historical Review*, XII (1944), 136–150. In that article, Durham specifically proposed that a study of the Council of Fifty be made. A year later, in 1945, Fawn Brodie revealed a sophisticated understanding of that organization in her brief references to it in *No Man Knows My History*, pp. 356–366. Yet another twelve years passed before historians began to pick up the thread again, most likely spurred on by the publication, in 1955, of *A Mormon Chronicle: The Diaries of John D. Lee, 1848–1876*. In 1957, Alfred L. Bush and Klaus J. Hansen attempted to assess the significance of the political kingdom of God and the Council of Fifty in "Notes Towards a Definition of the Council of Fifty," multilithed copies privately distributed by the authors, copy at Brigham Young University Library. That same year, Thomas F. O'Dea revealed considerable knowledge of the Council of Fifty in his brief but perceptive analysis of Mormon church-state relationships in *The Mormons* (Chicago, 1957), pp. 165–171. In 1958 appeared Hyrum L. Andrus' *Joseph Smith and World Government* (Salt Lake City), in which the author attempted to link the political kingdom of God to the original intentions of the founding fathers of the American Republic. Leonard J. Arrington, in his *Great Basin Kingdom: An Economic History of the Latter-day Saints, 1830–1900* (Cambridge, Mass., 1958), assessed the role of the Council of Fifty in the economic development of the Mormon commonwealth. James R. Clark, "The Kingdom of God, the Council of Fifty and the State of Deseret," *Utah Historical Quarterly*, XXVI (1958), 130–148 is an excellent introduction to the subject. By the same author is "Church and State Relationships in Education in Utah" (doctoral dissertation, Utah State University, 1958), a superior study revealing the role of the Council of Fifty and the political kingdom of God in that knotty area of conflict. Klaus J. Hansen's "The Theory and Practice of the Political Kingdom of God in Mormon History, 1829–1890" (master's thesis, Brigham Young University, 1959) is a preliminary study toward a synthesis of the available information on that topic. Articles dealing with specific aspects of the political kingdom of God and the Council of Fifty are Klaus J. Hansen, "The Political Kingdom of God as a Cause for Mormon-Gentile Conflict" *Brigham Young University Studies*, II (1960), 241–260; Klaus J. Hansen, "The Making of King Strang: A Re-examination" *Michigan History*, XLVI (1962), 201–219; and J. Keith Melville, "Theory and Practice of Church and State During the Brigham Young Era" *Brigham Young*

University Studies, III (1960), 33–55. Juanita Brooks' *John Doyle Lee*, published in 1962, contains much significant information on the kingdom of God and the Council of Fifty. Robert Bruce Flanders' *Nauvoo: Kingdom on the Mississippi* (Urbana, 1965), is a superior study revealing, among other things, Joseph Smith's ambition to establish a temporal kingdom of God in Illinois.

Appendix

Membership Lists of the Council of Fifty, 1844–1880 *

Council of Fifty under Joseph Smith, 1844

Babbitt, Almon
Badlam, Alexander
Bent, Samuel
Bernhisel, John M.
Brown, Uriah
Cahoon, Reynolds
Clayton, William
Coolidge, J. W.
Cutler, Alpheus
Emmett, James
Fielding, Amos
Fullmer, John S.
Haws, Peter
Hollister, D. S.
Hunter, Edward
Hyde, Orson
James, Samuel
Johnson, Benjamin F.
Kimball, Heber C.
Lyman, Amasa
Marks, William
Miller, George
Page, John E.
Parker, John D.

Phelps, William W.
Pratt, Orson
Pratt, Parley P.
Rich, Charles C.
Richards, Levi
Richards, Willard
Rockwell, O. P.
Scott, John
Smith, George A.
Smith, Hyrum
Smith, John
Smith, Joseph
Smith, William
Snow, Erastus
Spencer, Orson
Taylor, John
Whasson, Lorenzo D.
Whitney, Newel K.
Wight, Lyman
Woodruff, Wilford
Woodworth, Lucien
Young, Brigham
Young, Joseph

Sources: History of the Church, VI, 260–261, 263, 267, 341; Johnson to Gibbs, *passim.*

Council of Fifty During the Exodus, 1846–47

Babbitt, Almon
* Benson, E. T.
Bent, Samuel
Bernhisel, John
* Bullock, Thomas
Cahoon, Reynolds
* Carrington, Albert
* Clayton, William
Cutler, Alpheus
Emmett, James
Fullmer, John S.
Grant, George D.
Grant, Jedediah M.
Haws, Peter
Hunter, Edward
Hyde, Orson
Johnson, Benjamin F.
* Kimball, Heber C.
Lee, John D.
Lewis, P. B.
* Lyman, Amasa
Miller, George
* Pack, John
Parker, John D.

Phelps, William W.
* Pratt, Orson
Pratt, Parley P.
Rich, Charles C.
Richards, Levi
* Richards, Willard
* Rockwell, O. P.
* Rockwood, Albert P.
* Roundy, Shadrach
Scott, John
* Shumway, Charles
* Smith, George A.
Smith, John
* Snow, Erastus
Spencer, Daniel H.
Spencer, Orson
Taylor, John
Turley, Theodore
Whitney, Newel K.
* Woodruff, Wilford
* Young, Brigham
Young, Joseph
* Young, Phineas H.

Sources: "Official Records and Diaries of John D. Lee, 1846," pp. 97, 103, 110, 163; Clayton, pp. 202–203.

* Members of first pioneer company to reach the Great Basin, 1847.

Council of Fifty in Colonial Utah, 1847–49

Babbitt, Almon
Benson, E. T.
Bent, Samuel
Bernhisel, John
Bullock, Thomas
Cahoon, Reynolds
Carrington, Albert
Clayton, William
Eldredge, Horace
Fielding, John
Fullmer, John S.
Grant, George D.
Grant, Jedediah M.
Haws, Peter
Heywood, Joseph L.
Hunter, Edward
Hyde, Orson
Johnson, Benjamin F.
Kimball, Heber C.
Lee, John D.
Lott, Cornelius P.
Lyman, Amasa
Morley, Isaac
Pack, John
Parker, John D.
Phelps, William W.

Pratt, Orson
Pratt, Parley P.
Rich, Charles C.
Richards, Franklin D.
Richards, Levi
Richards, Willard
Rockwell, O. P.
Rockwood, Albert P.
Roundy, Shadrach
Scott, John
Shumway, Charles
Smith, George A.
Smith, John
Snow, Erastus
Snow, Lorenzo
Snow, Willard
Spencer, Daniel H.
Spencer, Orson
Taylor, John
Turley, Theodore
Wells, Daniel H.
Whitney, Newel K.
Woodruff, Wilford
Young, Brigham
Young, John W.
Young, Joseph

Sources: Lee, *Mormon Chronicle*, I, 80–100.

Council of Fifty, 1880

Bernhisel, John M.
Bullock, Thomas
Burton, R. T.
Carrington, Albert
* Cannon, Angus M.
Cannon, George Q.
Clinton, John
* Cluff, W. W.
Eldredge, Horace
Fullmer, John S.
Heywood, Joseph L.
Hooper, William H.
Hunter, Edward
* Jennings, William
Johnson, Benjamin F.
Kimball, Charles S.
Kimball, David P.
Kimball, H. P.
* Little, Feramorz
* Lyman, Francis M.
* Nuttall, L. John
Pack, John
Parker, John D.
Pratt, Orson
Pratt, Parley P., Jr.
Preston, William B.

Rich, Charles C.
Rich, Joseph C.
Richards, Franklin D.
* Richards, Franklin S.
Richards, H. J.
Sharp, John
Shumway, Charles
Smith, Elias
* Smith, John Henry
Smith, Joseph F.
* Smith, Silas S.
* Smith, William R.
Smoot, Abraham O.
Snow, Erastus
Snow, Lorenzo
Stout, Hosea
Taylor, George J.
Taylor, John
Taylor, William W.
* Thatcher, Moses
Wells, Daniel H.
* Wells, Junis F.
Woodruff, Wilford
Young, Brigham, Jr.
Young, John W.
Young, Joseph

Sources: Minutes of the Council of Fifty, 1880.
* New Members.

Members of the Council of Fifty, 1844–1880

Babbitt, Almon
Badlam, Alexander
Benson, Ezra Taft
Bent, Samuel
Bernhisel, John M.
Brown, Uriah
Bullock, Thomas
Burton, Robert T.
Cahoon, Reynolds
Cannon, Angus M.
Cannon, George Q.
Carrington, Albert
Clayton, William
Clinton, Jeter
Cluff, W. W.
Coolidge, Joseph W.
Cutler, Alpheus
Eldredge, Horace
Emmett, James
Fielding, Amos
Fielding, John
Fullmer, John S.
Grant, George D.
Grant, Jedediah M.
Haws, Peter
Heywood, Joseph L.
Hollister, D. S.
Hooper, William H.
Hunter, Edward, Jr.
Hyde, Orson
James, Samuel
Jennings, William
Johnson, Benjamin F.
Kimball, Charles S.
Kimball, David P.
Kimball, Heber C.
Kimball, H. P.
Lee, John D.

Lewis, P. B.
Little, Feramorz
Lott, Cornelius P.
Lyman, Amasa
Lyman, Francis M.
Marks, William
Miller, George
Morley, Isaac
Nuttall, L. John
Pack, John
Page, John E.
Parker, John D.
Phelps, William W.
Pratt, Orson
Pratt, Parley P.
Pratt, Parley P., Jr.
Preston, William B.
Rich, Charles C.
Rich, Joseph C.
Richards, Franklin D.
Richards, Franklin S.
Richards, H. J.
Richards, Levi
Richards, Willard
Rockwell, Orin Porter
Rockwood, Albert P.
Roundy, Shadrach
Scott, John
Sharp, John
Shumway, Charles
Smith, Elias
Smith, George A.
Smith, Hyrum
Smith, Joseph
Smith, Joseph F.
Smith, John
Smith, John Henry
Smith, Silas S.

Smith, William
Smith, William R.
Smoot, Abraham O.
Snow, Erastus
Snow, Lorenzo
Snow, Willard
Spencer, Daniel H.
Spencer, Orson
Stout, Hosea
Taylor, George J.
Taylor, John
Taylor, William W.
Thatcher, Moses

Turley, Theodore
Wells, Daniel Hanmer
Wells, Junius F.
Whasson, Lorenzo D.
Whitney, Newel K.
Wight, Lyman
Woodruff, Wilford
Woodworth, Lucien
Young, Brigham
Young, Brigham, Jr.
Young, John W.
Young, Joseph
Young, Phineas H.

Index

Index

Index

INDEX

Sugar Creek, Iowa, 110
Sword of Laban, 17

Talmage, James C., 185–6
Tauner, Thomas, 165
Taylor, John, 35, 39, 59, 61, 118, 129, 136, 168, 173, 174, 177
Teacher's Quorum, 8
telegraph, 166
Texas, 82–9, 94, 108, 113, 114
Texas Congress, 82, 84, 86
"Theo-Democracy," 40
theocracy, 24, 42, 61–2, 99–100
Theocratic Party, 190
Thompson, Charles B., 96
Times and Seasons, 51, 59, 74
Tocqueville, Alexis de, 37
Tolstoi, Leo, Count, 24
Tomlinson, Homer, 190
treaty of Guadalupe Hidalgo, 112, 125
treaty of Velasco, 83
Troeltsch, Ernst, 188
True Believer, The, 122
Tullidge, Edward W., 150, 182–3
Turner, Frederick Jackson, 113, 188

Union College, 140
Union Pacific Railroad, 143
United Firm, 48
United States Government, 22
United States President, 79
United States Topographical Engineers, 133
University of Deseret, 143
University of Pennsylvania, 140
Upshur, Abel P., U. S. Secretary of State, killed, 84
U.S.S. *Princeton*, 84
Utah Commission, 175
Utah Manufacturing Company, 144
Utah Territory, 34, 71, 132, 143, 163, 165, created, 136, influx of Gentiles, 146
Utah War, 164–5
Utopian Societies, 35

Velasco, treaty of, 83

Van Buren, Martin, 41, 74–5, 79, 80, 84
Van Leuven, F. M., 138
Vancouver Island, 109
Victoria, Queen, 3, 4, 10, 23
Voree, Wisconsin, 98

Walker, Charles, 167
Walker, Cyrus, 75–6
Warsaw Message, 51
Warsaw Signal, 156, 157, 159
Wells, Daniel H., 61, 133, 136, Chief Justice of State of Deseret, 136
West, Ira, 70–1
Whigs, 43, 75–6, 79, 84
Whitaker, John Mills, 180
White, Andrew Dickson, 24
Whitmer, Peter, 5
Whitney, Newel K., 59, 129, 136
Wight, Lyman, 48, 82, 94
Wilson, William, 157
Winter Quarters, Iowa, 62, 94, 96, 110, 111
Winthrop, John, 12
Wood, Reese, Doniphan, and Atchison (legal firm), 48
Woodruff, Wilford, 49, 63, 174, Manifesto ending polygamy, 176, 177, 178
Woodworth, Lucien, 59, 82, 85, 86, 88, 108,
"Word of Wisdom," 144

Young, Brigham, 4, 5, 10, 11, 34, 35, 38, 42, 49, 61, 62, and James Emmett's Missouri expedition, 93, and U. S. Government, 117, torial governor, 136, attempts to establish iron industry, 142, ceased convening legislature of kingdom of God, 169, death of, 172–3, decision to leave Illinois, 107–8, elected governor, 129, his only revelation recorded in *Doctrine and Covenants*, 110, importance of economic indepen-